Power Shuffles and Policy Processes

The Japan Center for International Exchange wishes to thank

The Nippon Foundation

Power Shuffles
and
Policy Processes

Coalition Government
in Japan in the 1990s

edited by
Ōtake Hideo

JCIE

Tokyo • Japan Center for International Exchange • *New York*

The surnames of the authors and other persons mentioned in this book
are positioned according to country practice.

Copyediting by Pamela J. Noda
Contributing editors: Frank Baldwin (chapters 1 and 5), Jane Singer (chapters 2,
6, and 7), Suzy Trumbull (chapter 3), and Micheline Tusenius (chapter 4).
Cover and typographic design by Becky Davis, EDS Inc., Editorial &
Design Services, Tokyo. Typesetting and production by EDS Inc.
Cover photograph © 1996 The Studio Dog/PhotoDisc, Inc.

Printed in Japan.
ISBN 4-88907-035-4

Distributed worldwide outside Japan by Brookings Institution Press,
1775 Massachusetts Avenue, N.W., Washington, D.C. 20036-2188 U.S.A.

Japan Center for International Exchange
9-17 Minami Azabu 4-chome, Minato-ku, Tokyo 106-0047 Japan

URL: http://www.jcie.or.jp

Japan Center for International Exchange, Inc. (JCIE/USA)
1251 Avenue of the Americas, New York, N.Y. 10020 U.S.A.

Contents

Foreword

I N the spring of 1996, the Japan Center for International Exchange (JCIE) launched the Global ThinkNet program, a multipronged cluster of policy research and dialogue activities designed to contribute to strengthening the Asia Pacific as well as the global intellectual network and, at the same time, to foster more active Japanese participation in such collaborative intellectual efforts. As a key element of the Global ThinkNet activities, JCIE began a series of study projects involving emerging intellectual leaders of Japan to encourage them to prepare for more active participation in international intellectual networks. Recognition had been growing in Japan and abroad that Japan has been underrepresented in international intellectual cooperative efforts largely because of a paucity of domestic independent policy research institutions and human resources.

One project under the Global ThinkNet program focused on the theme of "Japanese Politics in the New Era," under the direction of Ōtake Hideo, professor of political science at Kyoto University and a leading scholar on Japanese politics. The project reflected an awareness of the difficult constraints that domestic politics often place on effective Japanese participation and leadership in international affairs. A group of ten young political scientists was divided into two teams, each studying the two fundamental systemic changes in Japanese politics since 1993: the introduction of a new electoral system for the House of Representatives and the emergence of coalition governments. The volume of essays by the first team, titled *How Electoral Reform Boomeranged,* was published in 1998.

The second team of young political scientists focused on analyzing the impact of coalition politics on the policy-making process. In the course of their field studies, the group members gathered in Tokyo,

7

Kyoto, and Osaka for monthly joint workshops with the participation of resource persons, including leading political figures, bureaucrats, political reporters, and senior academicians.

With the collapse of one-party dominance by the Liberal Democratic Party in the summer of 1993, politics in Japan entered the era of coalition governments. By tracing the steps in decision making on specific policies, the group members examined how the policy process had changed under the coalition governments compared with that during the period of one-party dominance. Some scholars also discussed how policy changes contributed to the political realignment, or party system change, seen in the 1990s. The essays contained in this volume represent the efforts of the scholars of the second team and were published in 1998 in Japanese as a special issue of *Leviathan* (summer).

The project that resulted in this publication could not have been possible without the generous financial support provided by the Nippon Foundation. JCIE wishes to express its sincere gratitude for the continuing support of the foundation and for its encouragement and support for the efforts to bring emerging intellectual leaders in Japan into the growing international network through the Global ThinkNet activities.

YAMAMOTO TADASHI
President
Japan Center for International Exchange

Overview

Ōtake Hideo

F ROM a historical perspective, the 1990s in Japan can be called a time of political upheaval on a par with the decade after the end of World War II. In 1993, the Liberal Democratic Party (LDP), which had monopolized power for 38 years, was ousted in the House of Representatives (Lower House) election and Japanese politics entered a coalition era. During the period of one-party dominance from 1955 to 1993, the LDP had only once needed to ally with another party. Having secured only a marginal majority by recruiting some conservative independents after the 1983 Lower House election, the LDP formed a coalition government with eight members of the New Liberal Club (NLC), a splinter of the LDP. The coalition dissolved in the summer of 1986, when the LDP absorbed the NLC.

The coalition governments of the 1990s, however, are far more significant politically than the LDP-NLC coalition of the 1980s. From 1993 to the first half of 1999, three types of coalition governments were organized. The first one was a non-LDP coalition with eight parties installed under Prime Minister Hosokawa Morihiro in August 1993. The Hosokawa government succeeded in passing a controversial political reform bill through the Diet in early 1994, but Hosokawa's sudden decision to resign as prime minister in early April that year left most other issues on the government's docket unresolved. After some maneuvering within the coalition, Hata Tsutomu formed a minority government following the withdrawal of both the New Party Sakigake (*sakigake* means "pioneer") and the Social Democratic Party of Japan

(SDPJ) from the coalition. The Hata cabinet was forced to resign in June 1994, when the LDP, the SDPJ, and Sakigake tried to introduce a motion of no-confidence against the Hata cabinet.

The second type of coalition government was a three-party coalition with the LDP, the SDPJ, and Sakigake, which replaced the non-LDP coalition at the end of June 1994. The LDP returned to power by agreeing to support the SDPJ's chairman, Murayama Tomiichi, as prime minister. The SDPJ, formerly named the Japan Socialist Party (JSP), and the LDP were longtime rivals, and their alliance stunned the electorate. When Murayama resigned abruptly in January 1996, he was replaced by LDP President Hashimoto Ryūtarō. Immediately after Murayama's resignation as prime minister, the SDPJ changed its name to the Social Democratic Party (SDP) and tried to increase its appeal to the electorate by presenting itself as a party adaptive to the new situation in the post–cold war era.

The 1996 Lower House election—the first election under the new electoral system—seriously damaged the LDP's coalition partners, the SDP and Sakigake. The former won 15 of the 500 seats in the Lower House, and the latter won just two—far fewer than its preelection strength of nine seats. Although both parties agreed to stay in the coalition with the LDP, they declined representation in the new cabinet formed after the election. The LDP won 239 seats, or fewer than half of the Lower House seats. Later, however, some former LDP members returned to the LDP one by one, giving it a majority in the fall of 1997.

At the end of May 1998, the SDP and Sakigake announced they would leave the coalition to prepare for the House of Councillors (Upper House) election. Although the LDP then dominated power in the Diet for the first time since 1993, stable rule was brief. The LDP suffered a stunning defeat in the Upper House election in July 1998, forcing it to form a new coalition. In November, the LDP reached agreement with the Liberal Party (LP), and their coalition government—the third type—was installed in January 1999.

The coalition era of the 1990s was also a period of change in the party system. Many political parties appeared on and disappeared from the political stage. The Japan New Party (JNP) was established in 1992. Sakigake and the Japan Renewal Party (JRP) were formed by politicians who split from the LDP when the Lower House was dissolved in June 1993. In late 1994, the New Frontier Party (NFP) was established through a merger of six parties, including the JRP, the JNP, Kōmeitō (Clean Government P arty), and the Democratic Socialist Party (DSP). These four parties had supported the Hata government, which fell from power in June 1994. The NFP broke up into six political parties and groups at the end of 1997. After the Democratic Party of Japan (DPJ) was established in September 1996, many members of the SDP and Sakigake switched to the DPJ before the 1996 Lower House election. As a result of these mergers, splinters, and changes of allegiance, by the fall of 1998 only two parties, the LDP and the Japan Communist Party, remained of the nine that had existed in the summer of 1993.

How has the shift from LDP dominance to coalition governments affected the policy-making process? What factors brought about these political changes and power shuffles? The party system change and the coalition governments in the 1990s forced political scientists to reconsider the views on Japanese politics developed under LDP dominance, and to reconstruct the theoretical framework of Japanese politics.

In this book, seven political scientists present in-depth analyses of power shuffles and policy-making processes in Japan in the 1990s. The first three chapters offer case studies of policy making under coalition governments.

Chapter 1 discusses the establishment of long-term health care insurance for the elderly. Long-term health care insurance for the elderly was originally discussed by scholars and bureaucrats of the Ministry of Health and Welfare in the late 1980s as part of a new welfare vision for an aging society. The Hosokawa coalition government put this plan on its agenda in 1994, and the legislative process was initiated under the three-party coalition. Author Etō Murase Mikiko argues that the "three-party coalition lessened the influence of the LDP *zoku* [Diet members specializing in welfare policy]," whose main role under LDP rule was to act as intermediaries between bureaucrats and pressure groups. This setup had enabled the project team members of the ruling side to be involved in drafting the bill. Another influence on the policy-making process for long-term health care insurance was the involvement of new actors. In addition to the traditional pressure groups in welfare policy (such as the Japan Medical Association and the National Federation of Social Welfare Councils), labor unions, citizens' groups, and municipal governments were part of the process and affected its outcome.

Chapter 2 focuses on administrative reform of public corporations, or quasi-governmental organizations dealing with public finance and business operations. Public corporations had been criticized for their inefficiency and for interfering with private business activities, but reforms of those organizations were stymied by bureaucrats who had jurisdiction over them. Tatebayashi Masahiko argues that Murayama's three-party coalition put this issue on its agenda and achieved "more successful" reforms than the LDP government had in the early 1990s. At the time of formation of the coalition with the LDP, their former rival, the SDPJ and Sakigake needed a rationale for allying with the LDP. Sakigake was enthusiastic about reform and the SDPJ lent its support. Public-sector labor unions supporting the SDPJ could not help dampening their criticism of the government, because the SDPJ held the prime ministership. The LDP, which had defended the bureaucracy during its 38-years rule, had seen its ties with bureaucrats weaken during the ten months the party belonged to the opposition ranks. These changes under the three-party coalition "had a certain impact on the reform process."

Chapter 3 reviews telecommunications policy undertaken in tandem with the consideration of issues concerning the privatization and deregulation of the telecom giant Nippon Telegraph and Telephone Public Corporation (Denden-kōsha). Japan's three major public corporations, including Denden-kōsha, were privatized by the Nakasone LDP government in the mid-1980s. Although the other two public corporations were downsized or divided at the time of privatization, Denden-kōsha was privatized into Nippon Telegraph and Telephone Corporation (NTT) as a whole on condition that a review of its structure be undertaken within five years. Thus, NTT became the largest private company in Japan. In 1990, a final decision on NTT's structure was deferred another five years, causing the issue to be reviewed under the three-party coalition. Toyonaga Ikuko explains how NTT's trade union, which had exerted strong influence on the government in the late 1980s, became "marginalized" because Rengō (Japanese Trade Union Confederation), the new national center of trade unions, was weakened by the split of its supporting parties, the SDPJ and the DSP (later the NFP), between the government and the opposition after June 1994. Although the final decision on the structure of NTT was postponed again until after the 1996 Lower House election, the LDP government decided at the end of 1996 that NTT should be divided into three companies.

Chapter 4 considers the degree of similarity and difference among the policy-making processes of the LDP government and those of the various coalition governments. Decision making under the LDP government is characterized as bottom-up decision making because subcommittees of the committees in the party's Policy Research Council were monopolized by *zoku* members since the 1980s. Decision making under the Hosokawa eight-party coalition government, in contrast, relied on the leadership of Ozawa Ichirō, the key person behind the formation of the non-LDP coalition in the summer of 1993. The Hosokawa government succeeded where the LDP had failed in maneuvering the controversial political reform bill through the Diet. Ozawa's high-handed, top-down style of decision making, however, caused friction among the eight coalition partners, especially between the SDPJ and Sakigake. Nonaka Naoto argues that this antagonism motivated the formation of the SDPJ-Sakigake-LDP coalition that replaced the non-LDP coalition in June 1994. The Murayama government introduced the bottom-up style of policy making, by emphasizing the principle of "politics by consensus." It was "an effective return to how the LDP had governed under one-party dominance" before 1993.

Chapters 5 through 7 discuss the structural change in Japanese politics during the 1970s and 1980s that acted as the catalyst for the collapse of one-party dominance and party system change in the 1990s. In chapter 5 I present the backdrop to the political events of the last decade of the century by examining the impact of voter preference on party realignment and policy conflict from the 1970s to the present. The party system change that occurred in Japan after 1993 was not based on a bias alteration by a large segment of the population, or what is referred to as "party realignment" in political science. (In this book, we use the term political realignment or party system change, instead of party realignment, to explain the political change in Japan in the 1990s.) Three political parties newly founded in the early 1990s—the JNP, the JRP, and Sakigake—were led by three key figures, Hosokawa, Ozawa, and Takemura Masayoshi, respectively. They intended to "induce party realignment from the top" by offering their new policy packages with a clear axis of policy conflicts vis-à-vis other parties. The new stable left-right scale, however, failed to replace the traditional left-right scale between the LDP and the JSP, and these parties could not gain and stabilize support through new policy packages.

Chapter 6 discusses two decades of SDPJ structural reform, including the era before 1991 when the SDPJ was called the JSP. The JSP/SDPJ had a long tradition of intraparty cleavage between the leftists and the rightists since the 1950s, and the leftist groups were dominant within the party because of their strong influence in local chapters. As such, Marxism and constitutional pacifism deeply affected the JSP's policies until the early 1980s. Shinkawa Toshimitsu argues that the transformative process of overcoming the influence of Marxism was a consequence not of the JSP/SDPJ's own efforts for party reform, but of the labor unions' rightward shift in the mid-1980s. The party's adherence to "constitutional pacifism" was rather strengthened by the popular Chairperson Doi Takako in the early 1990s, but in 1994 the SDPJ suddenly abandoned constitutional pacifism when its chairman, Murayama, was named prime minister. The SDPJ's swing to the right, however, led to its splintering and weakening into a minor party in 1996.

Chapter 7 argues that new actors in Japanese politics facilitated the party system changes in the 1990s. Wada Shūichi focuses on two new types of actors: younger-generation politicians of the LDP and the JSP/SDPJ who were first elected to the Diet in 1986 and 1990, and forces raised outside the political establishment. Young politicians who entered politics after the mid-1980s were relatively free from traditional factions or ideological values. When faced with the criticism of the electorate over political scandals, they responded positively concerning political reforms. Forces outside the political establishment, including Rengō, advisory groups such as the Nongovernmental Ad Hoc Council for Political Reform, and the JNP (whose members were all newcomers to the Diet), hoped to influence the established political parties by calling for political reforms. Cooperation between these outside forces and the younger generation politicians on political reform caused discord within the established political parties. These movements weakened the traditional structure of the LDP and the SDPJ, thus leading to political change in the 1990s.

In the fall of 1999, another type of coalition government emerged between the LDP, the LP, and Kōmeitō. This new coalition is very powerful, holding 357 of the 500 seats in the Lower House. The second Lower House election under the new electoral system will be contested before October 2000. It is expected that retrospective voting rather than issue voting will characterize the election, as people will use their ballots to convey their judgement of the policy achievements of this new three-party coalition. Since the collapse of one-party dominance, voters' choices have shifted radically in every national election. In this context, politics in Japan is still in the process of "de-alignment" from the voting pattern under one-party dominance, and it could be difficult for a stable party system to emerge under the new electoral system.

Abbreviations

Denden-kōsha   Nippon Telegraph and Telephone Public Corporation
Dōmei   Japan Confederation of Labor
DPJ   Democratic Party of Japan
DSP   Democratic Socialist Party
EHI   Employee Health Insurance
IMF-JC   International Metal Workers' Federation–Japan Council
Jichirō   All Japan Prefectural and Municipal Workers' Union
JCP   Japan Communist Party
JMA   Japan Medical Association
JNP   Japan New Party
JNR   Japanese National Railways
JRP   Japan Renewal Party
JSP   Japan Socialist Party
Keidanren   Japan Federation of Economic Organizations
KDD   Kokusai Denshin Denwa Co., Ltd.
Kokurō   National Railway Workers' Union
LAFGO   Labor Federation of Government Related Organizations
LDP   Liberal Democratic Party
LP   Liberal Party
NFP   New Frontier Party
NHI   National Health Insurance
NLC   New Liberal Club
NTT   Nippon Telegraph and Telephone Corporation
OECF   Overseas Economic Cooperation Fund
Rengō   Japanese Trade Union Confederation
SCAP   Supreme Commander for Allied Powers
SDF   Self-Defense Forces
SDP   Social Democratic Party

SDPJ   Social Democratic Party of Japan
Second Rinchō   Second Provisional Commission on Administrative Reform
Sōhyō   General Council of Trade Unions of Japan
Tekkō Rōren   Japan Federation of Steel Workers' Unions
YKK   Yamasaki Taku, Koizumi Shin'ichirō, and Katō Kōichi
Zendentsū   All-Japan Telecommunications Workers' Union
Zenrōkyō   National Liaison Conference of Trade Unions

Power Shuffles and Policy Processes

The Establishment of Long-term Care Insurance

Etō Murase Mikiko

WELFARE and health care services for the frail or disabled elderly have been increasingly important items on the social policy agendas of governments in the developed countries since the 1980s (Organization for Economic Cooperation and Development [OECD] 1996, 13). Two distinct models emerged in Europe. In Scandinavia, welfare services, including universal health care, are funded mainly from general tax revenues and provided mainly by the state, whereas Germany, after lengthy debate, enacted a social insurance law in 1994 to provide long-term care for the frail elderly (OECD 1996, 247–259, 261–277).

The aging of Japan's population began two decades later than in Europe and North America, but is now extremely rapid. In the 1990s, the percentage of the total population comprised of the elderly—those 65 and older—has been comparable to that of the West. According to projections, by 2010 the elderly ratio of Japan's population will be the highest in the world. Three reasons are cited: life expectancy, already the world's longest, continues to lengthen; the birthrate is expected to decline; and the so-called baby boom generation, people born immediately after World War II, will become elderly about that year.

The Japanese public is fearful of heavy burdens in the future. Caring for elderly family members is already a hardship for many, an obligation vividly described in the media as a "nursing hell."

Nursing and other care services for the frail elderly in Japan have been provided mainly by family members, particularly women, in traditionally structured three-generation households. In the late 1970s, however, the prolonged recession caused by the oil crisis made welfare reform an important political issue. The government advocated a "Japanese-style welfare society" centered on families and local communities. The family was to retain major responsibility for the elderly.

By the mid-1980s, it was apparent that due to urbanization and other demographic shifts families would no longer be capable of providing care by themselves. Moreover, the large number of bedridden elderly who were in hospitals on a long-term basis, because no other institutions could provide adequate care, had driven up medical expenditures. How to achieve cost containment and provide additional facilities was the policy dilemma. In the early 1990s, the government responded with a new social service system to provide care for the elderly.

A long-term care insurance system for the elderly was first proposed by the eight-party Hosokawa Morihiro coalition government, which ended the Liberal Democratic Party's (LDP) monopoly on power in August 1993. The following coalition governments attempted to enact a bill: Hata Tsutomu's six-party coalition, and the Murayama Tomiichi and Hashimoto Ryūtarō governments, both composed of the LDP, the Social Democratic Party of Japan (SDPJ), and the New Party Sakigake (*sakigake* means "pioneer"). I shall describe the policy-making process in the health and welfare system during these three coalition regimes.

Policy making in the coalition governments is suitable for a case study. According to Japanese political scientists, health and welfare policy in the LDP era (1955–1993) was shaped in the ruling party by Diet members who specialized in this area, the *kōsei zoku*, or welfare experts (Inoguchi and Iwai 1987, 194–198; Nakano 1997, 81–85). This chapter compares the changes and continuities in health and welfare policy making during the coalition governments with previous LDP administrations. Among the questions addressed are: Were the coalition governments able to change long-established patterns and, if so, to what extent? Has the Japanese-style welfare trumpeted in the 1970s given way to a new model? The outlook for the new scheme enacted in 1997 will be discussed.

The analysis will examine the relevant political events at each stage of the policy process: agenda-setting, preparation of a draft bill, compromises in the proposal and consideration of the bill, and abandonment of the bill. Although I found no outstanding innovations in the policy process under the coalition governments, there were significant changes in the types of actors and how they interacted. In addition, the social insurance system created a new perspective in Japan on welfare for the elderly.

Systematic social welfare services for the elderly were established in 1963 by the Welfare Law for the Aged, which initiated free annual health examinations and provided for accommodations at nursing homes and low-fee homes for elderly people who could not remain at home because of their socioeconomic circumstances or their physical or mental condition.

In 1973, a free medical care system for those 70 and above replaced the copayment arrangement where medical costs were shared by patients and the national and local governments. The program boosted governmental spending on medical care for the elderly, making it a major portion of total medical expenditures.

Free medical care, however, was besieged by macroeconomic and demographic developments. The first oil crisis in 1973 triggered a recession and a fall in government revenues. The elderly population began to increase quickly, raising the demand for welfare services. Bureaucrats at the Ministry of Health and Welfare began to question the efficacy of continuing the free system and finally decided to abandon it. They convinced the LDP, which in June 1980 won control of both the House of Councillors (Upper House) and the House of Representatives (Lower House), that the system had to be altered (Campbell 1992, 282–300).

In 1982, the LDP-controlled Diet enacted the Health Care for the Aged Law. The legislation had three major features (Etō 1995, 102–103). First, free medical care was abolished, replaced by a copayment system that required beneficiaries to bear a certain amount of the expenses of medical services and was expected to make the elderly more aware of the costs of medical attention.

Second, in order to reduce the funds taken from general revenues to subsidize medical care for the elderly, the act allocated the costs among Japan's three health insurance systems: Employee Health Insurance (EHI) for most private-sector workers, Mutual Assistance Associations for employees of central and local governments, and National Health Insurance (NHI) for self-employed workers, farmers, and retired employees. EHI programs are of two types: government-managed programs for employees of small and medium-sized companies, and programs managed by private health insurance associations that cover employees of large companies. Through this redistribution pool the three systems pay 70 percent of the total medical expenditures for the elderly (the amount above the copayment), the central government subsidizes 20 percent, and prefectural and municipal governments pay the rest.

Third, the 1982 act created home health care services for the elderly, including visiting nurses, and called for health facilities to release elderly patients as soon as possible for continuing care at their own homes.

In late 1988, the Takeshita Noboru administration, claiming that additional revenue was needed for an aging society, passed a 3 percent consumption tax that went into effect on April 1, 1989. Angry voters turned against the LDP in the July Upper House election, and the Japan Socialist Party (the name of the SDPJ until 1991), which had fought the tax, substantially increased its seats.

To show the electorate how the money would be used and to justify the new tax, in December 1989 the LDP government announced a "Ten Year Strategy on Health and Welfare for the Elderly," known as the "Gold Plan," with an estimated total budget of ¥360 billion. Designed to improve the social infrastructure of welfare services for the elderly, the Gold Plan set specific goals to be attained by 1999. For example, it promised 100,000 home helpers and 240,000 beds in special nursing homes that would provide long-term care (Campbell 1992, 243–247).

The Health Ministry decided to delegate implementation of the Gold Plan to municipalities. The national government was responsible for all aspects of social welfare, from conception to implementation, until the 1980s, when responsibility was decentralized and municipalities were authorized to implement social welfare services. In order to achieve the Gold Plan's objectives, the ministry required each local authority to prepare a plan for health and social services for the elderly.

Despite the expansion of the programs for frail old people from the 1960s, there was widespread dissatisfaction with the system. Many elderly who fell sick or were disabled became bedridden because adequate care was unavailable, and the burden fell on their families. The welfare needs of the elderly had far outstripped the supply of services and trained personnel. For example, there were long waiting lists for admission to nursing homes.

Japan was aging so rapidly that the provision of services could not keep pace. More significantly, eligibility for welfare services was based on a means test that was supposed to balance demand for services with available supply. Municipal authorities decided who received services according to specified criteria, such as ability to perform routine activities, individual or family income, and household composition. Low-income elderly persons living alone had priority. The elderly with income above a certain level who lived with their family, especially if there were female members, found it difficult to qualify for welfare services, even if they were seriously disabled. But the frail or disabled old are not found only in the low-income bracket; in fact, most are in the middle-income range (Miura 1990, 11).

The welfare system had a built-in incentive for municipal authorities to suppress demand for services artificially. Actual need was rising but supply was inadequate, so they used eligibility standards to set welfare levels almost arbitrarily (Yashiro 1997, 8–9). While municipal officials limited demand to the supply of welfare services, nonprofit welfare organizations, many affiliated with religious organizations, also provided services. In many cases, municipalities subsidized providers to make services available.

POWERFUL PARTNERS

The policy community in Japan for health and welfare issues consists of Health Ministry bureaucrats, expert Diet members, and pressure groups.[1] John C. Campbell focused on bureaucrats in his study of the political process and aging policy, calling them the most important policy sponsors in most health and welfare policy changes (1992, 383–390). By contrast, Nakano Minoru, who analyzed policy making in terms of influence relationships among the main participants, emphasized the role of the health and welfare *zoku* members (1997, 65, 82–83).

Social policy making can be divided into two patterns depending on the issue and participants, according to Nakano. He argues that medical and welfare policies differ from pension policy. Various pressure groups, such as the Japan Medical Association (JMA), the Health

Insurance Association Union, and the National Federation of Social Welfare Councils, are involved in the former. In the case of pension policy, there are no intermediate groups and the role of special interests is not so evident. This distinction is applicable to other policy areas (Nakano 1997, 14–15).

Focusing on the interaction between politicians and bureaucrats, Nakano categorizes initiatives by *zoku* members as "interest politics." Bureaucratic initiatives, from agenda-setting to decision making in the Diet, are "technocrat politics."

Because of the sharp clash of interests in health and welfare affairs, Diet members representing pressure groups exercise a compelling influence on the policy process, including making compromises. Powerful organizations like JMA speak for themselves, but Diet members usually take the lead (Nakano 1997, 14–15).

The long-term care insurance system proposed in recent years was a new policy, not merely a revision of existing programs, and brought a variety of pressure groups with complicated relationships into the policy-formulation process. This makes it an interesting example of how the initiatives by *zoku* members differed under the coalition governments from those in LDP administrations.

Generally, during the LDP era bureaucrats in the Health Ministry set the policy agenda, with a few notable exceptions, such as the free medical care system for the elderly mentioned above (Campbell 1992, 144–153). In the early decades of LDP rule, the bureaucratic cognitive mode that focuses on a specific problem usually concentrated on how to secure equity by reducing benefit differentials, a problem that resulted from the variety of social insurance systems. In the 1980s, however, bureaucrats turned their attention to ways of ensuring stable insurance funding despite budgetary deficits (Hayakawa 1991, 153).

The usual procedure was for officials of the relevant bureau to draft a bill which was then considered by the appropriate advisory council (*shingikai*) in each ministry. After approval by the council, the draft was sent to the LDP's Policy Research Council where Diet members of the Social Affairs Division, the *kōsei zoku*, attempted to balance the interests of pressure groups and ministries. Once the LDP had agreed on the text, Health Ministry officials checked it and prepared a bill that was submitted to the Diet upon approval by the cabinet (Iwai 1988, 57–64).

While the bill was in committee in the Diet, *zoku* members

negotiated with the opposition parties and pressure groups to forge compromises and secure prompt passage. They also took the lead in revising the bill, though the process changed over time. In the 1970s, Diet members representing special interests simply pushed the Health Ministry for certain changes; the ministry's initial draft was often substantially rewritten. In the 1980s, however, they tended to share the same outlook on issues as the bureaucrats and urged pressure groups to make concessions, so drafts were often enacted with a minimum of revisions.

Writing of the leading LDP *zoku* members in the 1980s, Ōtake Hideo says they came to share the same broad national perspective as the bureaucrats, were very knowledgeable about technical details, and attained great influence and power. Ōtake calls this phenomenon the "technocratization of *zoku* members" and observes that, rising above local pressures and popular stands, they accepted a "logic of governance" as members of the party responsible for the nation (1994, 159).

In early 1994, the Hosokawa administration proposed a social insurance plan that added the responsibility of society as a whole to that of the family for care of the frail elderly. The proposal was made at the agenda-setting stage of the policy-making cycle, a stage I will describe in the section "Policy Streams" with the aid of John W. Kingdon's "revised garbage-can model." According to this model, the national agenda gets set by three process streams—problems, policies, and politics—flowing through the system (Kingdon 1984, 92–94).

CARING FOR THE ELDERLY

As noted above, an important problem in welfare for the elderly was eligibility based on a means test. Welfare bureaucrats and scholars had addressed the issue in the early 1970s. For example, in January 1971 the National Social Welfare Council submitted a report to the Health and Welfare Ministry urging revision of the no-fee system at welfare facilities for the elderly. The council pointed out the inequity between recipients of social welfare services in facilities on the one hand and the frail elderly being cared for at home on the other. The former received complete services paid for by the government; the latter were eligible for only a few, such as home helpers for a limited time per week.

From the mid-1970s, the concept of a Japanese-style welfare society emerged. Influenced by both neoconservatism and neoliberalism, it was posited on individual self-reliance and family and community solidarity, unlike the bureaucratic big-government programs of the West. The government reformed the social welfare system, requiring copayments by beneficiaries according to income. This was feasible because improved pension benefits had increased the elderly's ability to pay.

In 1980, there were several scandals involving for-profit welfare service providers, including the bankruptcy of a retirement home and the accidental death of a baby at a day-care center. For-profit facilities were not regulated under the 1951 Act for Social Welfare Institutions, and these incidents drew attention to shortcomings in the welfare system (Miura 1982, 14–15).

Ministry bureaucrats and some scholars also began to favor a universal and inclusive system that would cover both the poor and the middle class. They hoped the joint deliberations by the National Social Welfare Council, the Welfare Council for the Disabled, and the National Children's Welfare Council that began in January 1986 would result in revision of the eligibility criteria. Although the organizations studied the question for three years, the means test was maintained due to strong support by social welfare agencies and academic experts (Komuro 1989, 28–29). Why did these groups endorse the existing structure? They believed the system clearly prescribed the government's responsibility and the rights of beneficiaries, and that regulatory intervention could assure the quality of services (Furukawa 1997, 79–80).

Furthermore, welfare programs faced budgetary cutbacks. In December 1980, Prime Minister Suzuki Zenkō appointed the Second Provisional Commission on Administrative Reform (Second Rinchō), which called for financial restructuring without a tax increase, and the Ministry of Finance ordered each ministry to curtail spending. The Health and Welfare Ministry was obliged to submit a "minus ceiling" budget request in 1982 that cut outlays below the previous year. The ministry was hard pressed: Social programs included certain automatic increases and the aging of the population and higher personnel costs and prices overall were pushing up expenditures. The ministry skirted the immediate crisis by postponing the contribution to the national pension system and limiting medical expenditures. There was a limit to deferred payments and accounting gimmicks, however, and the bureaucrats began to seek new revenue sources. From late 1985 through early 1986, for instance, they created a specific account for the social security budget to separate it from the General Account allocation and avoid interference by the Finance Ministry (Yoshimura 1986, 17).

Regardless of the budgetary crunch, medical costs for the elderly soared in the 1980s. The common experience of developed countries is that as the population ages the number of frail elderly rises, which usually translates into higher medical expenditures. However, if facilities for the elderly are divided by functions into acute care and long-term care, medical costs can be lowered. Patients with acute problems are treated in hospitals and those with chronic conditions are cared for in nursing homes or in their own homes. Scandinavian countries have successfully cut medical expenditure this way (OECD 1995, 9; 1996, 165–176), and Germany hopes to achieve similar savings with its new long-term care insurance system (Alber 1996, 261–278).

In Japan, because of the shortage of facilities providing long-term care, such as nursing homes and home-care services, elderly patients with chronic illnesses who do not require acute treatment remain in hospitals for long periods. Referred to as "social hospitalization," this amounts to a waste of medical expenditures. The Health Ministry position was that "elderly persons with chronic conditions should not be kept in hospitals" (Okamitsu 1987, 6).

Pressure to reduce costs also came from other corners. The EHI associations, forced to contribute a great amount toward the medical costs of the elderly under the cross-subsidization scheme established in 1982, wanted relief. Corporations, which pay half the contribution for their employees, lobbied for reform on the grounds that rising contributions were an untenable financial burden. The Federation of National Health Insurance Associations and major business organizations like Keidanren (Japan Federation of Economic Organizations) demanded a new system that would cover medical costs for the elderly from public funds (Shakai Keizai Kokumin Kaigi 1988; Nikkeiren, Rengō, and Kemporen 1990, 27).

The cross-subsidization solution had reduced national expenditures for the elderly; it was impossible to restore the pre-1982 system unless the Finance Ministry relaxed its policy of ordering ministries to slash requests each year, which was not to be expected. But lowering costs would ease criticism of the cross-subsidization system. Health

Ministry bureaucrats recognized that cost containment required less occupancy of hospital beds by the elderly, which in turn meant a substantial expansion of welfare services, including those by for-profit suppliers. A new system was needed.

POLICY STREAMS

Kingdon notes that "The separate streams of problems, policies, and politics come together at certain critical times. Solutions become joined to problems, and both of them are joined to favorable political forces. This coupling is most likely when a policy window—an opportunity to push pet proposals or one's conceptions of problems—is open" (1984, 204). This coupling occurred in the agenda-setting process for a long-term care insurance system in Japan. Although the problems were clear, there were many policy streams, and social insurance was chosen from among several possible solutions.

The Health Ministry bureaucracy and social policy experts were well aware of the eligibility system's inadequacies. There was no formal policy debate. Instead, various alternatives were informally considered, and in the mid-1980s welfare bureaucrats and scholars began research on the long-term care insurance system under study in Germany (Tochimoto 1995, 28). A number of young bureaucrats, protégés of top-level ministry officials, organized a policy study group that in 1988 made public its findings in "A Proposal for a New System of Health and Welfare Administration in the Reform Period." The report recommended comprehensive home care programs funded by social insurance and a new service delivery format based on freedom of choice to replace the eligibility system.

At the time, some Health Ministry bureaucrats supported the Scandinavian model of funding health services from general taxation.[2] However, they concluded that the Scandinavian pattern was not feasible because municipal authorities and nonprofit organizations would object and the public would resist a tax increase.

Following the recommendations on deregulation of the Second Rinchō, the Nakàsone Yasuhiro administration privatized the Japanese National Railways, Nippon Telegraph and Telephone Public Corporation, and the Japan Tobacco and Salt Public Corporation. The Health Ministry followed by organizing the Promotion and Guidance Office on Private Services for the Elderly to encourage private firms to provide such services as home care and housekeeping. In 1985, life insurance companies began to market new policies that covered the cost for care if a person became mentally disordered or bedridden (Hori 1994, 12–17). Pro-deregulation bureaucrats endorsed private insurance for nursing expenses as an alternative to the publicly funded eligibility system (Niki 1995, 16).

Yet social insurance brings funds to the Health Ministry's coffers, enlarging its role and importance in the government and society at large. Commercial insurance leaves the money in the private sector and does not aggrandize bureaucratic interests. Also, under a public system, social insurance funds are allocated to a specific account separate from General Account funds and are not subject to strict review by the Finance Ministry. In the late 1980s, the Health Ministry's preference for public insurance was further strengthened by academic experts who said private insurance would only be effective with a mixed infrastructure of service suppliers. Private care was a supplement to public services, not a substitute for them (Miyajima 1994, 13–14). Ministry bureaucrats concluded that the government should fund welfare services for the aged that private companies would deliver (Zenkoku Shakai Fukushi Kyōgikai and Shakai Fukushi Kenkyū Jōhō Sentā, eds. 1989, 21–160).

From about 1987, many scholars and bureaucrats published articles on long-term care insurance. Two young officials advocated nursing insurance in a journal affiliated with the Health Ministry (Nishikawa 1987; Sawamura 1988) and Yamazaki Yasuhiko (1988), a prominent academic authority and a member of a Health Ministry advisory council, called nursing insurance the new frontier of social insurance. Such writings focused attention on long-term care insurance as the best solution.

In 1992, key members of ministry sections concerned with the elderly formed an informal working group to draw up an insurance system (Nihon Ishikai Sōgō Seisaku Kenkyū Kikō 1997, 12–13). The group's report, unofficially published, outlined a new system and listed potential problems such as insurance management and service delivery. According to Okamitsu Nobuharu, then director of the Department of Health and Welfare for the Elderly, after the younger bureaucrats presented their ideas members joined in a free-wheeling discussion (Kōseishō Daijin Kambō Rōjin Hoken Fukushi-bu 1992). The young bureaucrats were members of the policy study group mentioned earlier.

TAX REFORM

The policy window for long-term care insurance was opened when political streams converged. In our case they were a series of tax measures, from the 1989 consumption tax to the national welfare tax broached in 1994 by the Hosokawa administration.

As we have seen, the consumption tax led to the Gold Plan, which obligated municipalities to prepare health and welfare plans for the elderly. Another spillover effect was that latent welfare demands surfaced. Municipal service goals exceeded Health Ministry estimates in the Gold Plan. It called for 100,000 home helpers, for instance, but the municipalities wanted 170,000. Such disparities reinforced the ministry's perception that welfare services would require enormous funding.

A lesson from the consumption tax experience was that new levies could be justified in the name of welfare. The LDP and the Finance Ministry realized that the public would swallow a tax hike if it was told the money was for welfare purposes.

The final tap that opened the window was Prime Minister Hosokawa's proposal for a national welfare tax on February 3, 1994. The idea was formulated secretly by Ozawa Ichirō, secretary-general of the Japan Renewal Party (JRP), Ichikawa Yūichi, secretary-general of the Kōmeitō (Clean Government Party), and a few Finance Ministry bureaucrats. They persuaded Hosokawa that the government needed additional revenues. The governing coalition—the cabinet came from eight political parties—was not consulted. Takemura Masayoshi, leader of the New Party Sakigake and cabinet spokesperson, was not even informed (Katō 1997, 272–274). The cabal's main objective was to raise the consumption tax from 3 percent to 7 percent. Hosokawa called the hike a "welfare tax" but gave no indication how the money would be used. Questioned on this point by a journalist, the prime minister glibly responded that the health minister would elaborate on the welfare aspects.[3]

Enter the Welfare Vision Discussion Group, a private advisory body that had just been appointed to help Health Minister Ōuchi Keigo (Nihon Keizai Shimbun-sha 1994, 93). Each new minister has a panel of experts whom he can call upon for assistance, a perquisite of office that shows a new man is at the helm. Suddenly the group had the important task of justifying a 7 percent consumption tax rate. Hosokawa's press conference remark also gave Health Ministry bureaucrats a good opportunity to push the elderly up the policy agenda.

When other parties in the coalition government attacked Hosokawa's proposal on procedural grounds, it was immediately withdrawn. Nevertheless, the Welfare Vision Discussion Group, its mandate changed from rationalizing a tax increase to designing a grand plan for an aging society, went ahead with its work. The group's report, "A Welfare Vision for the Twenty-First Century," issued in March 1994, advocated socialized care for the elderly. In effect, the coalition government had in principle approved social insurance. Furthermore, "A Welfare Vision" confirmed the need to raise the consumption tax and called for a new Gold Plan to finance municipal health and welfare plans. Health Ministry bureaucrats had incorporated their ideas on welfare reform into the report.

THREE-PARTY COALITION GOVERNMENTS

The policy-making process examined below includes preparation of a draft bill for long-term care insurance, the struggles within the coalition over submission of the bill to the Diet, and abandonment of the bill. The process extended from the Murayama administration to the first Hashimoto cabinet under the three-party coalition formed by the LDP, the SDPJ, and Sakigake.

In April 1994, immediately after "A Welfare Vision" was made public, the Health Ministry organized a task force on elderly care measures, led by the vice-minister, that completed a long-term care insurance draft bill. In July 1994, the ministry appointed a Study Group on Care and Self-reliance for the Elderly that included experts on social policy and elderly care and directed it to make suggestions on socialized care. It should be noted that the ministry had already chosen social insurance. The scholars and experts were assembled to lend their authority and prestige to the bureaucrats' preferences. Not surprisingly, the group's report in December 1994 recommended what the ministry wanted.

A social insurance system for long-term care had already been proposed two months earlier in a report by the Committee for the Future of Social Security, a subgroup of the Social Security Systems Deliberation

Council. The council prepares reports for the prime minister and has substantial influence on decision making in the Health Ministry: the Health Ministry is not subordinate to the council, however. The two are usually in agreement on policy, and the council occasionally provides ideological support for the ministry. In this instance, too, the council endorsed the ministry's position.

In February 1995, the Health Ministry, having attained support for a social insurance system, opened discussions of a draft bill in the Council on Health and Welfare for the Elderly (hereafter the Elderly Health Council). The coalition government did not take up the issue, however. Conservative LDP members, admirers of the patriarchal family system—"a woman's place is in the home taking care of her family"—were not very interested in such insurance (Ikeda 1996, 63). The SDPJ, having backed a plan in 1990 for nursing care funded by tax revenues, hesitated to support social insurance. Yet no LDP politician opposed the objectives, which included containment of medical costs, a party goal. Nor were SDPJ politicians hostile to a plan that envisioned society sharing care for the elderly, a socialist tenet. During the LDP era, the ruling party never opposed Health Ministry proposals, largely because they were carefully crafted within the government's political capability. Ministry drafts were customarily revised during the LDP review.[4] The coalition government inherited this approach.[5]

When the Health Ministry conceives a new policy or revamps a current one, standard practice is to consult with the appropriate advisory council. Councils are organized by policy areas, and the draft bill fell under the purview of the Elderly Health Council. Its 26 members were drawn from groups involved in care and welfare services, as well as academicians and other experts in these fields. Among the groups represented were the Japan Medical Association, the Japan Dental Association, the Japan Association of City Mayors, the Federation of National Health Insurance Associations, business groups, and labor unions. Torii Yasuhiko, president of Keio University, was chairman.

The Health Ministry proposals laid before the council had seven key points (Kōseishō Kōreisha Kaigo Taisaku Hombu Jimukyoku 1996, 320–321): (1) financing to be half from social insurance contributions and half from national tax revenues; (2) municipal-level management; (3) premiums to be paid by everyone 20 years of age and older but beneficiaries limited to those 65 and older; (4) employers pay half of an employee's insurance premium; (5) no cash benefits to families caring for frail or disabled members; (6) 10 percent copayments for service costs; and (7) implementation on April 1, 1997.

The ministry intended to complete a draft bill by the end of 1995 and submit it at the ordinary Diet session in 1996. JMA had an enormous stake in the outcome because the bill threatened a constituent interest—the income of small hospitals—and strongly objected to the haste (Nihon Ishikai Sōgō Seisaku Kenkyū Kikō 1997, 23). The ministry was forced to slow down the proceedings.

"Deliberations" in an advisory council are often formalistic; members docilely follow the ministry's scripted scenario. Draft bills are usually approved in seven to ten sessions; a favorable outcome is a foregone conclusion. However, the Elderly Health Council met more than 20 times and carefully considered the seven key features. The ministry still hoped the council would ultimately approve the proposal, albeit with a few members dissenting on some points. Given the April 1996 deadline, the council would have to finish its work no later than December 1995. In fact, disagreements in the council derailed the ministry's timetable.

CONFRONTATION

Four points were particularly contentious: management of the system, minimum ages of the insured and beneficiaries, employer contributions to premiums, and cash benefits to families (Kyōgoku 1997, 26–37, 85–100).

Confrontation was sharpest on who would bear responsibility for running the system. The Japan Association of City Mayors, the National Association of Towns and Villages, and the Federation of National Health Insurance Associations were against local management. Their concern was twofold. First, fear that inadequate funding —subsidies—might force municipalities to cover the shortfall, as had occurred with national health insurance. Contributions to NHI are far less than expenditures because the enrollees have high rates of illness. In most municipalities the program is in the red and local governments have to make up the deficit. The Health Ministry proposal included a certain amount of subsidies, as are provided for NHI. Yet the mayors were afraid the insurance system would turn into crippling local deficits (Kōteki Kaigo Hoken Seido Kenkyūkai 1996a, 32).

Second, the mayors doubted their jurisdictions, so short on service infrastructure, could handle the anticipated wave of applications for various kinds of help. Enrollees were expected to demand services as a legal right as soon as the law took effect (Ikeda 1996, 64).

Ministry bureaucrats went through the motions of negotiating, suggesting management by the national government or a third party, but they insisted accessibility for citizens made local governments the logical entities to administer welfare. A separate program for the elderly would help to reduce the NHI deficits, the ministry said, and long-term care insurance should be seen as part of a series of reforms to improve health insurance finances.

The Elderly Health Council took up the issue of inequity between premium payers and beneficiaries in late 1995.[6] The Federation of National Health Insurance Associations and business groups, which wanted to reduce employer contributions, objected to premium payments from age 20 (Mizuno 1997, 8). Why should everybody be obligated to share costs for services they would not receive, the argument went, since not everyone would become bedridden or mentally incompetent (Ikeda 1996, 65).

The ministry refused to budge. The insurance scheme was designed to reduce medical expenditures for the elderly while also creating a new welfare system for an aging society. If only those 65 and older paid in, premium revenue would be wholly inadequate. Conversely, if frail people below 65 were entitled to benefits, the system would have been skewed completely away from the ministry's policy objective.

Related to eligibility was the question of employers paying part of employees' premiums. Management groups insisted that companies should not have to share the costs of caring for retired employees (Takanashi 1997, 10), and the Federation of National Health Insurance Associations agreed. Both had initially supported a long-term care insurance system because lower expenditures for the elderly would reduce their contributions,[7] but now the ministry plan entailed additional payments.

Rengō (Japanese Trade Union Confederation) took a neutral position on employer obligations.[8] Composed of companywide unions whose health insurance programs are based at each firm, the federation could not reach a consensus and just embraced the lofty principle that long-term care insurance should improve workers' lives.

Mayors opposed the Health Ministry's stricture against cash benefits for families providing care (Naruke 1997, 12), claiming it was contradictory to pay an outsider but not a relative who performed the same acts. The JMA agreed, citing the German system that permits cash allowances to the family. The underlying reason they sided with the mayors was the expectation that family members would have to fill the gap in trained care workers.

Female members of the Elderly Health Council led by Higuchi Keiko argued against cash allowances, convinced that such payments would keep elderly care a family responsibility, with women still the primary caregivers, and impede improvement of professional services (Kōteki Kaigo Hoken Seido Kenkyūkai 1996b, 35). The Health Ministry also saw payments as a barrier to development of a service infrastructure.

These conflicts over the draft bill split the Elderly Health Council into three factions. Faction A, comprised of scholars, women, and labor union representatives, basically favored the ministry draft with amendments, though they disagreed among themselves on some issues. They wanted socialized care for the elderly established as soon as possible. It should be borne in mind that the academic experts on the council would not have been chosen if their views differed from those of the bureaucracy, particularly the Health Ministry (Kusano 1995, 195–217). The labor unions, notably Jichirō (All-Japan Prefectural and Municipal Workers' Union), were especially important in this faction.

Jichirō, a national federation of unions for municipal and prefectural government employees, initially opposed social insurance. Many local welfare officials and care workers believed the eligibility system funded by tax revenues effectively protected the rights of their clients, whereas a new scheme might shortchange the poor (Hori 1994, 16). Discussion in the Elderly Health Council was premised on support for a social insurance system; its fundamental suitability was not subject to debate. Nonetheless, in the arena of public opinion the social insurance model was challenged by the Scandinavian model.

Jichirō unions were also concerned that long-term care insurance might lead to municipal deficits as national health insurance had. Nevertheless, the federation approved a social insurance system at its general meeting in May 1995, an about-face primarily inspired by loyalty to the Murayama administration, which was sponsoring the bill.[9] Not only had Jichirō unions long supported the SDPJ, but Prime Minister Murayama, chairman of the party, was a former member of the federation's Ōita prefectural branch.[10]

Faction B consisted of the representatives of municipalities, health insurance associations, and business groups. Not opposed to social insurance per se, they lobbied for a bill favorable to their constituencies.

Faction C, the nonprofit welfare organizations and the JMA, neither opposed nor supported the draft. What accounts for this behavior? The Elderly Health Council concentrated on insurance management and finance, matters of little interest to the nonprofit representatives.[11] The JMA was a covert activist that negotiated separately with the ministry. Having already secured its objectives, the JMA refrained from making demands at council meetings.

The JMA represented the interests of physicians who operated small and medium-sized private hospitals. Long-term care insurance was expected to change "social hospitalization"—shift elderly patients not requiring acute care to other facilities. Thus, some JMA members had a huge financial stake in the legislation. Yet the JMA president announced on April 9, 1996, that it "basically supported" long-term care insurance (Tsuboi 1996, 16). The explanation for this anomalous position is that JMA had changed its strategy in the 1980s "from acquisition to defense" (Takahashi 1986, 263), or, in the words of Ikegami and Campbell, "from enlarging the pie to securing vested interests" (1996, 61). Rather than rely on the *zoku* members to revise draft bills, the JMA sought concessions from the bureaucracy at the drafting stage.

In this case, the JMA held twice-weekly meetings with the Health Ministry parallel to the council meetings for a year (Nihon Ishikai Sōgō Seisaku Kenkyū Kikō 1997, 23). The JMA won the ministry's promise that long-term care hospitals used by bedridden elderly patients would be regarded as nursing homes and qualify for benefits under the new system (Ikeda 1996, 63).

Health Ministry plans to gain Diet approval in 1996 and implement the system in April 1997 were foiled when strong opposition to the draft bill prolonged the council meetings into 1996. The ministry had wanted the insurance system to start when the consumption tax rose from 3 percent to 5 percent on April 1, 1997 (Arioka 1995, 14). This was the understanding with the Finance Ministry, which saw long-term care insurance as the key to public acceptance of the tax increase, a lesson learned from the bitter experience with the initial levy in 1988 (Takiue 1995, 17). Social insurance funding was to be covered by premiums and governmental subsidies; the finance bureaucrats wanted to lay the groundwork for a higher consumption tax rate in the future. The Finance Ministry was positioning itself, and the Health Ministry had no choice but to go along. The end of April was the deadline for the Elderly Health Council's report. To spur the council on, ministry bureaucrats issued a detailed analysis on March 15, 1996, of each provision in the draft the council had covered so far.

COALITION DECISION MAKING

The LDP-SDPJ-Sakigake government had a four-tier decision-making structure, with the three parties represented at each level. Controversial issues were first discussed by a project team set up for each ministry, and then taken up by the Policy Coordination Committee composed of two members from each party. Next, issues were referred to the Executive Committee made up of key party members. Final authority rested with the Liaison Committee between the cabinet and the governing parties, the highest decision-making organ, comprised of party leaders (Nakano 1996, 77). The Welfare Project Team corresponded to the LDP's Social Affairs Division in its Policy Research Council, the pivotal group on welfare policy during the party's long hold on power.

Under LDP administrations, Diet members were not supposed to be formally involved until the Health Ministry had finished a draft bill based on an advisory council's report. When the Elderly Health Council's deliberations dragged on, the Welfare Project Team entered the picture. In mid-March 1996, Niwa Yūya, an LDP Diet member long concerned with welfare policy and a former minister of health and welfare, drafted a set of "private" suggestions that the team used in an attempt to achieve a compromise within the council.

Niwa's plan made two key concessions to opponents of the draft bill. First, municipalities would manage the insurance system, but implementation would start with home-care services and institutional services would be phased in as facilities became available. This was to reassure municipal authorities they would not be overwhelmed by demands for nursing home admissions, for example. Second, the age of the insurees was raised to 40 and over, an adjustment favorable to health insurance associations and business. Why from age 40? People at that age, according to the reasoning given, start to face the problem of care for their parents and look ahead to their own senior years.

In early January 1996, Murayama resigned and was replaced by Hashimoto Ryūtarō. The LDP, so experienced in governance, now led the coalition. Called a "potentate" by *zoku* members, Hashimoto had been involved with health and welfare policy since the 1970s, including a stint as minister of health and welfare. This shift in leadership paved the way for LDP initiatives.

Unable to reach a consensus, the Elderly Health Council submitted an inconclusive report, "Establishment of Long-Term Care Insurance for the Elderly: A Summary of Deliberations," to the Health Ministry on April 21, 1996, that merely identified points in dispute and enumerated different opinions. For an advisory body to end in such disarray was very rare.

The Health Ministry, still determined to get the bill through the Diet that session, offered a revised plan for an insurance system, based on Niwa's suggestions, to the Welfare Project Team on May 14. The major provisions were municipal management, insurees would be aged 40 and over, employers pay half of employee's premiums, initial provision of home-care services followed by gradual implementation of institutional services, and no cash payments to family members.

A joint meeting of the Welfare Project Team and the Policy Coordination Committee on June 11 failed to reach an agreement and referred the basic issues back to each party for consideration and decision. The Social Democratic Party (SDP) (formerly the SDPJ, which changed its name on January 19, 1996) and Sakigake agreed to submit the bill to the Diet. The Social Affairs Division of the LDP's Policy Research Council, however, could not reach a decision and delegated the matter to Yamasaki Taku, chairman of the council. On June 13, the council decided to consult with the coalition government's Policy Coordination Committee.

On the afternoon of June 14, the three party representatives in the Policy Coordination Committee—Yamasaki, Itō Shigeru (SDP), and Tokai Kisaburō (Sakigake)—met informally with leading members of the Japan Association of City Mayors and the National Association of Towns and Villages and appealed unsuccessfully for their support of the bill. That evening Yamasaki, Itō, and Tokai conferred with the Welfare Project Team. No consensus was possible, and the stalemate moved to the Executive Committee of the Ruling Parties, where the buck was supposed to stop in the coalition government. On the morning of June 17, the Executive Committee failed to resolve the conflicts. That evening the three parties abandoned efforts to bring the bill to the Diet immediately.

The coalition government was divided over presenting the bill to the Diet, with the SDP and Sakigake in favor and the LDP unenthusiastic (Mochizuki 1997, 169–170). There was a pro-submission group in the LDP, junior Diet members on the Welfare Project Team and others who wanted to continue the three-party coalition, but they were unable to win over senior *zoku* members, and the most influential LDP politicians stayed aloof from the battle. LDP members who were antagonistic to the partnership with the SDP and Sakigake and wanted a coalition with the conservatives in the New Frontier Party (established in December 1994) strongly opposed submission because the other coalition members favored it.

The impending Diet dissolution and general election were also factors. In the new single-seat district system combined with proportional representation introduced in 1994, nearly all Lower House members' districts correspond to municipal jurisdictions. Desirous of mayoral support, many LDP politicians shied away from a bill that would alienate local leaders (Arai 1996, 12).

In contrast, the SDP and Sakigake persistently backed the bill in order to have a tangible accomplishment from participation in the coalition. The SDP was also pressed by Jichirō, which had collaborated with the Health Ministry in drafting the bill, while Sakigake was supporting a member, Kan Naoto, then minister of health and welfare.[12]

CONCLUSION

Did the emergence of coalition governments change the policy-making pattern on welfare? Nakano contends that the LDP pattern continued with some variations in form (1996, 89). It is true that the basic process —set an agenda, draft a bill, and reconcile differences—remained the same. Yet new actors joined the health and policy community and the balance of power shifted.

Before, a few pressure groups, including the JMA and the National Federation of Social Welfare Councils, were dominant. Now, municipal governments, the Health Insurance Association Union, Keidanren, and Jichirō vigorously promoted their agendas, with city mayors and heads of towns and villages especially forceful. Organized labor, a newcomer through Jichirō and Rengō, became deeply involved and supported the Health Ministry.

At the popular level, the Committee of 10,000 Citizens for a Public Care System was organized and encouraged public discussion of a long-term care insurance system. Two influential figures represented the organization. They were Higuchi Keiko, a commentator and member of the Elderly Health Council, and Hotta Tsutomu, a former public prosecutor who had organized a group of welfare volunteers.

What induced these changes in the decision-making process? Marsh and Rhodes point out that policy communities are often a "major source of policy inertia, not innovation" and are "resistant to change." (1992, 261). By the same token, however, a new policy can destabilize a policy community. In Japan, the shift from eligibility criteria to long-term care insurance mobilized new participants.

Jichirō's strong ties with the SDPJ, especially the fact that the party chairman Murayama was prime minister, obligated the labor federation to endorse the legislation. Institutional linkages carried weight. That municipal governments and health insurance associations gained influence at the expense of LDP members was also important.

Furthermore, the Hosokawa administration championed transparency in government proceedings, opening the minutes and records of advisory council meetings to the public. Freedom of information forced ministries to transform the councils from superficial deliberations under bureaucratic control to forums for genuine discussion where interests clashed in full view. The Health Ministry had special cause to modify its behavior and image. Kan, minister of health and welfare in the first Hashimoto cabinet, had taken the lead in investigating and identifying officials who knowingly failed to stop the distribution of blood contaminated with the HIV virus. The emergence of such an unconventional minister curtailed bureaucratic secrecy and arrogance.

Did power shifts in the policy community affect the stages of policy formulation? No basic change was discernible in setting the agenda. Health Ministry bureaucrats perceived the problems in elderly care and seized an opportunity to open the policy window for a long-term care insurance system. According to Campbell, the mass media has played a significant role when the ministry altered policies (1990, 49–74; 1992, 140–144) and also influenced the agenda for a new system. It was not, however, because of human interest stories and television programs on the plight of family members trying to care for elderly relatives, the tales of hardship and sacrifice that put human faces in the issue. Rather, the bureaucrats, who saw spiraling medical expenses as more serious than the burden on families, used the media to advance their policies. They released survey data selectively, for instance, to show public demand for service facilities, and gave journalists reports showing that Japan lagged behind other industrialized countries in care of the elderly. The bureaucracy also retained control of the second stage, preparation of a draft bill.

Substantial changes occurred at the next stage—the reconciliation of interests. The advisory council and the governing parties functioned quite differently from the past.

Advisory councils in the LDP era meekly reviewed ministry proposals; discussion was formalistic, with members deferring to the bureaucracy. Under the coalition governments, however, there were often violent arguments, disputes over crucial points in the draft bill were fully aired, and the confrontations persisted despite intervention by politicians. The final draft of the bill was modeled after Niwa's memorandum and bore little resemblance to the ministry version.

Why did the Elderly Health Council operate so independently? The most obvious factor was that social insurance was a new system that demanded a different working style.[13] This also happened in the legislative process leading to the 1982 Health Care for the Aged Law. Lacking a clear-cut policy, the ministry gave the Social Security Systems Deliberation Council carte blanche to draft the bill (Watanabe 1992, 1,175).

The political inexperience of bureaucrats in the ministry's Headquarters for Elderly Care Measures suffers by comparison with the savvy of officials in the 1980s. At that time, Insurance Bureau Chief Yoshimura Hitoshi and Pension Bureau Chief Yamaguchi Shin'ichirō, both skilled political operators, successfully promoted reform of health insurance in 1984 and the public pension system in 1985, respectively. During the coalition government period under review, the bureaucrats in charge were in their late 30s to early 40s and lacked both knowledge and experience.[14] In effect, they lost control of the Elderly Health Council.

How did the coalition governments affect the advisory council? First, the very fact of a new regime changed its makeup and work style.[15] The presence of former opposition parties and a new party in the government brought new blood into the council. This point is contested by a Health Ministry bureaucrat who denies that the advent of a coalition government affected council appointments. Prior to convening the council, he says, the ministry had contacted the Rengō and Jichirō unions to sound out municipal officers and workers, because the proposed new system involved was such sweeping innovation.¹⁶ Nevertheless, since these unions were long-time supporters of the SDP, how could they have been kept off the council?

The three-party coalition lessened the influence of the LDP *zoku* members in the health field. Their main role had been as intermediaries, mediating between policy-making bodies and pressure groups (Nakano 1997, 81–85). With the LDP reduced to a coalition partner, their influence declined and they had to accommodate others. The Health Ministry gained power over welfare policy at the expense of LDP members. The venue for horse trading and deals among the policy players shifted from the LDP Social Affairs Division to the Elderly Health Council.

Politicians became more involved in policy formulation, for instance, regarding the eligibility of persons under 65. The Welfare Project Team worked on the draft bill at the same time as the Elderly Health Council and had a hand in revising it. According to Arai Satoshi (Sakigake), a member of the Welfare Project Team, the coalition government itself decided on the skeleton of a bill (Arai 1996, 12). Gotō Masanori (SDP) and Kan corroborated Arai's description.¹⁷ All three stressed that politicians were actively involved in the drafting process, a stage bureaucrats once initiated and controlled.

One case is insufficient to generalize about policy making in the coalition governments. However, the experience with social insurance shows that it was far more chaotic than the orderly process in the 1980s, which many observers consider the norm of governance. Confrontations in the Elderly Health Council were the functional equivalent of the compromise-making by *zoku* members in the LDP era. The only difference was at what stage the politicians undertook to revise the bureaucrats' draft bill.

The fact-finding function in the coalition governments was closer to the LDP style of the 1970s than the 1980s. Did LDP *zoku* politicians abandon their governance responsibility because they were in a coalition with other parties? Why did the smooth policy making of the 1980s break down?

Uncertainty and disorder in the coalitions stimulated public discussion through the mass media and forums established by the Health Ministry. Experts wrote extensively about the pros and cons of social insurance, and people who represented a variety of opinions participated in Health Ministry groups. As noted, the Committee of 10,000 Citizens promoted social insurance, activism on a welfare issue unprecedented in Japan.

Nevertheless, coalition government itself was clearly not the crucial factor in establishing long-term care insurance. That honor goes to the issue of a tax increase, specifically raising the consumption tax, which was the decisive factor in setting the agenda. A new insurance system could have been proposed if the LDP had continued in power and needed to justify a tax hike.

The Long-Term Care Insurance Bill was introduced to the Diet with slight amendments in the autumn of 1996, approved by the Lower House in the spring of 1997 and by the Upper House in that autumn. It was enacted on December 9, 1997, and goes into effect April 1, 2000.

Will the new system improve care of the elderly? When "A Welfare Vision for the Twenty-First Century" was released, many people had high expectations. This optimism gradually withered away as the content of the new scheme became clearer.

The first point that betrayed public expectations was that few additional welfare services will be provided under the insurance system. At present welfare is funded from tax revenues; under the new system individuals will pay monthly premiums. The consumption tax went up 2 percent in April 1997, and there will be other outlays. The manager of a private nursing home calls the new plan essentially a "second consumption tax" (Takiue and Yokouchi 1995, 18). Whether the supply of services will be sufficient is unclear.

Yet many people also strongly hope—even expect—that long-term care insurance will solve some problems in the present welfare system. Okamoto Yūzō, a physician whose hospital has had a high percentage of bed occupancy by the frail elderly, contends that the obligation to provide some benefits protects the rights of the insured (Okamoto 1996, 151).

The new system is expected to facilitate deregulation, enlarge services, and increase the number of providers. The more the insured exercise their rights, the more services will be available. If business opportunities increase in the long-term care market, additional suppliers will enter the field. At present, recipients can receive services only from suppliers approved by the municipal authorities. The new insurance will offer many options, from public facilities and nonprofit welfare organizations to for-profit companies and other nonprofit groups. Freedom of choice should stimulate competition among suppliers.

Although it is too early to predict outcomes, as insurees Japanese have acquired additional channels to articulate their interests. This may prove to be the most significant aspect of all.

NOTES

1. See Marsh and Rhodes (1992, 1–26) for a discussion of "policy community" and "policy networks."

2. Interviews with Satō Nobuto, a Health Ministry official, in Tokyo on October 17, 1997, and with Asakawa Tomoaki, also a Health Ministry official, in Tokyo on November 7, 1997.

3. Interview with Yakushiji Katsuyuki, of the *Asahi Shimbun*, in Osaka on February 28, 1997.

4. Interview with Miyashita Tadayasu, a former official of the Legislative Bureau, House of Councillors, in Tokyo on July 19, 1997.

5. Interview with Asakawa.

6. Interview with Asakawa.

7. Interview with Ikeda Shōzō, a representative of Jichirō (All-Japan Prefectural and Municipal Workers' Union) on the Elderly Health Council, in Tokyo on April 11, 1997.

8. Interview with Ikeda.

9. Interview with Ikeda.

10. Interview with Ikeda in Tokyo on May 15, 1997.

11. Interview with Asakawa.

12. Interview with Gotō Masanori, Lower House member and former SDPJ/SDP member of the Welfare Project Team, in Tokyo on June 19, 1997.

13. Interview with Kan Naoto, former minister of health and welfare in the Hashimoto administration, in Tokyo on July 11, 1997, and interviews with Satō and Asakawa.

14. Interview with Ikeda, April 11, 1997.

15. Interview with Miyashita.

16. Interview with Asakawa.

17. Interviews with Gotō and Kan.

BIBLIOGRAPHY

Alber, Jens. 1996. "The Debate about Long-Term Care Reform in Germany." In Organization for Economic Corporation and Development, ed. *Caring for Frail Elderly People: Policies in Evolution.* Paris: Organization for Economic Cooperation and Development.

Arai Satoshi. 1996. "Jiki Kokkai niwa hōan yōkō-an no naiyō de teishutsu kanō" (Will the nursing insurance bill be submitted to the next Diet session?). *Gekkan Kaigo Hoken,* no. 5: 12.

Arioka Jirō. 1995. "Mittsu no shingikai no teigen o yomu: Kaigo hoken no sōsetsu to kōreisha no futanzō no dōji kecchaku ga nerai ka" (Three advisory council proposals: Is the objective simultaneously to establish nursing insurance and increase the elderly's share of health costs?). *Shakai Hoken Jumpō,* no. 1883: 13–16.

Campbell, John C. 1990. "Media to seisaku tenkan: Nihon no kōreisha taisaku" (The mass media, policy change, and the Japanese elderly). *Leviathan,* no. 7: 40–74.

———. 1992. *How Policies Change: The Japanese Government and the Aging Society.* Princeton, N.J.: Princeton University Press.

Etō Mikiko. 1995. "Fukushi kokka no shukushō saihen to kōsei gyōsei" (Health and welfare administration in the reconstruction of social policy). *Leviathan,* no. 17: 91–114.

Furukawa Kōjun. 1997. *Shakai fukushi no paradaimu tenkan* (A paradigm change in social welfare: Theory and practice). Tokyo: Yūhikaku.

Hayakawa Sumitaka. 1991. "Fukushi kokka o meguru seiji katei: Hachijū-yon nen kenkō hoken hō kaisei katei no jirei kenkyū" (The political process and the welfare state: A case study of the 1984 health insurance revision). *Hōgaku Ronshū,* no. 43: 111–159. Published by Komazawa University.

Hori Katsushirō. 1994. "Sochi seido no igi to kongo no arikata" (The outlook for means-test eligibility). *Gekkan Fukushi* (April): 12–17.

Ikeda Shōzō. 1996. "Kōteki kaigo hoken o tsubushita no wa dare da" (Who killed the social insurance bill?). *Ronza,* no. 28: 62–67.

Ikegami Naoki and John C. Campbell. 1996. *Nihon no iryō: Tōsei to baransu kankaku* (Health care in Japan). Tokyo: Chūō Kōron-sha.

Inoguchi Takashi and Iwai Tomoaki. 1987. *Zoku giin no kenkyū: Jimintō seiken o gyūjiru shuyakutachi* (A study of policy tribes: The politicians who run the Liberal Democratic Party). Tokyo: Nihon Keizai Shimbun-sha.

Iwai Tomoaki. 1988. *Rippō katei* (The legislative process). Tokyo: Tokyo Daigaku Shuppan-kai.

Katō Junko. 1997. *Zeisei kaikaku to kanryōsei* (Bureaucrats, politicians, and tax reform). Tokyo: Tokyo Daigaku Shuppan-kai.

Kingdon, John W. 1984. *Agendas, Alternatives, and Public Policies.* New York: HarperCollins.

Komuro Toyomitsu. 1989. "Shakai fukushi kaikaku no shōten" (Focus on welfare reform). *Gekkan Fukushi* (March): 26–33.

Kōseishō Daijin Kambō Rōjin Hoken Fukushi-bu, ed. 1992. *Kōreisha tōtaru* puran kenkyūkai hōkoku shiryōshū (Report and documents of the study group for a "total plan" for the elderly). Tokyo: Ministry of Health and Welfare.

Kōseishō Kōreisha Kaigo Taisaku Hombu Jimukyoku, ed. 1996. *Kōreisha kaigo hoken seido no sōsetsu ni tsuite: Kokumin no giron o fukameru tame ni* (The establishment of nursing insurance for the elderly: The public debate). Tokyo: Gyōsei.

Kōteki Kaigo Hoken Seido Kenkyūkai. 1996a. "Kōteki kaigo hoken seido no shikumi o megutte" (Framework of nursing insurance for the elderly). *Gekkan Kaigo Hoken*, no. 4: 32–36.

———. 1996b. "Hi-hokensha no han'i o megutte" (Nursing insurance premiums: Who should pay?). *Gekkan Kaigo Hoken*, no. 6: 32–36.

Kusano Atsushi. 1995. *Nihon no ronsō: kitokuken no kōzai* (Vested interests vs. the public interest). Tokyo: Tōyō Keizai Shimpō-sha.

Kyōgoku Takanobu. 1997. *Kaigo hoken no senryaku: Nijū-isseiki-gata shakai hoshō no arikata* (Long-term care insurance: Social security in the 21st century). Tokyo: Chūō Hōki Shuppan.

Marsh, David, and R. A. W. Rhodes. 1992. *Policy Networks in British Government*. Oxford: Clarendon Press.

Miura Fumio. 1982. "Saikin no shakai fukushi no dōkō to jyakkan no kadai" (Recent issues in social welfare). *Gekkan Fukushi* (January): 8–15.

———. 1990. "*Shakai fukushi no atarashii nagare: Fukushi kankei 8 hō no kaisei ni yosete*" (Social welfare trends: Amendments to eight laws). *Shakai Hoken Jumpō*, no. 1703: 10-14.

Miyajima Hiroshi. 1994. "Kōreika shakai no kōteki futan no sentaku" (Options in public funding for the aged). In Noguchi Yukio, ed. *Zeisei kaikaku no shin sekkei* (Tax reform: The new design). Tokyo: Nihon Keizai Shimbun-sha.

Mizuno Hajime. 1997. "Nijū-isseiki o kangaeru kaigo hoken no seiritsu o (Establishment of long-term care insurance is necessary for the welfare in the 21st century). *Gekkan Kaigo Hoken*, no. 10 (January): 6–9.

Mochizuki Kōichi. 1997. "Kōteki kaigo hoken seido: Towareru seiji no chikara" (Long-term care insurance and political leadership). In Yomiuri Shimbun-sha, ed. *Chō-kōreika jidai* (The aging era). Tokyo: Yomiuri Shimbun-sha.

Nakano Minoru. 1996. "Seikai saihenki no rippō katei" (The changing legislative process in the age of party realignment). *Leviathan*, no. 18: 71–95.

———. 1997. *The Policy-Making Process in Contemporary Japan*. London: Macmillan Press Ltd.

Naruke Heisuke. 1997. "Hantai wa shinai ga kongo mo shūsei o yōkyū" (Not opposition, revision). *Gekkan Kaigo Hoken*, no. 10: 12.

Nihon Ishikai Sōgō Seisaku Kenkyū Kikō. 1997. *Kaigo hoken dōnyū no seisaku keisei katei* (Long-term care insurance: The policy-making process). Tokyo: Nihon Ishikai.

Nihon Keizai Shimbun-sha, ed. 1994. *Kanryō: Kishimu kyodai kenryoku* (Creaking giant: The bureaucracy). Tokyo: Nihon Keizai Shimbun-sha.

Niki Ryū. 1995. "Kōteki kaigo hoken no mittsu no ronten: Rōkenshin chūkan hōkoku ni kaketeiru mono" (Three issues in long-term insurance: The Elderly Health Council's interim report). *Shakai Hoken Jumpō*, no. 1888: 22–25.

Nikkeiren, Rengō, and Kemporen. 1990. *Rōjin hokenhō kaisei ni tsuite no yōbōsho* (Recommendations on long-term care for the elderly). *Shakai Hoken Jumpō*, no. 1700: 27–29.

Nishikawa Tōzō. 1987. "Kaigo mondai o kangaeru: Tokuni hiyō futan no shiten kara" (The cost of long-term care). *Kōsei Fukushi* (19 December): 2–4; (23 December): 2–9; (26 December): 2–5.

Organization for Economic Cooperation and Development, ed. 1995. *New Direction in Health Care Policy*. Paris: Organization for Economic Cooperation and Development.

———, ed. 1996. *Caring for Frail Elderly People: Policies in Evolution*. Paris: Organization for Economic Cooperation and Development.

Okamitsu Nobuharu. 1987. "Iryōhi tekiseika no shiten" (Health costs reconsidered). *Shakai Hoken Jumpō*, no. 1567: 6–7.

Okamoto Yūzō. 1996. *Kōreisha-iryō to fukushi* (Elderly health care and welfare). Tokyo: Iwanami-shoten.

Ōtake Hideo. 1994. *Jiyūshugiteki kaikaku no jidai* (The era of neoliberal reform). Tokyo: Chūō Kōron-sha.

Sawamura Yukio. 1988. "Kaigo hiyō o dō chōtatsusuru ka: Nishikawa rombun no keishō to shinka o mezashite" (Paying for long-term care: On Nishikawa Tōzō's proposals). *Kōsei Fukushi* (29 June): 15–30.

Shakai Keizai Kokumin Kaigi. 1988. "Kōreika shakai no iryō hoshō ni kansuru teigen" (Proposal for health care security in an aging society). *Shakai Hoken Jumpō*, no. 1625: 28.

Takahashi Hideyuki. 1986. "Nihon Ishikai no seiji kōdō to ishi kettei" (The Japan Medical Association: Decision making and political behavior). In Nakano Minoru, ed. *Nihon-gata seisaku kettei no hen'yō* (Changes in Japanese policy making). Tokyo: Tōyō Keizai Shimpō-sha.

Takanashi Shōzō. 1997. "Jigyōnushi futan no gimuzuke wa tōtei yōnin dekinai" (Companies can't pay more). *Gekkan Fukushi*, no. 10: 10.

Takiue Sōjirō. 1995. "Kōsei gyōsei, 21 seiki e no tembō: Rōjin hokenhō to kaigo hoken" (Health and welfare in the twenty-first century: The health care law for the elderly and long-term care insurance). *Shakai Hoken Jumpō*, no. 1867: 15–17.

Takiue Sōjirō and Yokouchi Masatoshi. 1995. "Kaigo hoken towa nani ka" (What is long-term care insurance?). *Shakai Hoken Jumpō*, no. 1891: 18–21.

Tochimoto Ichisaburō. 1995. "Doitsu ni okeru kōteki kaigo hoken no dōnyū to wagakuni no taiō" (The relevance of Germany's long-term care insurance system to Japan). *Gekkan Fukushi* (February): 28–35.

Tsuboi Eitaka. 1996. "Tsuboi nichi-i shinkaichō shoshin hyōmei" (Statement of Tsuboi, new JMA president). *Gekkan Kaigo Hoken,* no. 5: 16.

Watanabe Yoshiki. 1992. "Rōjin hokenhō no rippō katei" (The politics of health care for the elderly). *Hokudai Hōgaku* 42(4): 1161–1225.

Yamazaki Yasuhiko. 1988. "Shakai hoken ni yoru kaigo e no taiō" (Social insurance and elderly care). *Shakai Hoken Jumpō,* no. 1636: 6–8.

Yashiro Naohiro. 1997. "Sōgōteki seikatsu hoshō shisutemu" (Comprehensive social security system). In Yashiro Naohiro, ed. *Kōreika shakai no seikatsu hoshō shisutemu* (Private care providers and the aging society). Tokyo: Tokyo Daigaku Shuppan-kai.

Yoshimura Hitoshi. 1986. "Kōreika shakai e mukau iryō seisaku" (Health care policy for an aging society). *Shakai Hoken Jumpō,* no. 1527: 12–17.

Zenkoku Shakai Fukushi Kyōgikai and Shakai Fukushi Kenkyū Jōhō Sentā, eds. 1989. *Kaigo hiyō no arikata* (Nursing care costs). Tokyo: Chūō Hōki Shuppan.

The Reform of
Public Corporations

Tatebayashi Masahiko

ON June 30, 1994, the Liberal Democratic Party (LDP) regained control of government when it formed a ruling coalition with the Social Democratic Party of Japan (SDPJ) and the New Party Sakigake (*sakigake* means "pioneer"). The LDP had been the ruling party from 1955 to 1993, but it was ousted from office after the general election of the House of Representatives (Lower House) in July 1993. After unhappily sojourning with the opposition for almost 11 months while two consecutive non-LDP administrations, the Hosokawa and Hata cabinets, held power, the LDP allied itself with the SDPJ and Sakigake and recommended SDPJ Chairman Murayama Tomiichi as their joint candidate for prime minister. Two weeks after this three-party coalition government was created, it issued a package of policy initiatives that had originally been proposed by the SDPJ and Sakigake. One of the major components of the plan was administrative reform, especially the reorganization of *tokushu hōjin,* or public corporations.[1] These quasi-governmental organizations dealing with public finance and business operations have been the focus of public criticism for their inefficiency and for "interfering" with private business activities.

On February 24, 1995, the Murayama administration decided its public corporation reform plan, proposing that of the approximately 90 public corporations one be dissolved, three be privatized, and 14 be reorganized to form seven corporations.[2] This plan led to considerable public resentment. Why so little change, said critics, despite the broad public call for "small government"? The plan would only reduce by 11 the total number of public corporations, while their functions would largely be continued by transferring them to the surviving public corporations or to their previously affiliated ministries or agencies. Critics concluded that the reform initiative meant "almost nothing" (Matsubara 1995, 113), and "ended miserably" (Ōtake 1997, 20). However, I believe that this severe criticism actually reflected the gap between the high public expectations generated by Prime Minister Murayama's initial reform proposals and the blueprint later agreed upon by the three parties.

If one takes a historical perspective in examining administrative reform in Japan, the Murayama public corporation reform plan can be regarded as having been relatively successful. Japanese administrations had attempted several reform schemes in the previous three decades, with little success. The most recent prior to Murayama, an initiative by the Third Provisional Council for the Promotion of Administrative Reform (Third Reform Council) in 1993, which will be described in detail later, failed completely.[3] By these standards, the Murayama reform effort made considerable progress. The number of public corporations eliminated by the Murayama reform plan also compared favorably with past reform schemes, and was as ambitious in this respect as the well-regarded Ōhira administration reform plan of the late 1970s, which reorganized 13 of the public corporations.

The Murayama plan undoubtedly influenced all the public corporations by issuing guidelines for upgrading their activities and organization. Most significantly, Murayama's initiative can be regarded as having set the agenda for administrative reform by the three-party coalition. This compelled the succeeding LDP government of Prime Minister Hashimoto Ryūtarō, who replaced Murayama in January 1996, to commit itself to administrative reform as a major policy. It was noted at the time that the Murayama reforms actually restricted the specific policy choices of the Hashimoto administration (Ōtake 1997; Mikuriya and Watanabe 1997, 181).

Thus, the Murayama reform plan for public corporations, while not an unqualified success, at least equaled the achievements of past LDP administrations. In this chapter, I will examine how the Murayama administration formulated its reform plan and will analyze the pattern of policy making by the three-party coalition. The chapter will address particularly such questions as whether the shift from a one-party government to a coalition government brought about any changes in the policy-making process or outcomes.

Two currently prevailing approaches to these questions both emphasize the continuity of the political structure in post–World War II Japan. Both regard major political developments in the 1990s, including party reorganizations and electoral reform, as merely superficial changes. Analysts adopting one of these approaches have emphasized the LDP's dominance in the three-party coalition government, assuming that the LDP could maintain its influence to almost the same degree as it had under prior single-party rule. The "failure" of the Murayama public corporation reform plan was attributed to interference by LDP *zoku* politicians who tried to defend their special interests. (The term *zoku* refers to middle-ranking Diet members who have considerable influence in a specific policy area, related to a particular ministry or agency.)

Other political observers have emphasized the dominant role of bureaucrats in policy making. If the bureaucrats are assumed to have maintained continuous dominance over the policy-making process, then one could infer that there would be no major change in public policies, even with a change in party control and cabinet formation. This approach posits that the LDP had gradually strengthened its control over bureaucrats as LDP politicians accumulated knowledge in policy areas. The formation of the non-LDP coalition in 1993, however, increased bureaucratic power in policy making, because few of these politicians had experience in working with bureaucrats to make policy (Nakano 1996). The "ineffectual" Murayama reforms were also regarded as evidence of continuing bureaucratic dominance, as the bureaucrats labored to protect their turf and thwart attempts at reform.

However, I would argue that these interpretations do not explain why the Murayama reforms were much more successful than the Third Reform Council initiative announced 18 months earlier. In this chapter, I will present a third interpretation to explain the positive aspects of the Murayama reforms, emphasizing the changes in the policy-making process under the coalition system. I will argue that changes in party politics transformed public corporation reform policy formation in two opposing directions, thus neutralizing the impact that each would have, and bringing about a similar outcome to those of past reform attempts.

On one hand, party reorganization and the formation of succeeding opposition and LDP coalition governments seemed to stimulate LDP politicians to adopt new policy preferences and provided them with stronger incentives to carry out administrative reform. The coalition framework forced the LDP to compete with its coalition partners to claim credit for new policies and, at times, to compromise with its partners in policy decisions. In the case of public corporation reform, Sakigake took an opposing stand, strongly insisting that more than one-third of the approximately 90 public corporations be reorganized or privatized.

Moreover, because the LDP had been thrown out of office for the first time in its almost 40-year history, due to party reshuffling, LDP politicians now became concerned that with the adoption of new electoral reform laws they would lose control of the government again in the future. These changes seemed to loosen the close cooperative links between the LDP and bureaucracy that had been forged during the LDP's long-term rule. Geddes (1994) uses several Latin American nations as examples in arguing that government leaders in a two-party system are more likely to carry out administrative reform than those under one-party dominance. She claims that the two-party system, where ties with the bureaucracy are fairly evenly distributed among the major parties, provides political leaders with more incentives to carry out reform. I would argue that LDP politicians, correctly or not, interpreted the new electoral system to be a simple "Westminster" model, e.g., single-seat districts with plurality rule. Thus, they seemed to display obsessive concern that the electoral reforms would result in a two-party system in the future.

On the other hand, however, the coalition government increased bureaucratic autonomy and made administrative reform more difficult. The principal-agent theory posits that multiple principals enlarge the manipulatable space that agents can enjoy. Hammond (1994) writes that the differing policy preferences of the various governing parties in a coalition cabinet create a large policy space within which bureaucrats can maneuver. In the case of the Murayama cabinet, I would argue, the bureaucrats took advantage of this "manipulatable space" to defend their interests and dilute the proposed public corporation reforms.

The next section of this chapter will review the chronology of public corporation reform plans under earlier LDP rule and during the Murayama administration. The chapter will then examine the reform process by the three-party coalition, in terms of the strategies of the respective participants and the procedures for decision making.

COMPARING MURAYAMA REFORMS WITH PAST EFFORTS

Although the three-party coalition under Murayama was certainly the driving force behind public corporation reform, we cannot say that a coalition government is a necessary prerequisite for reform of public corporations, since such reform attempts have been made several times by LDP administrations as well. The Murayama reforms actually resemble earlier efforts in scale and scope. Over the years, criticism of the inefficiency of public corporations gradually increased and events such as bribery scandals, which flared up intermittently, would act as a catalyst to a new reform initiative. The LDP was not itself inclined to carry out administrative reform, since many LDP politicians maintained strong links with public corporations, regarding them as a political resource. Thus, outside pressure was sometimes needed to force the LDP to commit itself to administrative reform.

Administrative reform cannot be carried out via the routine process of policy making (March and Olsen 1989). In other words, because it requires special mechanisms to accomplish reforms, each reform process inevitably differs from others. However, it seems to be possible to roughly categorize the various attempts at public corporation reform in Japan into two types.[4] One is reform from outside the bureaucracy administering the corporations. Administrative reform by the Second Provisional Commission on Administrative Reform (Second Rinchō) in the early 1980s is an example of this type. In the case of public corporations, the reform process began with the establishment of a deliberation council for administrative reform—the Third Reform Council. The council then presented a specific reform plan, which the cabinet adopted and executed through coordination with the ministries. While LDP leaders were consulted by council members in advance, lower-ranking LDP Diet members, who are more positive toward public corporations, were relatively isolated from the policy-making process.

The other type is reform from inside. Administrative reform in Japan was sometimes routinely carried out by bureaucrats themselves. Examples of internal reform of public corporations include efforts carried out under Prime Ministers Miki Takeo, Fukuda Takeo, and Ōhira Masayoshi in the 1970s. In all of these cases, the reform plan was actually drafted by the ministry concerned through consultations with the Administrative and Management Agency (the predecessor of the

Management and Coordination Agency). Especially in the case of the Ōhira administration's reform, each ministry was assigned a numerical goal for public corporations, requiring them to merge superfluous corporations when necessary. Since this type of dispersed decision-making resulted in fragmented policy, rank-and-file members of the LDP held veto power in the subdivisions of the LDP's Policy Research Council.

These two types of administrative reform proved effective in bringing about desired outcomes in some cases but not others. There seemed to be no causal relationship between the type of policy making and its outcome. For example, reform of public corporations under the Ōhira cabinet, which was driven by public criticism over bribery scandals involving the Japan Railway Construction Public Corp. and Japan's international telephone carrier, KDD (Kokusai Denshin Denwa Co., Ltd.), succeeded in rapidly reducing the scale and number of public corporations. The Second Rinchō was also able to carry out dramatic reforms, with the partial privatization of three major public corporations: the Japanese National Railways, Nippon Telegraph and Telephone Public Corporation, and Japan Tobacco and Salt Public Corporation.

RECENT PUBLIC CORPORATION REFORM EFFORTS

Third Reform Council

This advisory council, which was organized by the Prime Minister's Office and operated from the fall of 1990 to the fall of 1993, discussed reform of public corporations. After being asked to do so by Prime Minister Miyazawa Kiichi in September 1992, council members discussed the role of government and organizational problems in the bureaucracy. The council suffered from an early failing: Its members tried to identify problematic public corporations at the beginning and propose specific reform plans for them, rather than creating a general guideline for reform.

From February to April 1993, the council held hearings to which it invited bureaucrats representing each ministry holding jurisdiction over the problematic public corporations it had previously identified.[5] On April 6, the council publicized an interim report that included specific names of 34 public corporations that had been discussed during the hearings. This report attracted a great deal of attention from the mass media, raising public expectations that the council would subsequently issue a drastic reform plan. However, in the final report publicized in October, the council declined to identify by name those public corporations needing reorganization; it simply advised the government to review the role of the public corporations and desirable reform. Drafting of actual reform proposals was left to the bureaucrats.

This "retreat" from reform was caused by the combined resistance of the bureaucrats, LDP politicians, and the public corporations themselves. Politicians have their own special interests concerning public corporations, since these corporations receive considerable budgetary funding and funds from the government's fiscal investment and loan program. Although the council tried to hold a second round of hearings after publicizing its interim report, it was unable to do so because ministry bureaucrats and public corporation representatives universally refused to attend them. Reportedly, Hashimoto, then chairman of the LDP's Policy Research Council, and other influential LDP members not only were in support of this stonewalling, they had initiated it.

The failure of the council's reform efforts has also been attributed to the ineffective strategies that it adopted. Bureaucrats did not cooperate with the council, some analysts say, because they felt it had failed to legitimize the first-round hearings. The bureaucrats complained that the council arbitrarily selected 34 of the 92 public corporations as their targets for reform. However, no matter on which side the fault lay, the basic problem was the mutual hostility between bureaucrats and council members that was present from the beginning. Since fall 1992, the council had been organized as a means of attacking the bureaucracy. Few former bureaucrats were selected to serve as council members, as had been the case in prior reform councils. A subcommittee system was abolished, since it had provided former bureaucrats with additional influence in the past. In addition, the council broadened its focus beyond the issue of public corporations. In its interim report, the council proposed more aggressive plans, including the reform of personnel affairs and the fiscal investment and loan program, and the reorganization of ministries. Bureaucrats thus assumed that the peripheral issue of public corporation reform spurred proposals for more significant administrative reform.

The other major problem that the council faced was the lack of support from government leaders and external groups. Prime Minister

Miyazawa placed priority on deregulation and decentralization; he displayed little enthusiasm for restructuring the bureaucracy. Business leaders also failed to pay particular attention to administrative reform. The chairman of the Japan Chamber of Commerce and Industry even expressed some anxiety as to whether the reform plan would affect financial organizations for small and medium-sized businesses.

Hosokawa Administration

Members of the Third Reform Council expected that the Hosokawa administration, which was formed by an eight-party coalition, would revitalize the reform initiative begun by the council. Prime Minister Hosokawa Morihiro himself was chairman of one subcommittee of the council until May 1992, when he ran for the House of Councillors, and he had publicized his determination to carry out administrative reform. However, it was too late to revise the Third Reform Council's final plan. As already mentioned, the council's report, issued in October, two months after the Hosokawa administration was formed, merely included guidelines for formulating reform plans and allowed each ministry to devise its own plan.

The Hosokawa administration approved its "General Program of Administrative Reform," based on the final report of the Third Reform Council, in a cabinet meeting held on February 15, 1994. It requested that each ministry examine all public corporations under its jurisdiction and address their problems within two years. This was a surprisingly muted response by the Hosokawa administration, considering the prime minister's earlier stated commitment to administrative reform. This is partly because he was forced to concentrate his efforts on electoral reform for the first six months of his administration. At the start of his administration, Hosokawa also focused on the issue of government deregulation, which allowed him to claim some positive results. For example, the deregulation of the beer industry, which led to the rise of many small local brewers, was widely covered by the mass media. However, Hosokawa apparently procrastinated on issues, including reforming public corporations and the postal savings system, that were controversial among the ruling parties. The slow response of the Hosokawa administration was also due to the failure of the Third Reform Council's initiative. The Hosokawa cabinet's "General Program" appeared to represent a new start after the failed efforts of the earlier report.

After the "General Program" was approved, the eight ruling coalition parties discussed public corporation reform in some interparty organs, such as the subcommittee for administrative and financial affairs of the Tax Reform Council of the coalition parties. However, this failed to accelerate the slow process of reform. The final report of this subcommittee added little to the "General Program" except for shortening the time allotted to the ministries for tackling their public corporation problems from two years to one year. At that time, it was clear that a two-year time limit was allowing ministries to defer any efforts to examine or carry out reforms of their public corporations. The only action taken had been by the Administrative Management Bureau of the Management and Coordination Agency, which has jurisdiction over administrative reform. The bureau had examined public corporations in terms of their routine management of bureaucratic organizations in general.

POLICY MAKING BY THE
MURAYAMA ADMINISTRATION
The LDP-SDPJ-Sakigake Coalition

The stagnating reform process was finally revitalized by the launch of the LDP-SDPJ-Sakigake coalition. As part of an initial agreement among the three parties, they concluded that administrative reform was a necessary precondition for garnering public acceptance for an increase in the consumption tax rate. They organized a task force to tackle administrative reform in July 1994. In the early summer, at the start of the new coalition government, the media paid considerable attention to a reform plan proposed by Sakigake which proposed privatization of 13 public corporations, including the Japan Development Bank, the Japan Highway Public Corporation, the Housing and Urban Development Corporation, and the Housing Loan Corporation; eliminating three public corporations, including the Livestock Industry Promotion Corporation; and reorganizing 31 corporations into 14. It also proposed decreasing the share of government holdings of the Nippon Telegraph and Telephone Corporation and Japan Tobacco Incorporated, both of which had been privatized in the mid-1980s, and delegating authority to local governments for regulating three public corporations, including the Hokkaido-Tōhoku Development Corporation.

The reform plan by Sakigake attracted much public attention, as it concretely identified the public corporations targeted for reform by name and proposed dramatic steps in privatizing and eliminating public corporations, and unifying those that were under the jurisdiction of more than one ministry. Bureaucrats criticized this plan as unrealistic. The party's coalition partners, the LDP and the SDPJ, also regarded it as fanciful. Sakigake itself did not seem to take it seriously. Tanaka Shūsei, one of the founders of Sakigake, wrote that this plan was never officially authorized by Sakigake's organization (Tanaka 1995, 157–159). However, the Sakigake plan had a large impact on the ensuing policy-making process. Later plans issued by the coalition government were always compared unfavorably with the Sakigake proposal and criticized as representing a retreat from reform. The mass media came to regard the Sakigake plan as an ideal model for reform.[6]

The task force formed by the three parties decided on its "Basic Plan for Administrative Reform" in September 1994. The coalition parties decided to shorten the time allotted for reform to one year. Based on this plan, the Management and Coordination Agency made a more detailed reform schedule, directing each ministry to submit an interim report to the agency by November 25 and a final report by February 10 of the following year.

Task Force Discussions

Membership in the 12-person task force was allocated to the ruling parties as follows: six for the LDP, four for the SDPJ, and two for Sakigake. The smaller parties were overrepresented compared with their numerical strength. Three chairmen—one from each party—served in one-month rotations.

After deciding on a basic plan, from October to November the task force held hearings on the public corporations, to which it invited bureaucrats and corporation representatives. These hearings were said to be comprehensive and intensive, examining everything from the routine work of each public corporation to the possibility of it being dissolved. This exhaustive approach was probably adopted by the project team due to the fact that the Third Reform Council had engendered resistance from the bureaucrats by identifying problematic public corporations before holding their first round of hearings.

The Ministry of Finance seemed to take a wait-and-see approach to the proceedings. In the past, the ministry played an important role in administrative reform by pressing other ministries to cooperate. The

Finance Ministry had its own organizational goal of cutting budget deficits by implementing administrative reforms. At this time, however, the ministry bureaucrats argued that rationalizing or merging public corporations would not improve the government's finances one whit. The Finance Ministry seemed to be wary of being a target of reform itself, since there were several major public corporations under the ministry's jurisdiction, including the Japan Development Bank, the Export-Import Bank of Japan, and the People's Finance Corp.

The Management and Coordination Agency was responsible for coordinating efforts by the other ministries to draft their own reform plans. When the coalition parties decided to shorten the time period to one year, the agency directed the other ministries to start examining their affiliated public corporations. After announcing the time schedule, eight directors-general for management[7] in the administrative management bureau of the Management and Coordination Agency invited and interviewed heads of bureaus or sections that directly oversaw their respective public corporations. These agency interviews were held independently of those conducted by the task force, although agency bureaucrats sometimes consulted with task force members to hear their views on what kind of questioning would be appropriate.

Each of the ministries formed its own internal task force to examine affiliated public corporations. The composition of these task forces varied; in some ministries the task force was led by the vice-minister, while in others it was directed by the director-general of the ministry's or agency's secretariat, or the director of the general affairs division in the ministry's secretariat. The bureaucrats in each minister's secretariat, who are sometimes said to be more pro-reform than officials directly responsible for the public corporations, were responsible for coordinating with these officials. Some ministries established examination committees inside the public corporations and let them draft their own reform plans.

Interim Report

In response to pressure from the task force and the Management and Coordination Agency, each ministry submitted an interim reform plan to the agency by November. It was notable, however, that not a single ministry proposed dramatic reforms, such as merging, dissolving, or privatizing public corporations. The ministries all claimed that none of the public corporations satisfied the criteria for applying these extreme reform measures that had been specified in the governing coalition's basic plan. Some ministries even insisted that their public corporations be maintained in their current form. For example, the Economic Planning Agency reported that "since the function of the Overseas Economic Cooperation Fund (OECF) is to supply public funds for development to areas where it is difficult to attract private capital, privatization would not be effective. Because no other organizations like OECF exist which can supply developmental loans, merging OECF with other institutions would not bring about greater efficiency, either" ("Koshi no omoi no ga" 1994, 3). The National Land Agency asserted that the Fund for the Promotion and Development of Amami Island was similarly essential: "This is a critical organization which provides funds on a continuing basis for promoting small businesses in the Amami islands. Since special measures are required to develop this area, it would not be appropriate to delegate national authority to the local government" ("Jigyō kakudai motomeru" 1994, 2). Moreover, the Science and Technology Agency claimed increasing demand for the services of the Japan Information Center of Science and Technology.

Some ministers followed their ministry's or agency's stance in appearing to be unenthusiastic about the prospect of reform of public corporations. For example, Kōmura Masahiko, director-general of the Economic Planing Agency, and Hashimoto, who was then minister of international trade and industry, strongly insisted on the continuation of the public corporations under their jurisdictions.

Most of the ministries seemed to be marking time, waiting to see how the other ministries would respond. Bureaucrats of the Management and Coordination Agency claimed that they had expected to encounter such passive responses by the ministries. However, Murayama and his political staff seemed to regard the report with trepidation, since it made them recall the failures of the Third Reform Council, which had been severely criticized by the mass media. Murayama said at a breakfast meeting on December 5 with leaders of Keidanren (Japan Federation of Economic Organizations), "If we continue to allow the ministries to draft their own reform plans, I am afraid that they will just keep repeating, incessantly, that 'this public corporation is indispensable.' I think we should have the chief cabinet secretary and the director-general of the Management and Coordination Agency [both ministers] identify the problematic public corporations"

("Shushō, tokushu hōjin minaoshi" 1994, 3). In other words, he suggested the adoption of a top-down approach to this problem.

On December 26 and 27, 1994, Igarashi Kōzō, chief cabinet secretary, and Yamaguchi Tsuruo, director-general of the Management and Coordination Agency, held detailed discussions with all of the ministers about the reform issue. Some ministers finally mentioned specific names of public corporations targeted for reform and detailed their reform plans, Igarashi said, noting that "this represented a certain degree of progress from when the interim report was issued" ("Taishoku-kin kyōsai" 1994, 1, evening edition). However, the overall approach remained bottom-up, not top-down. It was reported that Igarashi and Yamaguchi barely revealed their own plans to the other ministers, but instead just listened to the presentations by the ministries.

By this time, some ministries indicated that they were planning to restructure the public corporations under their jurisdiction. The Ministry of Transportation conceived a scheme to merge the Maritime Credit Corporation and the Railway Development Fund. The Ministry of Agriculture, Forestry and Fisheries reported that it was considering merging two of its six affiliated public corporations, the Japan Raw Silk and Sugar Price Stabilization Agency and the Livestock Industry Promotion Corp., and the Science and Technology Agency announced that it was considering merging two of its six public corporations. The Ministry of Construction publicized its plans to downsize the Housing and Urban Developmental Corp., while the Ministry of Home Affairs revealed its intention to privatize the Finance Corp. for Local Public Enterprises.

While some ministries presented concrete reform plans, most of the ministries merely reiterated their findings from the interim report. Bureaucrats from the Ministry of International Trade and Industry were especially vocal in criticizing the prime minister and his staff, claiming that the goals of the reform initiative were not clearly defined.

Labor unions that would be affected by the initiative actively lobbied SDPJ politicians against administrative reform in order to protect their members' interests. The leaders of the Labor Federation of Government Related Organizations (LAFGO) met with SDPJ member Yamaguchi and Yagi Toshimichi, a vice-minister of the Management and Coordination Agency, in December, requesting that the government initiate a mechanism that would allow laid-off workers from eliminated public corporations to find jobs in other public corporations.

Yamaguchi acceded to their request, eliminating LAFGO's primary objection to administrative reform. LAFGO, which is part of Rengō (Japanese Trade Union Confederation), then changed its position, becoming more tolerant of reform in general. LAFGO's more flexible position on public corporation reform was criticized by anti-Rengō labor unions. The administrative reform task force representing the three parties later agreed to honor the agreement between the SDPJ and LAFGO by promising that there would be no firing.

Final Decisions

What was the task force on public corporation reform doing while the ministries drafted their own reform plans? Members of the task force actually pressed the ministries to draft more positive plans, but they never proposed their own, sufficiently detailed alternatives. They wanted to lead the reform policy-making process, but because they were overly concerned about engendering the opposition of affected business groups and labor unions, they were unable to decide on details. They delegated execution of reforms to the bureaucrats in order to avoid criticism from their political supporters.

The three-party coalition government decided to move the date of their decision on the reform plan to February 10, 1995. They wanted to finalize the plan to enable them to prepare for Diet debate on the issue, as the New Frontier Party, the largest opposition party, was planning to place priority on administrative reform as part of its tactics for the upcoming Diet session.

Two important factors, which influenced policy making in the final stage, should be noted. One was the Great Hanshin-Awaji Earthquake of January 17, 1995, and the other was the emerging issue of reorganizing public financial institutions. The disastrous earthquake in Kobe increased demand for assistance from public corporations involved in reconstruction activities. The Small Business Finance Corp. and the Japan Development Bank stated publicly that they were considering urgent measures for earthquake recovery. The Hanshin Expressway Public Corp., which had been a target for reform, undertook a large amount of reconstruction work. While members of the coalition's task force argued that the need for public corporations in the long term should be discussed separately from the short-term impact of the earthquake, many business leaders, especially those in the Kansai area, became more supportive of the public corporations.

The reform of public financial institutions also began drawing public attention in January. Only in its initial proposal did Sakigake insist
on a drastic reform plan for public financial institutions. The party's
initial plan included calls for the privatization of the Japan Development Bank and the Housing Loan Corp. as well as a merger of the
Export-Import Bank of Japan and the OECF. Except for this early proposal by Sakigake, the reform of financial institutions had rarely been
discussed by the three-party coalition. But now suddenly some politicians, mainly in the LDP, insisted on the necessity of including financial institutions in the reform plan in the final stage.

The LDP officially proposed the merger of the Japan Development
Bank and the Export-Import Bank, both of which were under the Finance Ministry's jurisdiction, to the policy coordinating committee
of the ruling coalition on February 8. Sakigake criticized the LDP
proposal as inefficient, and party members presented their own counterproposal to merge the two banks with the Hokkaido-Tōhoku Development Corp. They also proposed combining the People's Finance
Corp., the Small Business Finance Corp., and the Environmental Sanitation Business Corp. into one entity. While the LDP plan focused on
public corporations under the jurisdiction of the Finance Ministry,
whose minister was Sakigake head Takemura Masayoshi, the Sakigake plan involved several different ministries. Sakigake's scheme,
however, met resistance from the LDP, because the Hokkaido-Tōhoku
Development Corp., the People's Finance Corp., the Small Business Finance Corp., and the Environmental Sanitation Business Corp. were
all tied to the electoral interests of incumbent LDP members. Negotiations between the LDP and Sakigake on the reform issue became
deadlocked, while the SDPJ took a neutral stance, concerned that the
coalition would break up.

Hashimoto, the minister of international trade and industry, consulted with Takemura and proposed a compromise that would establish an advisory organization to discuss the reform of public financial
institutions, including the fiscal investment and loan program. His
proposal, however, was criticized by Katō Kōichi, chairman of the
LDP's Policy Research Council, and it soon foundered.

On February 10, the deadline for making a final decision, coalition
members proposed several compromise plans to bridge differences
between the LDP and Sakigake positions. But they were unable to
reach an agreement and finally postponed a decision about financial

institutions for one month. Late that evening, Chief Cabinet Secretary Igarashi and Director-General Yamaguchi of the Management and Co-ordination Agency organized talks with the policy division chairmen and task force heads from each coalition party, pursuing a final compromise. This political party maneuvering, however, resulted in a draft reform plan that differed little from the proposals already drafted and publicly announced by the ministries. To reach a compromise on reform of public financial institutions, the coalition parties formed another task force for this issue. At the end of February, the LDP and Sakigake agreed on a plan to divide the Export-Import Bank into two parts, with one part merging with the Japan Development Bank and the other joining the OECF. This compromise decision was again revised during discussions at the cabinet level in March. Faced with the strong objections of the Ministry of Finance against dividing the Export-Import Bank, the coalition government gave up the idea and authorized a plan to merge the bank with the OECF.

Summary and Analysis of Murayama Reforms

How can we characterize the public corporation reforms of the Murayama administration, particularly in relation to past reforms and the failure of the aforementioned Third Reform Council?

First of all, the Murayama reforms were for the most part initiated by party politicians. There appeared to be little public demand for reform of public corporations. The business community was more interested in the issues of deregulation and decentralization than public corporation reform. For example, even after the various ministries had already issued their interim reports, in early 1995, the chairman of influential Keidanren stated that his group lacked a concrete plan "identifying which public corporations should be reformed" ("Tokushu hōjin no minaoshi" 1995, 2). While the business world professed indifference, labor unions strongly opposed public corporation reform. The Japan Postal Workers' Union, LAFGO, and Rengō lobbied against reform, mainly to SDPJ politicians. It could be said that the reform efforts were only possible because politicians wanted them to be carried out and they received the support of the mass media.

Even though the interests and strategies of the three parties widely varied, they agreed on implementing reform of public corporations. Sakigake members wanted to aggressively promote their party platform to the public via this administrative reform initiative, since they were a small party and had joined in a coalition with the LDP, which they had previously criticized and from which their members had originally defected. Sakigake actually took the initiative in the reform efforts early on by publicizing its own reform scheme. However, the Sakigake plan proved too extreme to serve as the basis of the task force or the ensuing policy-making process. In sum, Sakigake's role in public corporation reform seemed to be limited to setting the agenda.

SDPJ politicians also tried to initiate public corporation reform. At the time, they were seeking a rationale for cooperating with the LDP, their former enemies, and acquiescing to an increase in the consumption tax. However, the SDPJ did not seem to be able to play a leadership role in the reform efforts. Although the ministers of ministries involved in administrative reform were all SDPJ members, they were constrained from playing key roles. A major factor in this decision was the opposition of labor unions. Moreover, some SDPJ members, especially those from outlying districts, expressed support for public corporations due to the benefits they provided. Clearly, the LDP was not the only party involved in pork-barrel politics.

The LDP, on the other hand, which had previously defended the bureaucracy, was pro-reform this time. The LDP had obviously changed its stance: LDP politicians had been responsible for ensuring the failure of the Third Reform Council's efforts, and they had helped bureaucrats and public corporations maintain the status quo a year earlier. While they were out of office, however, LDP members came to understand the harsh truth that bureaucrats always fall in love with the party in office. Many LDP members thought that they had been betrayed by the bureaucrats. Moreover, the LDP realized that in a three-party coalition it could no longer claim credit for every action the government took. The LDP had to compete with coalition partners in claiming credit for policy making. Since Sakigake was enthusiastically advocating administrative reform, and the SDPJ had lent its tacit support, the LDP had no choice except to proceed with reform efforts. Participation in the three-party coalition's decision-making procedures made it easier, however, for the LDP to justify having adopted this altered stance to opposing rank-and-file members. Members of the subcommittees of the party's Policy Research Council lost much of the veto power they had enjoyed during earlier reform efforts. Task force members and party leaders could now take the lead in policy making, since they could legitimatize their relatively centralized decisions in terms of the need to bargain with coalition partners in order to stay in office.

A second characteristic of the Murayama reforms was that it allowed bureaucrats relative autonomy in decision making. This statement appears to contradict the prior assertion that party politicians led this process. However, bureaucrats were clearly delegated authority to decide the specific details of the reform plan. Coalition politicians wanted to effect administrative reform, as noted above, but they did not relish assuming responsibility for specifying which public corporations should be reformed and how reform should be accomplished. This was especially true of LDP and SDPJ members. Thus, they delegated the decision-making specifics to the bureaucrats and they tried to shirk the blame for these decisions from affected businesses and labor unions.

Ministries try to the best of their ability to protect the public corporations under their jurisdiction because they provide respectable jobs for many retired bureaucrats and because public corporations receive large government subsidies and assistance from the fiscal investment and loan program. Specific public corporations are seen as being part of a ministry's turf, resulting in escalating interministerial rivalry. Should the public corporations affiliated with one ministry undergo more dramatic reforms than those of other ministries, the supervisory bureaucrats in that ministry would be criticized, lessening their chances for future promotion. Nevertheless, ministries are not always obstinately protective of their public corporations. High-ranking bureaucrats are sometimes amenable to dissolving highly inefficient public corporations, as they are unwilling to shoulder continuing responsibility for their performance.

We can find examples of both of these general attitudes by the bureaucrats involved in the Murayama reform initiative. Ministries attempting to protect their own public corporations worked to ameliorate the impact of the Murayama reform efforts. Although they could not succeed in killing off the reform plan in the face of strong political demand, they succeeded in limiting the reforms to mergers of a reduced number of public corporations, while forestalling their privatization or dissolution. Moreover, the decisions on which public corporations to merge seemed to be affected by ministries' preferences. They seemed to have targeted either small public corporations that would not have much impact on the ministries, or clearly inefficient corporations whose performance might generate adverse criticism.

The Management and Coordination Agency's interest in reforms was by nature different from that of the other ministries, since the agency is charged with the task of carrying out administrative reform. However, in practice, agency personnel rarely act as progressive reformers, since they are lifetime bureaucrats who engage in mutually beneficial relationships with those in other ministries. The agency staff also includes many bureaucrats who are on loan to the agency from other ministries for limited assignments. The Management and Coordination Agency tried to play a conciliatory role in resolving conflicts between the politicians and the ministries, by withdrawing from contention the most objectionable of the individual ministries' reform plans.

CONCLUSION

In sum, a comparison with past public corporation reform plans suggests that the Murayama reforms represented a mixture of the two above-mentioned types of reform, those efforts from outside the bureaucracy, and those from inside.

Ruling coalition politicians clearly indicated to the bureaucrats their commitment to carrying out reform of public corporations. Party leaders were able to use the three-party coalition's relatively centralized decision-making procedure as a means for stymieing any opposition from *zoku* Diet members. In this respect, the reform efforts seemed to be external, like those initiated by the Second Rinchō. But unlike with the Second Rinchō, politicians involved in the Murayama reforms tried to shirk responsibility for the details of the reforms by delegating authority to the bureaucrats to write concrete reform plans. The final plan for reform, except for the merger of the Export-Import Bank and the OECF, was basically a compilation of the plans of the individual ministries. In this respect, the Murayama reforms appeared to be an internal undertaking.

The conspicuous distinction between the Murayama reforms and earlier efforts was that the Management and Coordination Agency seemed to enjoy great autonomy in this situation. The political parties failed to draft a specific reform plan, unlike in the case of the Second

Rinchō, but the *zoku* politicians were unable to exercise much veto power over the proposals, like they had in the case of reforms under the Ōhira administration and other unsuccessful attempts.

The results of the Murayama reform plan, as I mentioned before, were not much different from the administrative reforms under earlier LDP single-party governments. There were important changes in the approaches taken by the major players and the decision-making procedures, and these changes had a certain impact on the reform process. However, I would argue that these two kinds of changes pushed the reform process in two opposing directions, thus neutralizing their impact on each other. The change in the LDP's stance on administrative reform made the Murayama reforms possible, but the increased autonomy of the bureaucracy prevented any dramatic reforms from taking place.

NOTES

1. Public corporations are established by special government law to serve as instruments for state activities. However, unlike government agencies, they are not directly controlled by the regulations that apply to state organizations or public officials. Many high-ranking bureaucrats take positions at public corporations after retirement, in a practice called *amakudari*, or "descent from heaven." The number of public corporations increased in the 1960s and 1970s but decreased thereafter, in response to rising criticism.

2. The reform plan for public financial institutions was announced in March. If its proposals are included in the tally of final reforms, the reform plan resulted in the reorganization of 16 public corporations to eight.

3. The Third Reform Council was preceded by the Second Provisional Commission on Administrative Reform (Second Rinchō), which operated from March 1981 to March 1983. The Provisional Council for the Promotion of Administrative Reform was organized three times to follow up on the Second Rinchō report: the first convened between July 1983 and June 1986, the second between April 1987 and April 1990, and the third between October 1990 and October 1993.

4. This characterization was first suggested in 1984 by Tsuji Keiichi, a former vice minister in the Management and Coordination Agency (Gyōsei Kanri-chō Shi Hensan Iinkai 1984).

5. Almost all the ministries have at least one public corporation under their jurisdiction.

6. However, according to Tanaka (1995), because the final reform plan fell

far short of the Sakigake proposals, in the end both Sakigake and its head, Takemura Masayoshi, suffered negative repercussions.

7. Each of the eight directors-general is responsible for two or three ministries and/or agencies.

BIBLIOGRAPHY

Geddes, Barbara. 1994. *Politicians' Dilemma.* Berkeley and Los Angeles, Calif.: University of California Press.

Gyōsei Kanri-chō Shi Hensan Iinkai. 1984. *Gyōsei kanri-chō shi* (The history of the Management and Coordination Agency). Tokyo: Gyōsei Kanri-chō.

Hammond, Thomas. 1994. "Formal Theory, Comparative Bureaucracy, and the Institutions of Governance." Paper prepared for the annual meeting of American Political Science Association, New York City.

"Jigyō kakudai motomeru rei mo: Tokushu hōjin minaoshi, kaku shōchō no chūkan hōkoku" (Interim reports by the ministries and agencies: Some requests to expand areas of activity). 1994. *Asahi Shimbun* (29 November, evening edition).

"Koshi no omoi no ga yakunin-ryū?" (Are bureaucrats unwilling to reform themselves?: Interim report of public corporation review). 1994. *Asahi Shimbun* (25 November).

March, James G., and Johan P. Olsen. 1989. *Rediscovering Institutions: The Organizational Basis of Politics.* New York: The Free Press.

Masujima Toshiyuki. 1996. *Gyōsei kaikaku no shiten* (Perspectives on administrative reform). Tokyo: Ryōsho Hukyū–kai.

Matsubara Satoru. 1995. *Tokushu hōjin kaikaku* (The reform of public corporations). Tokyo: Nihon Hyōron-sha.

Mikuriya Takashi and Watanabe Akio. 1997. *Shushō kantei no Ketsudan: Naikaku kambō hukuchōkan Ishihara Nobuo no 2600 nichi* (Decision-making in the Prime Minister's Office: Ishihara's 2600 days as deputy chief cabinet secretary). Tokyo: Chūō Kōron-sha.

Nakano Minoru. 1996. "Seikai saihenki no rippō katei: Henka to renzoku" (The changing legislative process in the age of party realignment). *Leviathan,* no. 18: 71–95.

Ōtake Hideo. 1997. *'Gyōkaku' no Hassō* (The ideology of administrative reform). Tokyo: TBS Buritanika.

"Shushō, tokushu hōjin minaoshi, taishō o nazashi ni" (Prime minister to point out the public corporations that need reorganizing). 1994. *Asahi Shimbun* (6 December).

"Taishoku-kin kyōsai no tōgō mo" (Two retirement pension public corporations unified?) 1994. *Asahi Shimbun* (26 December).

Tanaka Shūsei. 1995. *Jidai o miru* (A look at the times). Tokyo: Daiya-mondo-sha.

"Tokushu hōjin no minaoshi ni sekkyoku-teki: Keidanren kaichō hōshin o tenkan" (President of Keidanren positive on public corporation reform). 1995. *Asahi Shimbun* (10 January).

Tokyo Shimbun Gyōkaku Shuzai–han. 1982. *Kokka hasan: Gyōkaku wa nihon o sukueruka?* (Bankruptcy of the state: Can administrative reform save Japan?). Tokyo: Gyōsei Mondai Kenkyū-sho.

The Battle over the Breakup of NTT

Toyonaga Ikuko

I N 1985, the Nippon Telegraph and Telephone Public Corporation (Denden-kōsha), one of Japan's three major public corporations, was privatized, becoming the Nippon Telegraph and Telephone Corporation (NTT), the nation's largest company. But that was just the beginning of the story. Various powerful interests waged a war over division and deregulation of the telecom giant for many years thereafter.

This chapter will analyze developments in telecommunications policy under successive coalition governments from 1993 to 1996. During that period, telecom policy underwent critical review, especially in regard to NTT, which retained considerable monopoly power. The key issue, whether to break up NTT, was not resolved until after the Liberal Democratic Party (LDP) regained power in its own right as a result of the October 1996 general election of the House of Representatives (Lower House). I will introduce two hypotheses to account for the policy making and political decision-making process revolving around the NTT issue during the coalition period. The first, which yields a static snapshot of the process, is the hypothesis of the politics of public opinion, whereby public opinion and the nonpolitical actors behind it enjoy a significant influence on policy making. The other, which provides a dynamic, historical interpretation of recent developments in Japanese politics, is the hypothesis of a failed attempt at corporatism, an experiment tried in Japan 10 to 15 years later than in such industrialized countries as Britain.

By corporatism I mean a political arrangement that meets three criteria: first, the existence of a labor or social democratic party that is firmly identified with union power and is assumed to have the bulk of the nation's labor movement under its control; second, a record and/or realistic prospect of that party actually forming a government; and third, the existence of an institutional arrangement whereby labor and big-business leaders meet and secure their influence on policy making.[1] If we confine our consideration to the third criterion, Japan can be said to have a long tradition of a kind of corporatism, with representatives of labor and other sectoral interests invited to take part in government advisory councils assigned to particular policy areas (Satō and Matsuzaki 1986, 166–167; Shinoda 1992, 265–266). I would argue, however, that the first two criteria are far more important, and more relevant, to recent developments in Japanese politics. As this chapter will demonstrate, telecom policy provides an ideal case study, one that corroborates both the "politics of public opinion" and the "failed corporatism" hypotheses.

THE BACKGROUND

The seeds of the long and drawn-out war between NTT and the Ministry of Posts and Telecommunications over the future structure of NTT were sown in the period of reform enthusiasm ushered in by the Second Provisional Commission on Administrative Reform (Second Rinchō), chaired by Dokō Toshiwo, a former chairman of Keidanren (Japan Federation of Economic Organizations). Second Rinchō was active from 1981 to 1983, and its initiative led to the 1985 privatization of Denden-kōsha. Privatization was effected by the fixed-price sale of tranches of government-held shares, thereby creating 1.6 million individual NTT shareholders and stimulating public enthusiasm for investing in stocks. Denden-kōsha's privatization was the major item in the privatization program promoted by Second Rinchō and Prime Minister Nakasone Yasuhiro. One crucial question was left unresolved, however: whether to keep the newly privatized corporation together or divide it into independent companies. This would remain the chief focus of concern for policymakers and the relevant actors until late 1996.

Second Rinchō is said to have begun work on the understanding that Denden-kōsha management would accept breakup upon privatization. But management changed its mind and joined forces with the company union, Zendentsū (All-Japan Telecommunications Workers'

Union), which adamantly opposed any division of the company (Iio 1993, 124; Nakasone 1996, 516; Suzuki 1996, 44–45, 59–63). The Posts and Telecommunications Ministry, meanwhile, marginalized at the outset of the Second Rinchō–led privatization debate, began by opposing privatization and then gradually shifted its position to stressing the need for a competitive environment for the telecom industry as a whole, maintaining that privatization of NTT should go hand in hand with dissolution of its monopoly (Iio 1993, chap. 5).

A temporary resolution was reached when Second Rinchō published its report on telecom privatization in July 1982. A tone of compromise was obvious: Denden-kōsha was to be privatized as a whole. A resolution to the privatization bill passed in December 1984 stipulated a review of the company's structure (that is, the question of its division) within five years of privatization. This review was duly undertaken. On March 2, 1990, the Telecommunications Council, a government advisory panel reporting to the minister of posts and telecommunications, submitted a report recommending that NTT's services be divided into two—a nationwide network service and a local network service—for the time being, with the possibility of further division to be left for future consideration. After much behind-the-scenes political wheeling and dealing, however, the government announced on March 30—just a day before the deadline—that the decision on breaking up NTT would be deferred to another review, to be concluded by the end of fiscal 1995 (April 1995 through March 1996). Accordingly, the war between pro- and antidivision forces was expected to reach its denouement in fiscal 1995 with the issuing of another set of Telecommunications Council recommendations. As it happened, the denouement did not come until December 1996 and was rather anticlimactic, owing to political developments under successive coalition governments.

The first coalition, formed in August 1993, after the July general election of the Lower House triggered by a no-confidence vote against the cabinet of Prime Minister Miyazawa Kiichi, comprised eight parties—all parties except the LDP and the Japan Communist Party. Led first by Hosokawa Morihiro (August 1993–April 1994) and then Hata Tsutomu (April–June 1994), that coalition was replaced in late June 1994 by a tripartite coalition that startled the nation, comprising as it did the LDP and its longtime rival the Social Democratic Party of Japan (SDPJ),[2] as well as the small New Party Sakigake (*sakigake* means "pioneer"). This coalition was headed by SDPJ Chairman Murayama

Tomiichi until his abrupt resignation in January 1996, whereupon the LDP's Hashimoto Ryūtarō took over.

The NTT war was fought on two fronts: public opinion and the political arena, specifically, political compromise. In the next two parts we will discuss the battles on each front, referring to the contextual factors shaping them.

THE POLITICS OF PUBLIC OPINION

The war over NTT policy was fought first on the front of public opinion. Interestingly, the actors appealing eagerly to public opinion were not politicians but senior bureaucrats, labor unions, and big-business leaders. Two arguments can be advanced to explain this phenomenon. One is to say that this was typical of the preliminary stage of policy making in Japan, when politicians as a rule play a minimal role, leaving bureaucrats and other players who have direct interests in the policy-making process a great deal of room to maneuver. The other is to assume that public support was actually perceived as the ultimate stake by those pursuing competing policy objectives. Analysis of a single example of the telecom policy-making process does not yield sufficient evidence to bear out the former interpretation, but the sequence of events outlined below demonstrates how public opinion can be seen as an important stake by policymakers and other interests and how it can be incorporated in the policy-making process even when its influence is not being mediated by representative institutions, such as political parties and elected officials.

The First Battle: Targeting the Stock Market

The battle for public opinion is seen most clearly in debate over countless reports on NTT issued by stakeholders, often with the intention of molding public opinion. The Second Rinchō report of 1982 was undoubtedly the most important, since it put the issue on the agenda and probably conditioned the way the war was fought. After this report, all stakeholders became more sensitive to reports produced by "authoritative" bodies and were eager to exert an influence on the drafting process. The Posts and Telecommunications Ministry was especially keen, since it had been shut out of the process of drafting the Second Rinchō report at first and had had to scramble to catch up with what was going on. Having learned a harsh lesson, thereafter the ministry enthusiastically promoted the prodivision cause to ensure that its stance would be reflected in subsequent reports.

The ministry targeted stock market analysts even before its Telecommunications Council began discussions for the fiscal 1995 review, since there was a perception that it had lost the previous phase of the war by March 1990 in the face of pressure from NTT shareholders and the Ministry of Finance, which was being blamed for a plunge in the value of NTT shares and was strongly concerned to keep the stock market stable. The stock market had slumped because of the collapse of the so-called bubble economy. The value of NTT shares had dropped accordingly, betraying shareholders' speculative expectations and feeding a deep sense of anxiety. It was thought that breaking up NTT would prompt a further drop in the share price, inflicting damage on the stock market as a whole (Iio 1993, 195–196).

The ministry therefore embarked on its fiscal 1995 campaign by contacting influential think tanks and analysts, especially those affiliated with major securities firms both at home and abroad. They were encouraged to produce optimistic reports on the impact of breaking up NTT. The price of NTT shares actually rose on the assumption that dividing up the company would increase its competitiveness. NTT executives, finally becoming aware of the atmosphere surrounding the market in November 1995, scrambled to recover lost ground and had a quiet word with some influential individuals in the securities industry. As a result, the industry clammed up on the NTT issue, producing no further reports assessing the impact of dividing NTT. It has been said that NTT could lean on securities firms by threatening to withhold the right to handle transactions in the imminent stock flotation for its newly spun-off company in the mobile telephone business (Fujii 1996, 20–24; Nikkan Kōgyō Shimbun 1996, 101).

The ministry's strategy of targeting stock market spokespeople was successful in that it kept the Finance Ministry away from events and prevented interference from shareholders. It could make no further gains, however, for counterpressure was soon focused on the same targets, effectively muzzling them. The ministry's effort thus failed to decisively sway public opinion, or at least market opinion.

Division versus Deregulation

The way in which the ministry was forced reluctantly to announce a policy of further deregulation of the telecom industry is another eloquent example of the actors' keen concern with public opinion. In the course of the heated debate over reports, NTT came to realize that its exclusive practices in relation to network access would harm its position in the eyes of report-producing bodies, which the company equated with public opinion. The ministry, meanwhile, suffered under a similar handicap in begrudging further deregulation.

NTT made the first move. In September 1995, it suddenly announced that it would open up network access to all other telecom companies, thus outflanking the ministry, which had been criticizing NTT for exclusive, discriminatory management of network access. NTT was now able to argue that there was no reason to break up the company and that a competitive environment for the industry as a whole should be created by removing the ministry's regulatory power.

Sentiment immediately shifted in NTT's favor, putting the ministry on the defensive. The ministry had been chivied into a position in which it had had to clarify its attitude toward further telecom deregulation. Up to that time, the ministry had maintained that NTT had to be broken up before further deregulation took place, otherwise the new telecom companies that had so far been protected by government regulation would be mowed down by mighty NTT.

The bureaucrats of the ministry's Telecommunications Bureau were most reluctant to play the card of further deregulation, though this now appeared essential to restore the ministry's standing in the eyes of the public. Antagonism toward NTT within the Telecommunications Bureau had escalated to the point where all channels of communication with the company were closed off, unlike the leadup to the previous review, when they had been kept open. Consequently, a sense of crisis grew within the ministry, along with criticism of the Telecommunications Bureau. In the end the minister was called on to resolve the issue. In December 1995, he announced (without, it was rumored, going through the Telecommunications Bureau) the ministry's intention to promote further deregulation, irrespective of NTT's management structure.

The ministry also tried to woo public opinion by suggesting a further step. At the time there was speculation that the ministry's real aim was to break up NTT in order to bring about a proliferation of telecom companies, since this would create more executive posts into which senior bureaucrats could step after retiring from the ministry (the practice of *amakudari*, or "descent from heaven," whereby retired bureaucrats take up high-ranking jobs in companies in the sector under the ministry's jurisdiction). To dispel such suspicions and give an appearance of neutrality, the ministry suggested publicly that it might introduce some form of self-regulation of *amakudari* to new telecom companies. The possibility of self-regulation was put on the agenda in early 1996, as the fiscal 1995 review process was drawing to a close. It was clear that the ministry was desperate to appeal to public opinion, though in the end it stepped back from the brink, unable to commit itself to such a self-sacrificing step (Fujii 1996, 58–64, 111–113, 121–125).

The Union versus Big Business

Zendentsū also used its abundant financial and organizational resources to appeal to public opinion. The union energetically organized seminars, symposiums, and other forums designed to sell its antidivision line, though most were packaged and presented as neutral, voluntarily organized functions. Zendentsū also asked its 230,000 members for additional donations (which amounted to ¥350 million) to finance operations to block the company's breakup, and later secured approval from the union's annual convention to use money from the ¥50 billion strike fund.

The union's most eye-catching action was the purchase of a full-page advertisement in a national daily on March 31, 1995, in which the head of Zendentsū, Kajimoto Kōji, and the president of NEC Corporation, Sekimoto Tadahiro, argued against the division of NTT. Some politicians felt this was going too far. There was definitely negative sentiment toward the union's attempt to throw its weight around in public (Fujii 1996, 90–91).[3]

NEC's Sekimoto gave the impression, in the newspaper ad, that he was speaking for Japanese big business. While many business leaders were sympathetic to the antidivision camp, the other side had allies, too. One was Suzuki Yoshio, director of the Asahi Research Center. At the time, he was a member of the Administrative Reform Committee, set up by the Prime Minister's Office in December 1994 to follow up the work of Second Rinchō. Earlier he had served on the secretariat of Second Rinchō. It was he, in fact, who persuaded the Posts and Telecommunications Ministry to play the deregulation card to save the prodivision cause. He also ensured that the recommendations of the Administrative Reform Committee's Subcommittee on Deregulation echoed the ministry's line. Not coincidentally, those recommendations were published the day after the minister's announcement of a policy of further deregulation (Fujii 1996, 119–120; Nikkan Kōgyō Shimbun 1996, 37–39; Suzuki 1996, 279).

The schism in big business was sharply reflected in various reports, especially those produced by Keidanren, which functioned mainly as the political front for big-business interests. Keidanren set up a special working group in 1994 to contribute to the fiscal 1995 review. At first the group took a fairly neutral stance, even in the eyes of Ministry of Posts and Telecommunications bureaucrats (Fujii 1996, 71). This may have sprung from a sense of noblesse oblige, which was quite common among business leaders and was the main motivation for such voluntary activities of Keidanren. But it was not long before pro- and antidivision interests clashed as the working group struggled to draft Keidanren's recommendations.

The Divided Business Sector

The rift within Keidanren reflected that between the so-called NTT family of companies and companies that had close ties (especially of capital) with the non-NTT telecom companies created after the privatization and partial deregulation of telecommunications. The NTT family of companies included NTT's "main banks" and electronics firms, such as NEC, that were its major suppliers. Together they constituted the bigger group within Keidanren. The other side, however, could mobilize sympathy from old-line heavy industries, which had been undergoing wrenching restructuring for many years due to intensified international competition and thus had good reason to resent NTT's privileged and protected status.

In September 1995, Keidanren published an interim report on the NTT issue. It stressed the necessity of deregulation without ever mentioning the possibility of dividing NTT. This was a humiliating blow to the ministry, which had tried hard to "assist" the working group. It had even helped arrange a research trip for working-group members to the United States, hoping that the recent successful breakup of AT&T would impress them. It is said that the ministry begged to the very end for the inclusion of at least a mention of division and even suggested that in return it might concede on deregulation policy.

As discussion proceeded to the upper echelons of Keidanren, however, the prodivision argument gained strength. Both camps mobilized all their forces in the series of discussions that ensued. The ministry also tried to secure influence by asking its former senior bureaucrats to attend important meetings. The top level of internal discussion was Keidanren's Committee on Information and Telecommunications Policy. Here antagonism between the two camps reached a peak, and strong words were exchanged. It seemed virtually impossible to produce any recommendations that would represent the united voice of Keidanren. Indeed, the final report on telecommunications policy, issued on January 8, 1996, contained no substantial opinion regarding NTT's future structure, a reflection of the deep schism within Keidanren (Fujii 1996, 67–86; Nikkan Kōgyō Shimbun 1996, 39–41).

Impotent Keidanren?

It was not surprising to find Keidanren participating in major policy debates. Ever since former Chairman Dokō Toshiwo had been appointed to head Second Rinchō, becoming a national figure symbolizing the administrative reform initiative, Keidanren had even seemed to bear the mantle of reform advocate. This was not always the case, however, as seen in the NTT policy debate. Its internal split over NTT deprived Keidanren of the chance to provide leadership in this heated policy debate and thus reinforce its image as a public-minded "wise men's group." The course of events also suggested that the world of big business could easily be divided by conflicting causes that reflected existing configurations of business liaisons and interests and that the primary concern of the business leaders in Keidanren was to win over the organization to their particular cause.

Other questions arise: What was at stake in regard to the Keidanren report? Why was the Posts and Telecommunications Ministry so frantic over it? Why were business leaders so ready to fight one another, even to the extent of exposing Keidanren's disunity to the outside world? The report would have no binding force, comprising merely the recommendations of a voluntary organization. It was quite certain, however, that the report would have an important effect on public opinion. Was that the only reason for its perceived importance? To answer these questions, we need to examine Keidanren's political power.

Keidanren had long been the main conduit for the flow of money from big business to political parties. It provided donations through an organization called the Kokumin Seiji Kyōkai (Association for National Politics), and had a fund-raising committee to control the flow of political donations from its member companies to the LDP, as well as to the opposition Democratic Socialist Party (DSP).[4] What is important here is that Keidanren's member companies were discouraged from funding parties directly, although there were no constraints on corporate donations to individual factions and politicians. Keidanren had introduced this integrating arrangement to ensure a united stance of capital vis-à-vis the labor movement and to sustain the rule of the LDP as the guardian of the capitalist order. Consequently, Keidanren had placed itself in a rather difficult position in terms of ensuring that the LDP, and politics as a whole, reflected its own organizational interests effectively (Ishikawa and Hirose 1989, 178–181).

It is likely that the wrangling within Keidanren was motivated by concern over the report's effect on public opinion rather than its direct impact on policymakers. Their preoccupation with public opinion led Keidanren members to air their differences publicly. It is also possible that those within Keidanren who participated actively in the debate were allied with different groups of politicians and/or branches of the civil service and waged a surrogate battle on their behalf.

Keidanren's activities as an organization were not specifically designed to exert strong leverage in order to promote its particular concerns at any given time. Instead, individuals who gained prominence in Keidanren received the "fringe benefit" of gaining the friendship of important politicians and making the maximum use of these personal relationships either to satisfy their own infatuation with politics, which is quite common among Japanese business leaders, or to further their particular business interests (Ōtake 1996, 176, 186–187). Some studies suggest that peak business organizations offer high-ranking members opportunities to mingle with important policymakers (Tsujinaka 1988, 212–213; Kabashima 1990, 17–19) and that business leaders are inclined to cultivate long-term, regular interaction with high-ranking politicians and/or bureaucrats because this is the best way of exerting influence over politics and policy making (Tsujinaka 1988, 212–213; Ōtake 1996, 184–186).

This organizational inclination to encourage individuals to nurture ties with high-ranking policymakers exposed Keidanren to partisanship, especially after it relinquished its role in soliciting business donations to the LDP in 1994 as a consequence of the LDP's split. Keidanren gave up this role after upheaval in the LDP in 1993 over political reform policy had divided business leaders between those sympathetic to Ozawa Ichirō and his followers, who bolted the LDP and set up the neoconservative Japan Renewal Party (JRP) just before the general election, and those supportive of the old guard that remained within the LDP. It is also believed that this partisanship also affected some parts of the civil service, mainly through personal connections between politicians and senior bureaucrats.[5] In short, personal relationships between business leaders and high-ranking politicians and/or bureaucrats may have played a part in dividing Keidanren. Even if that was the case, however, public opinion was still the only conceivable stake in this surrogate battle that would affect NTT's policy.

The Telecommunications Council report was published on February 29, 1996. It recommended dividing NTT into one national long-distance carrier and two local carriers. Unsurprisingly, the council's orientation coincided with that of the Posts and Telecommunications Ministry, which had been able to manipulate proceedings and the appointment of members of the council. Nevertheless, by then the ministry had lost points with public opinion as a result of its earlier intransigence over deregulation. It has been pointed out that the ministry should have conceded on deregulation at least a month earlier if it hoped to win the fiscal 1995 battle (Fujii 1996, 133). Public opinion had been shown to have the power to pick winners.[6]

THE POLITICAL FRONT

After publication of the Telecommunications Council report, as well as other reports by governmental and nongovernmental bodies presenting arguments for and against breaking up NTT,[7] the company's destiny was handed over to the politicians, who dealt with the issue in a confidential, low-key manner, in sharp contrast to the highly public debate of the preceding phase. The government was scheduled to deliver its decision by the end of fiscal 1995. On the very day of the deadline, however, the government announced that it would defer its decision so that it could submit legislation during the next ordinary session of the Diet, which would start in January 1997.

The politicians' immobility was no doubt influenced by the political situation that emerged with the rise of coalition governments. In the following I will discuss the logic that shaped politicians' handling of the NTT issue and evaluate their final output in terms of the hypothesis of a failed attempt at corporatism. Before exploring the implications of this hypothesis, however, we need to review developments

surrounding the privatization of Denden-kōsha, since the seeds of attempted corporatism seem to have been sown at that time.

The Seeds of Corporatism?

The major actors remained more or less the same from privatization
into the coalition period, at least until the LDP-SDPJ-Sakigake coalition replaced the eight-party coalition. First, we must mention Yamagishi Akira. The president of Zendentsū at the time of Denden-kōsha's
privatization, he became the president of the peak labor organization
Rengō when it incorporated public-sector unions in 1989. He left his
mark on all crucial political dealings regarding NTT and was unques-
tionably one of the key actors until the surprise formation of the LDP-
SDPJ-Sakigake government led to Rengō's marginalization.

Second, we must mention the politicians Kanemaru Shin and his
protégés Ozawa Ichirō and Hata Tsutomu. Kanemaru, chief lieutenant
of the powerful Takeshita faction of the LDP, had established himself
as an *éminence grise* within the party, though he disappeared from the
political scene after resigning from the LDP and giving up his seat in
the Diet in October 1992 following allegations of having received illegal political donations from the courier company Tokyo Sagawa Kyūbin. Ozawa and Hata were regarded as being among the most promising
young leaders of the LDP. They were instrumental in splitting the
party in 1993, when they broke away to establish the JRP, and they later
took the initiative in forming the eight-party coalition government.
These politicians had a hand in both critical developments in telecom
policy and the failed attempt at corporatism. Not surprisingly, all three
belonged to the Posts and Telecommunications *zoku* (a reference to
politicians with strong ties to one or another government agency) and
thus were well positioned to influence policy in this area. They also
shared the wish for institutional reform to bring about a true two-party
system that would enable alternation of the ruling party.

Political dealings over the privatization of Denden-kōsha served as
the catalyst for an enterprising union leader and reformist LDP politicians under the aegis of Kanemaru to cultivate contacts. It was also
this process that enabled Yamagishi to establish his reputation as a
shrewd labor leader. Yamagishi was greatly aided by his close ties with
Shintō Hisashi, the last president of Denden-kōsha and the first president of NTT. (Such ties were no surprise in a nation where enterprise
unions are the norm.) In the leadup to privatization, Shintō persuaded

Yamagishi to accommodate privatization, while Yamagishi persuaded Shintō to endorse the union's opposition to division (Nakasone 1996, 516).[8] In addition, the Nakasone government accommodated Yamagishi's demands. Zendentsū's focus was clearly on preventing the company's breakup, and the government had good reason to make concessions on this point, since it was in a hurry to pass legislation to implement privatization of Denden-kōsha, which had become symbolic of the government's entire privatization program.

Actually, Zendentsū was more bothered by the Japan Socialist Party (JSP), which was intent on blocking any privatization bill that would earn points for the LDP even though Zendentsū, having earned government concessions, clearly wanted it. While Yamagishi could still rely on those JSP Diet members whose main base of support was Zendentsū, it was felt that the JSP as a whole was disappointing and unreliable. (Actually, Zendentsū-backed JSP members were a help in that they mediated contacts between Yamagishi and some LDP members on the NTT issue.) The union leader was urged to realize the significance, and the future necessity, of direct communication with LDP politicians (Iio 1993, chap. 7). The fact that Kanemaru, a power in the Posts and Telecommunications *zoku* and at the time chairman of the LDP's General Council, acted flexibly in behalf of Zendentsū is suggestive.[9]

Thus, four groups of actors worked together toward creation of a privatized NTT: Denden-kōsha's labor union and management, some influential LDP politicians, and Zendentsū sympathizers within the JSP. In retrospect, the communication channels among the four groups were later to develop into a much broader force whereby some LDP and JSP politicians, and from time to time union and business leaders, would discuss the possibility of putting an end to the LDP's prolonged rule. The NTT issue served to catalyze this force, with Zendentsū and its leader an integral part of the process from the start.

The First NTT Review

The conclusion of the first review of NTT's structure by the scheduled deadline of the end of March 1990 revealed the discretion of politicians more clearly. The communication channels developed in connection with privatization appeared to be effective in influencing the government's decision, which was hammered out in the LDP Policy Research Council's subcommittee on telecommunications policy. Just before the deadline, the subcommittee decided that NTT's future structure should be reviewed again in fiscal 1995, overruling the Telecommunications Council report that had recommended dividing NTT into three companies. Hata was chairman of the subcommittee and is said to have delivered his judgment in the presence of representatives of both the Finance and the Posts and Telecommunications Ministries.[10]

As already mentioned, events surrounding the 1990 review featured another twist. It has been reported that when the Telecommunications Council began deliberations in 1988 the Posts and Telecommunications Ministry's Telecommunications Bureau was besieged for three days with phone calls from NTT shareholders anxious about a possible drop in the share price. Worried over the stock market, which had already fallen, and concerned to raise the maximum amount of money from the future sale of the remaining government-held shares of NTT, the Finance Ministry stepped in.

At first glance, this may seem to be just another example of the traditional rivalry between the two ministries, with the much stronger Finance Ministry likely to be the winner. However, the sequence of events can also be seen in the light of the following two contexts. First, the outcome of the review can be explained as a consequence of the personal relationship cultivated between Yamagishi and some LDP politicians since the time of privatization. It has been recalled that Yamagishi directly requested Hata to halt the prodivision forces.[11] It is also widely believed that Kanemaru, Hata's mentor, quietly engineered the political compromise regarding the 1990 review, thus rewarding Yamagishi for their long relationship (Fujii 1996, 94; Obi 1996, 108).[12] All this suggests that a certain group within the LDP on the one hand and Zendentsū and its leader on the other were committed to the outcome of the first review, auguring their far bolder enterprise three years later of engineering the formation of the first non-LDP government in 38 years.

Second, we must remember that the LDP was short of a majority in the House of Councillors (Upper House), which it had lost when the JSP made dramatic gains in the 1989 Upper House election thanks to the popularity of its chairwoman, Doi Takako. After that election, the LDP had no choice but to take into consideration the stance of the JSP, which had strengthened its position as the largest opposition party.

The emergence of Rengō was another significant factor. Rengō was formed in November 1987 as the Japanese Private-Sector Trade Union Confederation, the umbrella organization for major private-sector unions, including those belonging to Sōhyō (General Council of Trade Unions of Japan) and Dōmei (Japan Confederation of Labor), which thereupon disbanded. Rengō changed its name to the Japanese Trade Union Confederation when the public-sector unions affiliated with the former Dōmei and Sōhyō joined in November 1989, whereupon Sōhyō disbanded. The merger of Sōhyō, which supported the JSP, and Dōmei, which backed the DSP, into Rengō was expected to facilitate the rapprochement of the JSP and the DSP.[13]

Yamagishi was also the leader of the movement for united labor, and was expanded Rengō's first president. His design was for Rengō to urge cooperation among opposition parties, especially the JSP and the DSP; their united endeavor, backed by Rengō's powerful electoral machine, would pave the way for a non-LDP government.[14] The time seemed ripe for the emergence of a social democratic, labor-backed force, Doi's popularity and the emergence of Rengō being seen as powerful assets to challengers to LDP rule.

Given this context, the antidivision camp's success in modifying the Telecommunications Council's recommendations can be explained in terms of the opposition's power to block legislation in the Upper House and what appeared to be an unprecedented opportunity for labor (Rengō) to influence political decision making. This reflected the optimistic view of many center-left observers that labor could have a real influence by bringing about an end to LDP dominance and participating in an alternative government.

Rengō's Corporatist Ambitions

Rengō seemed to be advancing toward the anticipated corporatist era. Having unified private- and public-sector unions, the organization's leadership believed that it could now facilitate cooperation between the JSP and the DSP, which had been antagonistic toward each other for so long. The Kōmeitō (Clean Government Party) and Shaminren (United Social Democratic Party) as well as Upper House Rengō (a parliamentary group of Upper House members elected with Rengō's support in 1989), were also invited to cooperate in order to coordinate opposition control of the Upper House and increase opposition chances of wresting control of the Lower House from the LDP in a future general election. Rengō's stated aim was to create an alternative governing force, with the ultimate goal of creating a two-party system. To commit itself to this grand plan, it deliberately left the matter of electoral support for specific parties and candidates to the discretion of individual member unions while proclaiming its intention of "cooperation and collaboration" with the above-named four parties in particular (Rengō 1990, 200–201). Rengō also advocated a comprehensive policy approach rather than ad hoc, piecemeal support for member unions' policy concerns and repudiated the rigid ideological agenda that had preoccupied Sōhyō and the JSP for so long (Shinoda 1989, 123, 146).

Rengō's broad-church endorsement of center-left parties and its comprehensive and pragmatic approach to policy seemed to point to the possibility of its developing into the united voice of labor, catalyzing an alternative governing force through its inclusive and mediating approach to center-left parties, and achieving responsible participation in government. Reinforcing this outlook, Yamagishi became a national figure through active involvement in politics and frequent appearances in the media, recalling the shrewd political skills he had exercised in the privatization of Denden-kōsha and the creation of Rengō.

At the time, Yamagishi apparently had a somewhat corporatist image of party-labor partnership, whereby Rengō would assure electoral support to a group of parties (or individual politicians) committed to social democratic ideals in exchange for the prerogative of access to government decisions once those parties took power (Igarashi 1992, 342). The opposition's dominance of the Upper House no doubt encouraged such a vision. Later, however, Yamagishi came to believe that Rengō could not afford to wait for an alternative governing force to materialize from the array of opposition parties.[15] This was one cause of the gulf that would divide what had been anticipated as a step toward corporatism from what was actually being attempted with Rengō's backing.

Now that the combined opposition held the majority in the Upper House, the next question was how to build up a similar majority in the Lower House and topple the LDP from power. The following discussion will assume that Japanese social democratic forces were aware of the prospect of corporatism, which would enable them to influence government policies by having the parties they supported elevated to power.

The Eight-party Coalition Government

By the time the final settlement of the NTT issue was reached in December 1996, Japanese party politics had undergone its most dramatic change since 1955, when the LDP was formed through the merger of two conservative parties and the JSP was reunified (it had split into left- and right-wing parties in 1951). That was the birth of an eight-party coalition government excluding the LDP in 1993, followed by the even more unconventional phenomenon of the formation of an LDP-SDPJ-Sakigake coalition government in 1994. Under these coalitions, the SDPJ shared in government for the first time—as the largest party in the first coalition and the second largest in the second (in which it also provided the prime minister).

On the surface, the rise of a non-LDP government seemed to fulfill the ambition of Rengō and its allies in the social democratic bloc, since they had access to power as insiders for the first time. In fact, the coalition was in large part the brainchild of Rengō's leader, Yamagishi. He was one of the key figures who had masterminded a pact between the SDPJ and Ozawa's JRP aimed at wresting the Lower House majority from the LDP in 1993.[16] All Yamagishi's hard work seemed to have been rewarded.

The SDPJ-JRP pact that enabled this revolution was also notable in some other senses. It meant a formal end to the most important confrontation in Japanese postwar politics, that between proponents of disarmament and rearmament, since the JSP/SDPJ championed the former and Ozawa's group the latter. (As a member of the LDP, Ozawa had strongly advocated the use of Self-Defense Forces [SDF] personnel in United Nations peacekeeping operations.) At the same time, however, it meant a significant deviation from the original corporatist scenario envisioned by center-left observers, since the coalition incorporated an element most alien to any social democratic scenario—Ozawa's JRP, the "new right" group that had bolted the LDP.

Nevertheless, the fact that the coalition's self-declared mandate was limited to political reform could be said to legitimize its unconventional, even contradictory, composition. This mandate was fulfilled with the electoral reform of 1994 that introduced a single-seat district system for the Lower House in place of the multiseat system that had prevailed through most of the postwar period—an initiative pushed by Ozawa and his allies since 1992, on the grounds that it would lead to a two-party system. Because of the coalition's limited purpose, it is difficult to argue that it represented an attempt at corporatism. We can make a couple of observations, however. First, Yamagishi and Ozawa shared the vision of a two-party system in Japan, in which a labor-backed social democratic party would compete with a conservative party. On the basis of this common ground, Yamagishi threw his support behind Ozawa's design for electoral reform.[17] The promise of corporatism was still felt to exist beyond the anticipated reform.

Second, while conciliating other members of the coalition at first, Ozawa gradually revealed his domineering leadership style. Hosokawa Morihiro, chosen as prime minister because of the significant contribution his popular Japan New Party had made to the overthrow of the LDP in the 1993 Lower House election, soon turned out to be a mere figurehead. Ozawa's dictatorial and unpredictable maneuvers, coupled with his Machiavellian approach to potential allies in pursuit of a given goal, was precisely what made electoral reform possible, though it also made Rengō's participation in power subject to his whim or, at best, his personal contact with labor leaders. The viability of corporatism would have to wait to be tested until the eight-party coalition, with its limited reform mandate, had disbanded.

The LDP-SDPJ-Sakigake Government

The emergence of the LDP-SDPJ-Sakigake coalition in late June 1994 stunned the nation. Unlike the previous coalition, it was far from being the product of a corporatist initiative, for it had nothing to do with Rengō and its sympathizers. The tripartite coalition was the result, rather, of a revolt by left-wing elements of the SDPJ keen to revenge themselves on Rengō and its SDPJ collaborators for attempting to marginalize them.

The drive to marginalize and even eradicate the leftist, fundamentalist elements of the SDPJ actually predated the period of coalition governments. While strengthening its ties with certain LDP politicians, the center-right wing of the SDPJ had been urged to cut loose from its left-wing colleagues (Nakasone 1996, 16; Honzawa 1997, 40). This drive intensified after the SDPJ voted against the International Peace Cooperation Bill (which would enable SDF personnel to take part in UN peacekeeping missions) in June 1992 despite the center-right leadership of then-Chairman Tanabe Makoto, who had been expected to impose his pragmatic line on the party. This event dramatically exposed the party's inability to overrule its fundamentalist wing on such crucial matters as security, negating the party's credentials for government. It also reopened the gulf between the SDPJ and the DSP, which basically agreed with the LDP on security, thus destroying the effectiveness of Rengō's broad-church electoral endorsement in the July

1992 Upper House election. Those who had anticipated an SDPJ government in cooperation with the DSP in the near future were deeply disappointed. Yamagishi was no exception and had to discard the idea that the SDPJ could be assimilated as a whole into an alternative governing bloc.[18] In the July 1993 Lower House election, Zendentsū and some other powerful unions actively campaigned against left-wing SDPJ candidates, removing their names from their lists of endorsed candidates, and were responsible for the defeat of quite a few (Honzawa 1997, 57).

Naturally, outrage built up among left-wing SDPJ members. This, together with Ozawa's miscalculation, led to the irrevocable breakdown of the eight-party coalition. Ozawa tried to shed the SDPJ from the coalition, whereupon the party resigned from the cabinet, triggering the collapse of the coalition in June 1994 and, indirectly, the SDPJ's improbable alliance with the LDP later that month. In fact, SDPJ left-wingers had been in contact with some LDP members behind the scenes, frustrated and possibly resigned to their waning fortunes within the party as well as vis-à-vis the electorate (Nihon Keizai Shimbun-sha 1994, part 3; Kyōdō Tsūshin-sha 1996, 67–70). Ironically, the marriage of convenience between traditional enemies was brokered by the most leftist, fundamentalist members of the SDPJ and the mainstream conservatives of the LDP.

This new coalition marginalized the forces both within and without the SDPJ that had been committed to the previous coalition government, including Rengō (Nihon Keizai Shimbun-sha 1994, 126–30). The parties supporting Rengō were now divided between the government and the opposition. One of Rengō's major backers, the DSP, even disappeared when it was subsumed, together with all the other parties in the first coalition except the SDPJ and Sakigake, into the New Frontier Party (NFP), established in December 1994. The prospect of a new relationship between united labor and the government seemed to have faded. Rengō was also caught in a bind between member unions that supported SDPJ Chairman Murayama as prime minister of the LDP-SDPJ-Sakigake government and those, like Zendentsū, that were opposed.

Zendentsū and its sympathizers attempted to create a new party headed by the center-right SDPJ politician Yamahana Sadao (Kyōdō Tsūshin-sha 1996, 39, 98–99, 151), a move in keeping with Rengō's newly declared policy of launching a "third force" that would help pave the way for a two-party system (Rengō 1995, 64). But the timing could not have been worse. Catastrophic events—the Great Hanshin-Awaji Earthquake of January 1995 and the sarin nerve-gas attack in Tokyo subways by the Aum Shinrikyō cult in March 1995—plunged the nation into crisis mode, leaving no leeway for political games, and plans for a new party were aborted.

The Final Phase of the NTT War

The final phase of the war over NTT took place after Rengō had lost its sense of direction, its dream of corporatism shattered. This was also a time when politicians and various interests were maneuvering for greatest advantage under the new Lower House electoral system in preparation for the next general election, which it was felt could come at any time (in the event, it was held in October 1996).

In 1995, the LDP-SDPJ-Sakigake government embarked on the second review of NTT's structure, as had been scheduled in 1990. In the runup to the review, Zendentsū began trying to appease the LDP, which resented the union for its recent attempt to split the SDPJ and set up a new party under Yamahana. Zendentsū targeted Katō Kōichi, secretary-general of the LDP and a leading contender for leadership of the Miyazawa faction, and he appeared to be sympathetic. After all, Katō had consolidated his position in the party as well as in the Miya-zawa faction thanks to his close ties to the SDPJ, which at the time was a valuable asset to the coalition. There was good reason for consider-ing that Katō's personal interest in strengthening his position within the party and his faction might prompt him to contact interests re-lated to the SDPJ and thus cause him to listen to Zendentsū, as well.

Apart from that, the prospect of a Lower House election under new rules was Zendentsū's strongest card. The coalition's working group on the NTT issue gradually came under Zendentsū's influence as ex-pectations of an election grew. The best the working group could do was defer a final decision on NTT's structure to the next ordinary ses-sion of the Diet, starting in January 1997. This decision, arrived at just before the deadline for the review, was the initiative of the LDP mem-bers of the working group. Anticipating a general election, they wanted to avoid any complication of their relationship with Zendentsū, which was talking openly of lending its support to politicians who would op-pose the breakup of NTT.[19] In fact, Zendentsū was pressuring politicians of all stripes, offering its backing in the next Lower House election to candidates sympathetic to NTT and Zendentsū's antidivision cause (Fujii 1996, 91–92, 140).

This was a far cry from the days when unions had been identified with certain parties on a more or less permanent basis. It was also a big break from the time when Rengō had been preparing, by means of a broad-church endorsement of center-left parties, for the materialization of a social democratic bloc. In a sense it was, however, a logical extension of the selective endorsement policy Zendentsū had adopted vis-à-vis SDPJ candidates in the 1993 Lower House election.

As early as 1991, it was recognized that there were two schools of thought within Rengō regarding its relationship with political parties (Igarashi 1992, 342). One envisaged a long-standing, regular partnership with a particular party or bloc of parties. This was the approach embraced by Yamagishi. The other advocated issue-by-issue or policy-by-policy cooperation with various political parties. This is said to have been the preference of Washio Etsuya, Rengō's secretary-general from 1993 to 1997 and its president from 1997 onward, and also possibly that of Ashida Jinnosuke, Yamagishi's immediate successor as Rengō president.[20] Rengō was inclined toward the former type of relationship during the eight-party coalition period. But after the emergence of the LDP-SDPJ-Sakigake coalition, and not coincidentally after Yamagishi's resignation as president in October 1994, Rengō leaned toward the latter, piecemeal approach of policy-by-policy cooperation. This was a natural shift, in a sense, since Rengō could not wholeheartedly support the SDPJ after its internal upheaval had led to its unexpected alliance with the LDP (Rengō 1995, 64). This piecemeal approach soon came to be practiced in a rather aggressive, extensive way, leading Rengō to endorse even some LDP candidates in the 1996 Lower House election.

Washio's approach accorded with Zendentsū's behavior in regard to the fiscal 1995 NTT review, when it issued promises of support and threats to withhold support in the next general election on the basis of politicians' stance regarding the breakup of NTT. There is good reason to believe that this approach was effective at that particular time, since even the most established politicians were nervous over their chances in the first general election to be contested under the new system of single-seat districts. Naturally, Zendentsū took maximum advantage of its ability to deliver an organized vote. This may seem to prove the superiority of the piecemeal approach to party-labor relationships. But there was no guarantee that Zendentsū would be able to repeat its performance in subsequent Lower House elections, especially if the LDP reestablished its dominance under the new electoral system, which was thought to be advantageous to incumbents. (The 1996 Lower House election did in fact deliver victory to the LDP, which formed the next cabinet in its own right, though it maintained the façade of a coalition with the SDP and Sakigake for some time thereafter.)

When the deadline for settlement of the NTT issue was postponed, Zendentsū insisted in vain that the original schedule should be adhered to, wishing to maximize its influence before the next general election. By the end of 1995, however, both NTT and the Posts and Telecommunications Ministry were aware that the only way to bring about an end to hostilities was to divide NTT but create a single holding company. This idea, originating within big-business circles, was seriously discussed within NTT around the turn of the year, though the company did not suggest it to the ministry at that time, judging that a prodivision resolution in fiscal 1995 could be averted (Fujii 1996, 127–33).

The Settlement: Zendentsū Marginalized

The October 1996 general election enabled the LDP to reinforce its position as the largest party in the Lower House; it boosted its strength from 211 seats (out of 511 in the prereform Lower House) to 239 seats (out of 500 in the postreform Lower House) but failed to gain a majority. Meanwhile, the SDP made a disastrous showing, dropping from 30 to 15 seats, while Sakigake won only 2 seats, down from 9. After the election, the SDP and Sakigake agreed to remain in coalition with the LDP but declined representation in the new cabinet. Though the SDP was still a meaningful presence in the Upper House, in the July 1995 Upper House election for half the chamber's 252 seats the party's strength had plummeted from 41 to 16 of the seats contested, and there was no prospect of the party doing any better when the next Upper House election came due, in 1998. Zendentsū's marginalized position in the 1996 NTT settlement was curiously synchronous with the collapse of the SDP's influence.

In December 1996, the holding-company plan surfaced again, this time as the Post and Telecommunications Ministry's official policy. It came as a complete surprise to Zendentsū, though not to NTT, which had stayed in close touch with the ministry.[21] The settlement arrived at was the outcome of behind-the-scenes wheeling and dealing between

NTT and the ministry. It called for NTT to be divided into two local network companies (one for eastern Japan and one for western Japan) and one long-distance carrier that would be licensed to provide international services, as well. All three companies were to be under the control of a holding company. These changes were to be implemented within two and a half years of the enforcement of enabling legislation. This solution allowed both sides to save face: NTT maintained overall ownership, while the ministry secured the breakup of NTT's management and an increase in the number of executive posts.[22] The settlement was made known to the outside world only after the two sides had reached agreement, in dramatic contrast to the much-publicized battles that had characterized earlier phases of the telecom war.

Meanwhile, the LDP had regained control of the Lower House by enlisting the support of LDP-leaning independents while retaining the arrangement of consulting with the SDP and the Sakigake on major legislative issues because of its weakness in the Upper House. The LDP welcomed the announcement on December 6 of the ministry's new policy on NTT, since the party was eager to legalize holding companies, which had been abolished during the Allied occupation following World War II. The SDP's initial response was fairly negative, party spokespeople expressing reservations over possible damage to NTT's competitiveness. Curiously, Zendentsū made no comment for six days.[23] Later developments showed that Zendentsū swiftly shifted its focus to quibbling over details of the new structure, just as it had done when it capitulated to Second Rinchō's privatization plan.

Zendentsū pretended that the settlement did not necessarily represent a defeat for the union, but its members' future became far more uncertain, for it was not clear how the unions of the newly created telecom companies could take countermeasures against the holding company's management decisions. A simple division of NTT might have been better for the union in terms of its members' shopfloor rights, though the workers may have been happy at the prospect of increased competitiveness through more flexible management and the consolidation of capital. Zendentsū maintained an optimistic tone, as if it were more concerned with the fortunes of the enterprise as a whole than with its members' shopfloor rights. The union swiftly shrank to a mere enterprise union when it found itself marginalized in relation to the government as well as management.

CONCLUSION

The rise and fall of Japanese corporatist ambitions left a clear stamp on the development of NTT policy, which was swayed by shifts in the NTT union's position on the political front. The period of coalition governments aborted the promise of corporatism, and once-influential Zendentsū was reduced to a mere bystander in the end, excluded from the decision-making process.

The development of NTT policy also illustrates vividly how public opinion influenced the policy contestants. The way in which considerations of public opinion overruled policy arguments is especially noteworthy because that phase of the telecom war barely involved politicians, who as elected officials might be expected to be most attentive to public opinion. Politicians did step in to make decisions at a later stage, but they did not give public opinion as much weight as nonpolitical actors had earlier. Instead, they avoided public debate and relied on wheeling and dealing behind the scenes.

The policy making, or non–policy making, process seen in the course of the struggle over the breakup of NTT spotlights one notable pattern of the Japanese policy-making process that was probably shaped in the Second Rinchō period, when massive media coverage of Second Rinchō's activities and members brought policy debate closer to the public. This pattern consists of a curious combination of two contrasting phases. One is the phase wherein nonpolitical actors are major participants and public opinion is the ultimate stake: Much-publicized debate vies for public opinion, while politicians stay out of the debate until the final decision has been handed to them. The other is the phase after the final decision has been handed to politicians, when they deal with it in their usual behind-the-scenes, wheeling-and-dealing manner. This provides an opportunity for representatives of interest groups to influence parties and individual politicians using their political resources, such as an organized vote and personal ties. In sharp contrast to the much-publicized debate of the earlier phase, the logic behind the eventual outcome is unlikely to be announced to the public. In the case of NTT, the sequence of events in the second phase was affected by the course of the failed attempt at corporatism.

This pictures helps us identify different stages in a policy-making process wherein different factors, ranging from public opinion to an organized vote, carry the most weight. That helps us understand the course of action, and the strategy, of the actors involved in the process. We can plausibly say that public opinion has symbolic weight in the phase of setting the policy agenda—that is, setting a limited set of policy alternatives before politicians and the public—as does any organized vote (such as that of labor) whenever politicians' decisions are called for. Consequently, those actors who would be expected to be independent from public opinion, most notably bureaucrats, turn out to be attentive to public debate and sensitive to public opinion, while politicians enjoy relative independence from public debate despite their status as elected officials.

NOTES

1. Igarashi employs a similar definition of corporatism when he refers to the strategy pursued by Yamagishi Akira, president of Rengō (Japanese Trade Union Confederation) from 1989 to 1994, and the Rengō mainstream to establish "a labor party comparable to its European counterparts, and through it a labor voice in politics," which would enable "an effective corporatist arrangement to run the macroeconomy" (1992, 320).

2. Before February 1991, the SDPJ was known in English as the Japan Socialist Party (JSP). In January 1996 the party name was changed to the Social Democratic Party. In this chapter, for convenience' sake the party is referred to as the JSP before February 1991, as the SDPJ from February 1991, and as the SDP from 1996.

3. Some important members of the government working group formed in March 1996 to guide the government's decision on NTT shared this anti-Zendentsū, or more generally antiunion, sentiment. The major such figure was the LDP politician Nonaka Hiromu, who criticized "unions' infatuation with politics" (interview with Ogasawara Michiaki, Ministry of Posts and Telecommunications, March 18, 1997).

4. The DSP was formed in 1960, after a group of right-wing JSP members broke away because of disagreement over revision of the U.S.-Japan Security Treaty. The DSP espoused middle-of-the-road policies and generally supported the LDP's security stance.

5. Ozawa Ichirō, the de facto leader of the eight-party coalition, is said to have had close ties to a Posts and Telecommunications Ministry official who aggressively advocated division of NTT.

6. Public opinion as discussed here is not necessarily a concrete, objective phenomenon. Takeshita defines public opinion as "the particular body of opinion that is perceived to be influential in society by the policymakers concerned" (1990, 76). What interests us is that in the war over NTT, at least as

far as the fiscal 1995 phase is concerned, there is no evidence of widespread public concern. The favor of public opinion seems to have been merely a symbolic asset to policymakers, but clearly one they thought was worth pursuing.

7. Of reports by governmental bodies, that issued in November 1995 by the Fair Trade Commission's advisory committee on competition policy in the field of information and telecommunications, which appeared to side with NTT, became another important focus (Nikkan Kōgyō Shimbun 1996, 32–34). Many reports issued by private-sector bodies were in fact public relations exercises by Zendentsū, NTT, and other business interests in disguise and were clearly intended to influence public opinion via media coverage of their content (Nikkan Kōgyō Shimbun 1996, 40–41).

8. Those who had been associated with Second Rinchō saw this as an unforgivable "betrayal" by Shintō (Suzuki 1996, 58).

9. Nakasone recalls that Sejima Ryūzō, an influential politico-business fixer, persuaded Kanemaru to accommodate privatization despite the latter's initial reluctance (1996, 516). Iio suggests that the JSP's failure to accommodate Zendentsū's demands during Diet proceedings on the Denden-kōsha privatization bill paved the way for the subsequent realignment of the union world, which slipped out of the JSP's control and caused the party's marginalization (1993, 285).

10. Interview with Ogasawara, March 18, 1997.

11. Interview with Yamagishi Akira, July 11, 1997. Not coincidentally, in April 1994 Hata took over from Hosokawa as prime minister of the non-LDP coalition, a coalition orchestrated by none other than Yamagishi.

12. Interestingly, Kanemaru had established himself as a power in the Posts and Telecommunications *zoku* when he extended his influence to the field of telecommunications policy with his active involvement in Denden-kōsha's privatization (Iio 1993, 282).

13. See note 4.

14. This was termed the "SDP-Kōmeitō-DSP line" or the "strategy to consolidate social democratic forces."

15. Interview with Yamagishi, July 11, 1997.

16. Interview with Adachi Hiromichi, director of Rengō's Political Division, August 21, 1997.

17. Yamagishi is said to have opposed the idea of electoral reform at first. Ozawa, on the other hand, was a fervent proponent of a single-seat district system, which had been discussed within the LDP for some time and was seen by many as a shortcut to a two-party system. Outwardly, it was over this issue that Ozawa and his allies left the LDP. Ozawa then worked on winning over Yamagishi, which he did by insisting that the reallocation of Diet seats to smaller, single-seat districts would enable peaceful coexistence even between currently competing parties (interview with Yamagishi, July 11, 1997).

18. Interview with Yamagishi, July 11, 1997.

19. In the 1996 general election, the chair of the working group, the LDP's

Yamasaki Taku, secured the support of Zendentsū and defeated his NFP rival for the same seat.

20. Igarashi calls the former a "European" type of party-labor relationship, the latter an "American" type (1992, 342). The issue was whether what was anticipated was a two-party system consisting of a "radical" party and a "conservative" party, in which case the former would naturally monopolize labor support, or a system featuring two conservative parties, in which case individual candidates would matter more. Rengō's leaders themselves seemed confused by this terminology. Ashida, for example, seemed to be impressed by a German union leader who said that the DGB (Deutsche Gewerkschaftsbund), the German counterpart of Rengō, left the matter of party support to each individual's conscience ("Rōso wa kenzai" 1997). And Adachi Hiromichi, director of Rengō's political division, insisted that Washio's approach was more "European" than that of Yamada Seigo (secretary-general of Rengō from 1989 to 1993), who was inclined to shun involvement with politics and elections. At some point, however, Washio began to feel the necessity of supporting a social democratic party so that it could be presented to the Socialist International as the representative of Japanese labor (interview with Adachi on August 21, 1997).

21. Interview with Ogasawara, March 18, 1997; interview with Yoshiwara Yasunori, a member of Zendentsū's Central Executive Committee, August 21, 1997. It should be noted that in June 1996 NTT's chairmanship was taken over by a man who was both an NTT loyalist and a former Posts and Telecommunications Ministry official. This appointment was arranged by the LDP overriding the wish of the outgoing president, a tough antidivision fighter, for elevation to chairman (Fujii 1996, 161–164).

22. It was speculated that nearly 40 executive posts would be added as a result of the breakup (question by Kawamura Takashi, NFP, House of Representatives Standing Committee on Posts and Telecommunications, May 14, 1997).

23. Interview with Ogasawara, March 18, 1997. The statement finally issued by Zendentsū did not challenge the ministry's proposal or discuss the pros and cons of the proposed breakup. Zendentsū stated that it had approached the proposal as a totally new policy and merely questioned technical points that would be contained in the enabling bill (interview with Yoshiwara, August 21, 1997).

BIBLIOGRAPHY

Fujii Hajime. 1996. *Bunkatsu: NTT vs. Yūseishō—taigi naki tatakai* (Breakup: NTT versus the Ministry of Posts and Telecommunications—a war without justice). Tokyo: Daiyamondo-sha.

Honzawa Jirō. 1997. *Rengō no tsumi to batsu* (Rengō's sin and penalty). Tokyo: Piipuru-sha.

Igarashi Hitoshi. 1992. "Seiji, seitō to rōdō kumiai" (Politics, political parties, and labor unions). In Hōsei Daigaku Ōhara Shakai Mondai Kenkyūsho, ed. *"Rengō jidai" no rōdō undō: Saihen no dōtei to shintenkai* (The labor movement in the Rengō era: The path of realignment and new developments). Tokyo: Sōgō Rōdō Kenkyūsho.

Iio Jun. 1993. *Min'eika no seiji katei: Rinchō-gata kaikaku no seika to genkai* (The political process of privatization: The achievements and limits of Rinchō-style reform). Tokyo: Tokyo Daigaku Shuppan-kai.

Ishikawa Masumi and Hirose Michisada. 1989. *Jimintō* (The Liberal Democratic Party). Tokyo: Iwanami Shoten.

Kabashima Ikuo. 1990. "Masu media to seiji" (The mass media and politics). *Leviathan*, no. 7: 7–29.

Kyōdō Tsūshin-sha. 1996. *Murayama renritsu seiken gekidō no 561 nichi: Dokyumento seikai saihen* (The 561 turbulent days of the Murayama coalition government: Documenting political realignment). Tokyo: Kyōdō Tsūshin-sha.

Nakasone Yasuhiro. 1996. *Tenchi ujō: 50 nen no sengo seiji o kataru* (Reflections on 50 years in postwar politics). Tokyo: Bungei Shunjū-sha.

Nihon Keizai Shimbun-sha, ed. 1994. *"Renritsu seiken" no kenkyū* (A study of the coalition government). Tokyo: Nihon Keizai Shimbun-sha.

Nikkan Kōgyō Shimbun. 1996. *NTT ni mirai wa aru ka* (Does NTT have a future?) Tokyo: Nikkan Kōgyō Shimbun-sha.

Obi Toshio. 1996. *NTT saigo no sentaku* (NTT's final option). Tokyo: Kōdan-sha.

Ōtake Hideo. 1996. *Gendai Nihon no seiji kenryoku keizai kenryoku: Seiji ni okeru kigyō, gyōkai, zaikai* (Political and economic power in contemporary Japan: Companies, industries, and business circles in politics). Rev. ed. Tokyo: San'ichi Shobō.

Rengō. 1990. *Rengō hakusho: 90 shunki seikatsu tōsō no shiryō to kaisetsu* (Rengō white paper: 1990 spring labor offensive documents and commentaries). Tokyo: Rengō.

———. 1995. *Rengō no katsudō to kiroku: Rengō ninenkan no ayumi: '93.10–'95.9* (Rengō activities and records: The last two years, October 1993–September 1995). Tokyo: Rengō.

"Rōso wa kenzai, 'fuyōron' muyō" (Labor unions still in good shape: No need for claims that labor is useless). 1997. *Asahi Shimbun* (28 August): 8.

Satō Seizaburō and Matsuzaki Tetsuhisa. 1986. *Jimintō seiken* (LDP administrations). Tokyo: Chūō Kōron-sha.

Shinoda Toru. 1989. *Seikimatsu no rōdō undō* (The labor movement at century's end). Tokyo: Iwanami Shoten.

———. 1992. "'Rengō' jidai ni okeru 'seisaku sanka' no genjō to tembō" (The realities and prospects of labor participation in policy making in the Rengō era). In Hōsei Daigaku Ōhara Shakai Mondai Kenkyūsho, ed. *"Rengō jidai" no rōdō undō: Saihen no dōtei to shintenkai* (The labor movement in the

Rengō era: The path of realignment and new developments). Tokyo: Sōgō Rōdō Kenkyūsho.
Suzuki Yoshio. 1996. *Antō! NTT vs Yūsei-shō* (Secret Strife! NTT versus the Ministry of Posts and Telecommunications). Tokyo: Kōdan-sha.
Takeshita Toshirō. 1990. "Masu media to seron" (The mass media and public opinion). *Leviathan,* no. 7: 75–96.
Tsujinaka Yutaka. 1988. *Rieki shūdan* (Interest groups). Tokyo: Tokyo Daigaku Shuppan-kai.

Characteristics of the
Decision-making Structure of Coalitions

Nonaka Naoto

THE coalition government formed in late June 1994, the third since one-party rule by the Liberal Democratic Party (LDP) ended in 1993, particularly astonished the Japanese electorate. It comprised a previously unthinkable alliance of the LDP, the Social Democratic Party of Japan (SDPJ), and the New Party Sakigake, and Murayama Tomiichi, chairman of the SDPJ, was elected prime minister. The SDPJ, formerly called the Japan Socialist Party (JSP), had been the largest opposition party and the LDP's staunchest rival for nearly four decades. Its policies—especially on security matters—were vastly different from those of the LDP. Specifically, it suggested that the very existence of the Self-Defense Forces violated the Constitution and it advocated terminating the U.S.-Japan Security Treaty. The first coalition government, which was inaugurated less than a year previously, composed an alliance of eight parties that included the SDPJ but excluded the LDP. Hosokawa Morihiro was the prime minister of this unprecedented non-LDP administration.

Politics in Japan were chaotic and unpredictable in the coalition era as the rules and practices evolved during the period of LDP dominance no longer worked. The process leading to the formation of the Murayama coalition government was particularly unusual. The LDP swallowed wholesale the SDPJ-proposed conditions and principles for the coalition government, and yielded the post of prime minister to the SDPJ—even though it had nearly three times the number of House of Representatives (Lower House) seats than the SDPJ. For its part, the SDPJ broke a campaign pledge from the 1993 Lower House election when it switched allegiance from a coalition that excluded the LDP to one that included the LDP. Furthermore, after winning the prime ministership, the SDPJ abandoned its principles and reversed itself on its basic policies. In his first policy speech as prime minister in late July 1994, Murayama declared the Self-Defense Forces constitutional, voiced support for the security treaty with the United States as the basis of Japan's security policy, and endorsed policies advanced by the LDP until 1993. An SDPJ party convention ratified these policy positions that September.

This chapter compares the decision-making processes of the Hosokawa and Murayama coalition administrations with the policy-making processes of the LDP-dominated governments until 1993. Considering how the SDPJ had previously always considered itself to be the antithesis of the LDP, it is ironic that decision making during the Murayama administration more closely resembled that of the period of LDP dominance than policy making under the Hosokawa coalition government, which excluded the LDP.

The characteristics of decision making under the LDP-dominant system are discussed first, followed by examinations of the features of decision making in the Hosokawa and Murayama administrations. The respective policy-making mechanisms of the Hosokawa and Murayama governments are evaluated, transforming the methods of conducting politics is described, and then various conclusions are drawn.

POLICY MAKING IN
THE LDP-DOMINANT SYSTEM

For 38 years, no opposition party seriously threatened the LDP's political dominance. The lack of alternation in government meant that for a long time the LDP was effectively the party of government while the other parties were too weak to be regarded as legitimate opposition parties in the true sense of the term. As a consequence, even within the LDP, party discipline loosened and power dispersed. The lack of necessary competition and tension between the governing and opposition parties also resulted in general disinterest and apathy among the electorate.

LDP dominance encouraged and resulted in various operating mechanisms and patterns. A key characteristic was the decentralization of power and the role of local "pork barrel" politics for individual

LDP politicians. In budget making, LDP members had to focus on local public works needs in order to stand a chance of being reelected in their districts. Under the multiseat district system which prevailed before the 1996 election, an LDP candidate competed against LDP rivals as well as candidates of other parties. The electoral imperative of pork barrel politics and the LDP's dependence on deficit spending and the compiling of supplementary budgets were typical of the period of LDP-dominance.

The rise of *zoku* members—Diet members with special ties to specific government ministeries—was also important to decision making in the era of LDP dominance. This phenomenon increased the power of LDP politicians in the policy-making process relative to that of bureaucrats. Yet it also discouraged the LDP from aggregating interests. For example, the LDP's Policy Research Council included ministry- and issue-based select committees where matters of respective special concern were discussed. This process was in line with large umbrella organizations losing influence, such as Keidanren (Japan Federation of Economic Organizations) representing the interests of businesses, and Nōkyō (Japan Agricultural Cooperative Association) representing those of farmers. *Zoku* members formed an iron triangle with bureaucrats, industrial sector groupings, and powerful individual corporations (Curtis 1988, 110–112). *Zoku* members also changed the characteristics of LDP factions. As *zoku* members organized groups based on particular interests rather than factions, factional policy differences disappeared, with *zoku* members in each faction representing specific policy positions.

Yet faction leaders were also able to control members as cabinet and other high-level posts were shared proportionally between factions. Strong adherence to seniority meant that all senior LDP members had at least one chance of becoming a minister. Generally though, the power of factional leaders to control faction members became diluted, as did the policy orientation of each LDP faction.

The structure of the politico-administrative relationship and the stability it provided were also key to the decision-making process in the era of LDP dominance. Features included the vertical divisions and other organizational features of the bureaucracy, the central government's domination of local government, the interface between politics and the bureaucracy in the predominance of jurisdictional principles within the cabinet, and the interaction between bureaucrats and politicians such as the *zoku* Diet members. LDP governments typically also used certain types of nonpolitical deliberative organs to pave the way for policy recommendations. A notable feature of these deliberative councils is the important role that bureaucrats and ex-bureaucrats play in them.

As the power of the LDP decentralized, it relied on a "bottom-up" style of reaching consensus, rather than a "top-down" style of decision making. Its style of consensus building was also rooted in behind-the-scenes bargaining, politicking, and deal making with the opposition. This style of managing politics prevented the LDP from leading on controversial issues such as electoral reform in the early 1990s. Public discontent with the last LDP government—which neglected to pass the electoral reform bill—strongly informed the 1993 Lower House election.

DECISION MAKING IN
THE HOSOKAWA GOVERNMENT

It follows that political reform was the most crucial issue in 1993 for the newly formed Hosokawa coalition government. Prime Minister Hosokawa made a strong commitment to political reform at his first press conference on August 10, 1993, saying that he would resign if he failed to realize political reform by the end of that year. In his first policy speech in the Diet on August 23, Hosokawa also called his administration a "political reform government," underscoring his commitment to achieving political reform.

Coordinating policy with the eight ruling parties was crucial for the Hosokawa coalition government and a three-tier decision-making structure was established to achieve this (see fig. 1). The Party Representatives' Committee comprised the secretaries-general of the five major parties, namely the SDPJ, the Japan Renewal Party (JRP), Kōmeitō (Clean Government Party), the Democratic Socialist Party (DSP), and the New Party Sakigake (*sakigake* means "pioneer"). Under this committee was the Secretaries' Committee. This latter committee had two suborganizations: a political section and a policy section. The political section consisted of party whips and Diet affairs' chairmen, and the policy section comprised policy board chairmen.

Figure 1. Policy-making Structure under the Hosokawa Government

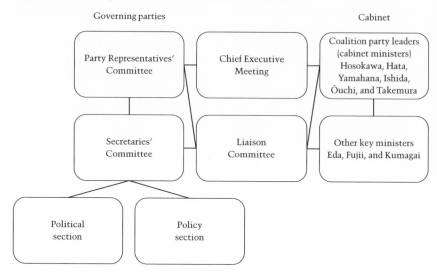

A Chief Executive Meeting and a Liaison Committee coordinated policies between the cabinet and the governing parties. The Chief Executive Meeting, the supreme decision-making body, was composed of 11 members. Six members were party chairs while the other five were party secretaries-general—in other words, the members of the Party Representatives' Committee.

The most important organ to coordinate policies among governing parties was the Party Representatives' Committee and, at the beginning of the Hosokawa government, this committee operated on the basis of unanimous decision making. Ozawa Ichirō, the secretary-general of the JRP, led the Party Representatives' Committee from September 1993 (Asahi Shimbun Seiji-bu 1994, 59–75).

In August 1993, the Party Representatives' Committee authorized an electoral reform plan based on an SDPJ proposal that combined a single-seat district system with proportional representation. Under this plan, each voter would have two ballots—one for the single-seat district system and the other for proportional representation—and 250 seats would be allotted each to the single-seat system and proportional representation. As the SDPJ knew it had little chance to win under the single-seat district system, it gave more weight to proportional representation. The JRP and Kōmeitō wanted to allot 300 seats for the single-seat district system and 200 seats for proportional representation, and allow each voter one ballot, but in the end they yielded to the SDPJ's proposal (Asahi Shimbun Seiji-bu 1994, 60).

Negotiations between the ruling parties and the opposition on the political reform bill focused on the schedule of deliberations. This was mainly attributable to the LDP's time-consuming filibusters, tactics that the SDPJ/JSP ironically developed in the 1950s and 1960s during the period of LDP dominance. Deliberations on the political reform bill only started in the Diet in mid-October, although the extraordinary session began on September 17.

Even worse, Hosokawa was faced with SDPJ members who failed to support their leadership in the push for legislation on political reform. Yamahana Sadao, the SDPJ's party chair who championed political reform, was blamed for the SDPJ's defeat in the Lower House election and Murayama Tomiichi, a left-winger who was cautious about electoral reform, replaced him in September. When the political reform bill was voted on in a plenary meeting of the House of Councillors (Upper House) in January 1994, the bill was rejected by 12 votes as 20 SDPJ members either voted against the bill or abstained from voting.

Hosokawa had tried to provide leadership in the final stage of decision making. In a mid-November 1993 Chief Executive Meeting, Hosokawa had asked Murayama, then SDPJ chairman, to allow him discretion regarding revisions to the electoral reform bill when meeting with LDP President Kōno Yōhei. In spite of the SDPJ's desire not to decrease the seats allotted to proportional representation, in his meeting with Kōno, Hosokawa proposed decreasing the number of seats for proportional representation from 250 to 224.

In trade policy, a final decision about opening Japan's rice market had to be made. The Uruguay Round of the General Agreement on Tariffs and Trade (GATT) was expected to conclude by the end of 1993, and the government had to decide by then whether or not to partially open Japan's rice market. When the LDP raised the issue in 1989, the shift of farmers' votes from the LDP to opposition parties led to the LDP's historic defeat in the Upper House election. After the 1989 election, the LDP shelved the issue for more than four years.

Among the eight governing parties, the SDPJ had been strongly critical of opening the rice market, because not a few of its members were elected from rural areas. Yet it was a dilemma for the SDPJ, because if it did not go along with the plan to open the rice market, the Hosokawa coalition government would collapse. After long, tumultuous discussions, the SDPJ reluctantly agreed to the policy in mid-December in the interests of maintaining the coalition.

In terms of relations with the United States, economic measures to raise domestic demand—such as deregulation of the economy and passage of a supplementary budget—were being called for. Although Hosokawa did not ignore the U.S. requests, he took the initiative to raise domestic demand in its own terms. In other words, he neither obeyed the U.S. government, nor utilized *gaiatsu*, as external or U.S. government pressure for domestic reform is known. Hosokawa proposed three budgetary supplements in fiscal 1993 to stimulate domestic demand and organized an advisory panel to discuss economic deregulation and restructuring policies. It was clear that his policy met U.S. government demands as well as those of the Japanese business sector, which was suffering fallout from the collapse of the "bubble" economy in the early 1990s.

These instances describe the policy-making process under the Hosokawa cabinet and they distinguish it from that followed by LDP governments. A different picture emerges if the Hosokawa government's achievements and the actual processes are considered. The advisory group on economic restructuring, which was chaired by Hiraiwa Gaishi, former chairman of Keidanren, and organized under the Prime Minister's Office from October to December 1993, was not free of bureaucrats' influence. Six of the group's 15 members were former bureaucrats. Although the Administrative Reform Promotion Headquarters was organized under the Prime Minister's Office in early 1994, it was heavily dependent on the Management and Coordination Agency.

Coalition partners resisted the top-down style of decision making. A typical example was the reaction to Hosokawa's initiative to introduce a 7 percent "national welfare tax" in early February 1994. Hosokawa himself, Ozawa, and Saitō Jirō, vice minister of finance, developed the idea. Yet many in the ruling coalition, including Takemura Masayoshi, the chief cabinet secretary, did not know about it until shortly before Hosokawa held a midnight press conference on February 3.[1] Many coalition partners—including Takemura and Ōuchi Keigo, the minister of health and welfare—criticized this new tax plan, and it was shelved within two days of a meeting of the ruling parties. On February

8, when the Hosokawa cabinet announced a ¥6 trillion tax cut, no plans were released to offset the revenue loss.

In sum, the Hosokawa coalition government relied on top-down initiatives in its decision-making process and, certainly in the cases of opening Japan's rice market and realizing electoral reform, succeeded in meeting its goals. Hosokawa's reliance on Ozawa's strong leadership, however, engendered a tenacious dissonance and distrust among the governing parties that ultimately led to the eight-party coalition's breakdown.

DECISION MAKING IN
THE MURAYAMA GOVERNMENT

The Hosokawa government was preoccupied with trying to realize political reform and open Japan's rice market, two issues which LDP governments had failed to resolve since the late 1980s. But Hosokawa suddenly announced his resignation on April 8, and then the subsequent Hata Tsutomu government fell in late June when a no-confidence motion was introduced in the Lower House.

Major diplomatic issues that the next government, the Murayama administration, had to deal with included trade disputes with the United States, concern about North Korea's development of nuclear weapons, obtaining a permanent seat on the UN Security Council, and accepting responsibility for aggression during World War II. Murayama also had to address many economic issues. These included increasing domestic demand following the collapse of the bubble economy, restructuring Japan's economic and social systems developed in the post–World War II era, and reforming the tax and social security systems to meet the needs of Japan's aging society. The Great Hanshin-Awaji Earthquake in Hyogo Prefecture in January 1995 placed the issue of ineffectual crisis management on the agenda, as well as that of how to finance reconstruction of the damaged Kansai area.

Rebellion against Ozawa's high-handed, top-down style in the Hosokawa government partly motivated the formation of the Murayama coalition government. So inevitably the structure for making decisions in the Murayama administration (see fig. 2) was different to that used under Hosokawa.

First, the coordinating organs had larger memberships than those of the Hosokawa government—nearly twice the number. The Executive

Figure 2. Policy-making Structure under the Murayama Government

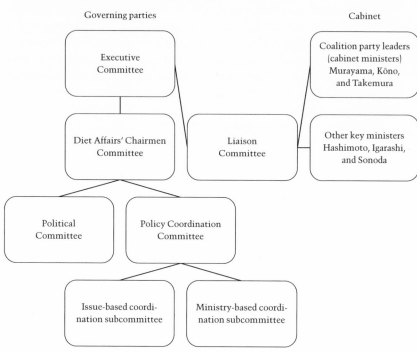

Committee—comparable to Hosokawa's five-member Party Representatives' Committee—comprised 11 members: three secretaries-general and representatives of suborganizations, including a representative
of Upper House members. A Policy Coordination Committee—comparable to the policy section of the Secretaries' Committee under Hosokawa—was composed of eight members: three from the LDP, three
from the SDPJ, and two from Sakigake. The Policy Coordination Committee, which reported to the Executive Committee through a Diet
Affairs' Chairmen Committee, also had two subcommittees. One subcommittee was organized according to ministerial functions and the
other was issue-based. Representatives of each party were involved in
the steering groups, and the chairs rotated monthly.

The Diet Affairs' Chairmen Committee under the Executive Committee operated on the basis of consensus. It comprised 20 members
—ten from the LDP, seven from the SDPJ, and three from Sakigake—
although any Diet members from the three governing parties could

observe meetings. These organizational features were the result of SDPJ and Sakigake requests to make the decision-making process more democratic and transparent than it had been in the Hosokawa government. For the LDP, this type of arrangement was similar in organization and function—although broader—to that of its General Council. The LDP's General Council is recognized as being the arena in which important policy and political issues are discussed; it too operates on a consensus basis.

A second contrast between the Murayama and Hosokawa governments' styles of decision making has been alluded to already—namely, the role of consensus building in the process. In principal, no policy was discussed in the Executive Committee without the unanimous agreement of the Diet Affairs' Chairmen Committee. The committee of Diet chairmen thus served as the common decision-making body among the ruling parties. The pitfall of this practice, however, was the sacrificing of effectiveness in decision making. Not surprisingly, the Murayama government ended up shelving many controversial issues.

A third contrasting characteristic of the Murayama government with that of Hosokawa was that the style of decision making was bottom-up. With few exceptions, the Executive Committee served to authorize decisions made by lower organs. This bottom-up style gave lower-level bodies such as the subcommittees of the Policy Coordination Committee a tangible role in the decision-making process.

In terms of policy itself under the Murayama government, four points can be noted.[2] First, some adopted policies reflected the SDPJ's position, including that of Murayama himself, but they were limited. Examples include compensation for foreign "comfort women" who were forced to provide sexual services to Japanese troops during World War II, legislation for financial aid to families of victims of the 1945 atomic bombings of Hiroshima and Nagasaki, and compensation for victims of "Minamata disease," those who have been suffering from nervous system problems since a chemical company dumped mercury in Minamata Bay in Kumamoto Prefecture in the 1950s. But the impact of these SDPJ-initiated policies on the electorate was very limited. Also, in the case of compensating the comfort women, the Murayama government established a nongovernment fund for this purpose— which was the same strategy that the LDP followed. Yet the SDPJ took some initiative in handling the budget allocation for fiscal 1995, with spending on social welfare increasing 9 percent over the previous year.

Nevertheless, the overall framework of the budget remained untouched and several supplementary budgets had to be drawn up, so the SDPJ's impact on the budget was quite limited.

Second, the SDPJ underwent a few drastic policy conversions, reversing itself profoundly on some of its basic policies. Examples include recognizing the Self-Defense Forces as conforming with the Constitution, maintaining the security treaty with the United States, accepting the national flag and anthem, endorsing nuclear power plants, and raising the consumption tax from 3 to 5 percent.[3] These issues are not just relevant to the core ideology of the SDPJ, but are fundamental to national security and the national treasury. The process whereby these SDPJ policy stances were changed was quite unusual. An extraordinary SDPJ convention was held on September 3, 1994, where, in a violation of normal intraparty debate, the changes were effectively presented as accomplished facts. Considering the particular stress laid on democratic procedures in the three-party coalition government in reaction to Ozawa's heavy-handed style in the Hosokawa administration, the forceful way in which the SDPJ made the policy changes was very surprising. While it is true that the SDPJ had always played the role of objector and had never prepared itself to assume responsibility and power, the party's sudden about-face on certain policies—without legitimate deliberation and process—was problematic.

Ironically, the SDPJ's policy reversals enabled the settlement of controversial issues which were deadlocked from the era of LDP dominance. These included issues relating to the U.S.-Japan Security Treaty, utilizing Self-Defense Force planes for the relief of Japanese abroad, revising the Basic Law against Calamities, and the question of increasing the consumption tax.

The third characteristic of policy making under the Murayama government was the strong tendency to postpone making difficult or controversial decisions.[4] Instances from international relations include the issue of the right of collective self-defense and Japan's role in the case of a regional emergency, both situations associated with suspicions about a North Korean nuclear weapons program. In terms of domestic issues, decisions on restoring a balanced budget and administrative reform were both postponed. Overall, the Murayama coalition government did not tackle the serious issues for which quick responses were needed. The sole exception might be the decision to raise the consumption tax to 5 percent from 3 percent, but this decision was in a sense more accepting something already set than taking the original tough decision.

A fourth characteristic of Murayama policy making was the way it imitated LDP methods. This included the practice of using certain types of influential nonpolitical deliberative and advisory organs. For example, a recommendation from the Tax System Research Council under the Prime Minister's Office was used to legitimate the decision to raise the consumption tax rate. Many other important issues such as economic deregulation and political decentralization were first discussed in these types of councils. While an actual situation required a fundamental innovation, the methods used to decide on policy were always biased toward maintaining the status quo.

Two other points should be made regarding the repetition of previously used methods for deciding policy. One concerns the tendency to react to pressures from the United States. It is quite revealing that economic structural reform was first pursued around the time of trade negotiations with the United States. The 1994 Basic Plan for Public Investment in terms of which ¥630 trillion would be spent in ten years to stimulate domestic demand was also influenced by requests from the United States.

The other aspect of the repetition is the excessive reliance on budgetary measures. A huge amount of public investment is dependent on government bonds and supplementary budgets, and the inclination to increase public infrastructure investment remains unchanged. Massive and sustained deficit spending suggests that the tendency to depend on budgetary measures is a quantitative problem as well as a qualitative one.[5]

In sum, the Murayama coalition government undertook very few SDPJ-inspired policy initiatives. If the Murayama government seemed to suggest that it managed legislation smoothly, it achieved this rather ironically by not putting forward its own policy proposals and by imitating LDP-derived patterns of governance. Indeed, the SDPJ totally renounced its own principles and committed effective policy suicide. Considering that the LDP had agreed unconditionally to join the SDPJ and Sakigake in forming the Murayama coalition government, this is surprising. Yet all three of the parties participating in the coalition compromised their principles in the process of forming a government together.

EVALUATION OF
THE POLICY MECHANISMS

The biggest goal of the Hosokawa coalition was passing political reform legislation. The coalition spent so much energy on realizing this policy goal and on achieving its lesser aim of opening Japan's rice market that other issues were shelved. The Murayama government, on the other hand, developed a much better track record of passing legislation. But can this difference in success rates only be explained in terms of the structure of the two coalitions' respective policy mechanisms?

The first distinguishing characteristic of the actual policy process in the Hosokawa government is the role of Ozawa Ichirō. Ozawa, then secretary-general of the JRP, in fact led decision making in the coalition government. At least three reasons explain why Ozawa was so powerful in the Hosokawa administration.

First, Ozawa's initiatives led to the formation of the coalition government. His strategic groundwork was critical to the process that led to the successful formation of a coalition that excluded the LDP (Ishihara 1997). His insights and understanding were vital in knowing the inclinations of those in Sakigake, for example, who had the casting votes to form a coalition either including or excluding the LDP. Given the role he played in the genesis of the coalition, it is not surprising that Ozawa acquired such a predominant position within the Hosokawa government.

Second, Ozawa's close relationships with various members, including the executive members of the Kōmeitō and the DSP, were crucial resources. He had developed solid relations with Ichikawa Yūichi and Yonezawa Takashi, secretaries-general of the Kōmeitō and DSP respectively, during his years in the LDP. Also, most members of the JRP, who had followed Ozawa when he left the LDP, were still under his tight control. In addition, Ozawa had a large network of sympathizers—even among bureaucrats. Consequently, with his political experience and policy knowledge, Ozawa easily distinguished himself from the many amateurish politicians of the other coalition parties.

Third, the structure of the Party Representatives' Committee, the supreme decision-making body of the coalition government, helped Ozawa actualize and then project his power. Although eight parties comprised the Hosokawa coalition government, only five of the six larger parties with seats in both the Lower House and the Upper House participated in the Party Representatives' Committee. A simple majority was needed to pass decisions in the committee so, with the support of Ichikawa and Yonezawa, Ozawa became the leader of the majority group within the committee. The fact that the Party Representatives' Committee was recognized as the supreme decision-making organ and that it effectively did not need to involve other bodies in policy making also constituted favorable circumstances for Ozawa. The status of the Party Representatives' Committee as the supreme decision-making organ therefore enforced Ozawa's dominant position in the ruling coalition, as did the fact that the presidents of the governing parties were effectively sidelined by being in the cabinet. Some contend that these arrangements were in fact intentional.

Ozawa's preeminent position in the Hosokawa government is confirmed by the observation that all important information was reportedly transmitted immediately to Ozawa when it was brought to the attention of Prime Minister Hosokawa.[6]

The second key characteristic of decision making in the Hosokawa government was its top-down style. Designating the Party Representatives' Committee to be the predominant decision-making body epitomizes this style. That bodies and procedures necessary for a bottom-up style of managing decisions were never introduced—or intentionally blocked from being introduced—is revealing.

The top-down tendency was particularly pronounced when the issue was important or controversial. In fact, the more important the issue and the more numerous the interest groups concerned, the fewer people were likely to be involved in policy making and the more obtuse the procedure. This was thought to be indispensable to policy innovation. Yet it was criticized—not only by Ozawa's opponents—as "secretive" and "despotic."[7]

In contrast, the decision-making style and procedures that the Murayama government followed were bottom-up. The subcommittees of the Policy Coordination Committee typically initiated the policy-making process, and the Policy Coordination Committee took decisions about what to pass to the next levels of decision makers, the Diet Affairs' Chairmen Committee and the Executive Committee. In this framework, those bodies that actually carried out the practical work and compiled the policy blueprints became influential.[8] Yet the Diet Affairs' Chairmen Committee, which had been expected to function as the supreme decision-making organ, failed completely in its performance (Nihon Keizai Shimbun-sha 1994, 68–70). Its dysfunctionality showed eloquently how the most effective work is typically done lower down the hierarchy in bottom-up policy making.

Bottom-up decision making in the Murayama government had the collateral characteristics of being more democratic and more transparent than decision making in the Hosokawa administration. But the Murayama coalition government also had the politicians' affliction of postponing making difficult decisions or not making them at all. Part of the problem in this particular case was the four-decades-long rivalry between the SDPJ/JSP and the LDP, and their having completely opposite basic policies. Also, the bottom-up, consensus-building approach prevented controversial divisive issues from being passed up the hierarchy. Even though Prime Minister Murayama reversed core SDPJ policies on the security treaty with the United States, the Self-Defense Forces, and nuclear power plants, the SDPJ still adhered to many other policy stances that were essentially different to those of the LDP. The SDPJ, for example, did not completely alter its position on economic and financial policies. Many issues were shelved in the interests of maintaining the three-party coalition.

Surprisingly though, the Murayama government achieved a 100 percent success rate in terms of passage through the Diet of government-sponsored bills. This suggests that, in some respects at least, the coalition managed policy making extremely well. Perhaps success in this area had to do with the SDPJ's dramatic reversals in policy once it became a governing party and its chairman became prime minster. While the SDPJ/JSP had previously objected to government's policies, it suddenly found itself in the fundamentally different position of having to lead government policy making. Perhaps the coexistence of a smooth routine legislation process and the endemic postponing of addressing difficult issues was not contradictory, but rather the result of both the sudden shift in the SDPJ's basic policies and a change in its political strategy.

The second characteristic of policy making in the Murayama government was the important role that the bureaucracy played. In bottom-up decision making, the power of the top politicians is inevitably curtailed. Instead of strong leadership from either the prime minister or a party leader, bureaucrats who support and cooperate with the bottom-up policy process can be very influential. Although the relationship between the bureaucracy and the governing party or parties can be detached due to the government changing, relations between the LDP's *zoku* politicians and sections of the bureaucracy were characterized by give-and-take during the era of LDP dominance. The SDPJ, however, was not experienced in governing, and the LDP was not used to negotiating openly with its political partners—LDP politicians were used to bargaining behind the scenes. As the governing parties were not accomplished in coordinating policy between them, bureaucrats were able to take the initiative, using their knowledge about policy and process. This helps explain the Murayama government's smooth handling of routine policies.

A final point about the Murayama government is the fact of the LDP gradually increasing its role and influence in the coalition. The LDP made fairly important concessions toward the SDPJ and Sakigake at the outset of the coalition. As their governing collectively continued, it became increasingly clear that the LDP members' long accumulated personal networks and knowledge of policy were crucial to helping manage the policy agenda.

TRANSFORMING THE METHOD OF CONDUCTING POLITICS

In trying to understand the transformation from the Hosokawa government to that of Murayama, the preeminence of Ozawa is crucial. The personal style and views of Prime Minister Hosokawa had some influence on the political scene during his government. But more fundamentally, Ozawa's methods and views guided the way in which many important decisions played out.[9] Ozawa once explained, "Leadership means after all top-down. The responsibility of a leader is to determine for himself, taking into account the opinions of followers. That is democracy" (Ozawa 1996, 22). He also opined, "Once we choose a leader, we should entrust things to him. There is a mandated term. This makes democracy different to despotism" (quoted in "Ozawa Ichirō no" 1997).[10] In his view, a leader of a political group has to have solid will, a sense of responsibility, and the capacity to carry out what he thinks is necessary, in some cases even without sufficient agreement or consensus. In his view, the more people and serious interests are involved in an issue, the more leadership is needed. The introduction of the national welfare tax plan suggests the influence of his views.

For one who had been at the center of LDP politics and policies for so long, the style of decision making Ozawa used in the Hosokawa government—the secretiveness and tendency to rely exclusively on close followers—was perhaps an attempt at policy innovation. Yet these radical methods had rather limited results. Regardless, the fact is that Ozawa's views and methods contrasted with the mechanisms previous LDP governments used (Satō and Matsuzaki 1986; Nonaka 1995).

The views and methods of the Murayama government were opposite to those of Ozawa and were very similar to those LDP governments cherished, with the stress on consensus building and avoiding top-down indiscretions. This style of governing evolved slowly for the LDP and, in the case of the Murayama government, emphasizing harmony and coexistence between and within the governing parties was clearly also effective.

The policy-making methods which evolved in the period of LDP governance could thus be said to have survived the challenge from Ozawa during the Hosokawa government and to have expanded their adherents to include the long-resisting SDPJ. The dynamics among the governing parties in the Murayama administration were different to those of *kokutai* politics, the complicated behind-the-scenes politicking and bargaining characteristic of the period of LDP dominance. But the principle of inner democracy, which the Murayama government insisted on, was long established within the LDP. So the shift from the Hosokawa government to the Murayama government symbolized a return to governance in the mold of the LDP.

It also normalized relations between the party that traditionally governed and those that were typically in opposition. That the Murayama administration was comprised of a coalition of parties had some unintended consequences for interparty relations.

First, the negotiating process leading to the formation of the coalition government was conducted more transparently than the usual intraparty bargaining among LDP politicians.

Second, a dynamic emerged which gave priority to maintaining the coalition. This dynamic kicked in when consensus building between the governing parties became difficult and the viability of the coalition was called into question. The threat of a coalition collapsing had not existed in the period of LDP dominance and, interestingly, the threat of collapse during the Murayama administration resulted in the LDP yielding to the SDPJ on controversial matters in the interests of maintaining the coalition.

Within the LDP, the influence of *zoku* politicians with long experience of government was well established. Yet they found themselves without opportunities for influence in the Murayama government because the LDP had made so many concessions while negotiating the policy coordination structure. There were not many *zoku* politicians among the SDPJ—except in the fields of social welfare and labor policy —while Sakigake only had 25 deputies in total.

Maintaining the coalition at all costs also related to another aspect of political activities. In the period of LDP dominance, the discretionary power of factional leaders on personnel affairs was a kind of last resort for controlling party members as policy making became more pluralistic.[11] But once the presumption of LDP dominance was broken, and dissident members of the LDP left the party and succeeded in occupying the key posts in the new non-LDP coalition government, inner party control mechanisms based on personnel affairs ceased to function. Maintaining the coalition above all else was a sort of substitute for this mechanism and its logic served to integrate the coalition, both within and without the LDP. The chairman of the LDP's Policy Research Council obtained significant new influence as the leader of the Policy Coordination Committee.

Third, in areas such as welfare and health care, several experts belonging to the former opposition parties became very effective players in the policy process. For example, during discussions about establishing long-term care insurance, SDPJ members played very important roles.

Fourth, the SDPJ accepted the cumulative policies of successive LDP governments, finally abandoning its traditional obstructionist role. Now all parties—except the communists—were potential allies in government. This was not a bad thing in itself. But because the SDPJ/ SPJ had reversed its policy positions so quickly and seemingly easily, the policy debate suffered. Indeed, there never was one, given the way in which the SDPJ changed policy. The lack of debate about the merits of existing policy was particularly regrettable as the LDP resumed its dominant position after the October 1996 Lower House election.

Finally, the New Party Sakigake behaved as a prototypical "policy-oriented political party."[12] Although party members did not succeed in achieving sufficient of their policy objectives, they conducted their politics and pushed their policy programs clearly.

It is not clear whether these changes are transitional or enduring and whether they will entail structural or institutional transformation. But, along with the newly introduced electoral system, these factors will exert future influence on politics in Japan.

CONCLUSION

As we discussed, the characteristics of the decision-making process under the Hosokawa non-LDP coalition government and the Murayama three-party coalition government contradict each other. Under the Hosokawa government, a group led by Ozawa tried to introduce a new top-down way of decision making which was different to that used by LDP governments. Although this new method succeeded in delivering the realization of electoral reform, it became a source of friction between the partners in the Hosokawa coalition. This antagonism fundamentally motivated the formation of the new LDP-SDPJ-Sakigake coalition in mid-1994. The new coalition stressed another way of conducting politics, which was an effective return to how the LDP had governed under one-party dominance. While the Murayama coalition government in some respects gave birth to a different logic and structure, in a more fundamental way it shared many characteristics with LDP governments.

That Ozawa was seen as a common political enemy is the first factor that explains the unprecented LDP-SDPJ-Sakigake alliance. For LDP members, he instigated the breakup of the LDP when he left the party with many of his followers. For the SDPJ, he was an aggressor whose strategy could realistically split the party. Opposing Ozawa was pure power politics as he was trying to establish a way of conducting politics in Japan that seriously threatened the interests and status quo of the LDP as well as the SDPJ.

"Politics by consensus," which dominated the Murayama government, was reflected in intraparty LDP politics, relations between political parties, relations between the bureaucracy and political forces, and also in the political process vis-à-vis, for example, pressure groups. "Politics by consensus" was a prudent and conciliatory way of coordinating interests, building consensus, and gradually developing policies. As a result, as the LDP became increasingly predominant since the 1960s, some opposition demands were already reflected in policies.[13] Policy coordination with opposition parties was thus institutionalized, even though this was done through behind-the-scenes *kokutai* politics.

Another aspect of "politics by consensus" under LDP governments was the important role the bureaucracy played with its legal knowledge, policy information, and regular contact with interest groups. Bureaucratic concurrence with the way in which the LDP made policy also explains how the Murayama coalition government continued LDP policies in such a strangely "natural" way.

Even for the LDP, conducting good politics with other potential and present coalition governing parties has been crucial. The subsequent importance of factional politics within the LDP has diminished since its period of dominance ended, and the rules of political competition and allegiance have changed fundamentally. Even though both the LDP secretary-general and the chairman of the Policy Research Council have obtained new resources due to their critical roles in maintaining coalitions, other party members have not yet recognized these power sources as legitimate. Power struggle in policy making has shifted from the closed arena within the LDP to the open space between the potential governing parties. The old order and the old political rules have changed radically, yet new integrating mechanisms have not formed.

NOTES

1. In contrast with Hosokawa and Ozawa, Takemura felt that the consumption tax should not be raised and that income tax should be reduced. Takemura is rumored to have had frequent contact with Mori Yoshirō and Mitsuzuka Hiroshi, both executive members of the LDP, so Ozawa and his allies were wary of him (Ishihara 1997, 100).

2. I am here indebted to Yakushiji Katsuyuki of the *Asahi Shimbun* for his classification of policies, although my categories differ somewhat from his (speech by Yakushiji Katsuyuki in Osaka on February 28, 1997).

3. On July 18, 1994, Prime Minister Murayama stated in a speech to the Diet that he would maintain the security treaty with the United States. In replying to opposition questions in the Lower House chamber, he then commented on the constitutionality of the Self-Defense Forces and suggested that both the Hinomaru (the national flag) and "Kimigayo" (the national anthem) had already taken root in the general public.

4. Mikuriya also discusses the problem of postponing decisions, but focuses on the weaknesses of politicians vis-à-vis bureaucrats (Mikuriya 1996).

5. The decision to commit ¥685 billion in public funds for the failed housing loan companies (*jūsen*) reflected this same tendency.

6. Interview with an anonymous bureaucrat who worked in the Prime Minister's Office during the Hosokawa administration.

7. This type of criticism was frequently made against Ozawa, and he and Ichikawa were often said to make decisions at some "unknown place outside the Diet." This way of involving only very few followers or high-ranked bureaucrats in decision making was also used by Tanaka Kakuei when he was minister of international trade and industry, especially in settling the textile trade dispute with the United States in the 1970s. See Ōtake (1979, especially the latter half of the third chapter).

8. As did the individuals involved. Katō Kōichi, then chairman of the LDP's Policy Research Council, distinguished himself as the leader of the Policy Coordination Committee and as a leading figure in the LDP-SDPJ-Sakigake coalition.

9. Takemura Masayoshi, then chief cabinet secretary and leader of Sakigake, was another pillar of the Hosokawa government. He and Ozawa often disagreed with each other. For example, on security policy, Takemura was a dove. The antagonism of these two key personalities was problematic for the Hosokawa government.

10. Ozawa's "despotic" style brings to mind another phenomenon, that of domination by the Takeshita faction. The Takeshita faction was dominant within the LDP and it had much influence over personnel affairs in the party. But there is a difference between controlling personnel affairs and dominating decision making.

11. The main characteristics of the pluralism in policy making within the LDP were the sharing of information and the variety of represented interests at the lower levels. Yet this pluralism slowed decision making, especially when difficult problems crept up. So executive LDP members utilized a kind of threat about personnel matters. This combination of a pluralistic, decentralized decision-making mechanism and a centralized personnel system seems to be found in many postwar Japanese firms. See Nonaka (1995) and Aoki (1988).

12. By using the term "policy-oriented political party," the aim is to differentiate it from the single-issue movements of the 1970s. The basic difference between the two is that the policy-oriented party is always conscious of national politics as a whole.

13. The most impressive example of this would be in welfare policies. Yet it also does not mean that there were no adversarial policies toward opposition parties. Pursuing the privatization of the Japanese National Railways would be a good example of the latter.

BIBLIOGRAPHY

Allison, Gary, and Sone Yasunori, eds. 1993. *Political Dynamics in Contemporary Japan*. Ithaca: Cornell University Press.

Aoki Masahiko. 1988. *Information, Incentives, and Bargaining in the Japanese Economy*. Cambridge, U.K.: Cambridge University Press.

Asahi Shimbun Seiji-bu. 1991. *Ozawa Ichirō tanken* (Explorations on Ozawa Ichiro). Tokyo: Asahi Shimbun-sha.

————. 1994. *Renritsu seiken mawari butai* (Turning stages of coalition government). Tokyo: Asahi Shimbun-sha.

Budge, Ian, and Hans Keman. 1990. *Parties and Democracy: Coalition Formation and Government Functioning in Twenty States*. New York: Oxford University Press.

Calder, Kent. 1989. *Jimintō chōki seiken no kenkyū*. Translated by Toshiko Calder. Tokyo: Bungei Shunju-sha. Originally published as *Crisis and Compensation: Public Policy and Political Stability in Japan, 1949–1986* (Princeton: Princeton University Press, 1988).

Curtis, Gerald. 1988. *The Japanese Way of Politics*. New York: Columbia University Press.

Hirano Sadao. 1996. *Ozawa Ichirō to no nijū-nen* (Twenty years with Ozawa Ichirō). Tokyo: Purejidento-sha.

Ishihara Nobuo. 1997. "Heisei no shushō kantei, dai 3 kai" (The Prime Minister's Office in the Heisei era, no. 3). *Chūō Kōron* 112 (3): 82–106.

Johnson, Chalmers. 1982. *Tsūsanshō to Nihon no kiseki*. Translated by Yano Toshihiko. Tokyo: TBS Buritanika. Originally published as *MITI and the Japanese Miracle* (Stanford: Stanford University Press, 1982).

Kitaoka Shin'ichi. 1996. "'Kensei jyōdō-ron' saikō: Yoyatō kankei no atarashii wakugumi" (Conventional procedures of constitutional democracy reconsidered: A new framework for ruling and opposition relations). *Chūō Kōron* 111 (5): 48–59.

————. *Jimintō: Seikentō no sanjū-hachi nen* (Liberal Democratic Party: Thirty-eight years as ruling party). Tokyo: Yomiuri Shimbun-sha.

Laver, Michael, and Kenneth Shepsle. 1996. *Making and Breaking Governments: Cabinets and Legislatures in Parliamentary Democracies*. New York: Cambridge University Press.

Mikuriya Takashi. 1996. "Ji-sha-sa kettei sakiokuri no kōzu." (Structural background of shelving decisions under the LDP-SDPJ-Sakigake coalition). *Chūō Kōron* 111 (4): 62–71.

Muramatsu Michio. 1994. *Nihon no gyōsei* (Public administration in Japan). Tokyo: Chūō Kōron-sha.

Narita Norihiko. 1995. "Seiji kaikaku hōan no seiritsu katei" (Legislative process of the political reform bills: Descriptions from the perspective of the Prime Minister's Office and the governing parties). *Hokudai Hōgaku Ronshū* 46 (6): 406–486.

———. 1997. "'Seiji kaikaku no katei-ron' no kokoromi: Dessan to shōgen" (On the process of political reform: Witness and analysis). *Leviathan*, no. 20: 7–57.

Nihon Keizai Shimbun-sha. 1994. *Renritsu seiken no kenkyū* (A study on coalition governments). Tokyo: Nihon Keizai Shimbun-sha.

Nonaka Naoto. 1995. *Jimintō seiken ka no seiji erīto* (Political elite under the LDP governments). Tokyo: Tokyo Daigaku Shuppan-kai.

Okimoto, Daniel. 1989. *Between MITI and the Market*. Stanford: Stanford University Press.

Ōtake Hideo. 1979. *Gendai Nihon no seiji kenryoku keizai kenryoku* (Political and economic power in contemporary Japan). Tokyo: San'ichi Shobō.

Ozawa Ichirō. 1996. *Ozawa Ichirō kataru* (Ozawa Ichirō speaks). Tokyo: Bungei Shunjū-sha.

"Ozawa Ichirō no seiji" (Politics by Ozawa Ichirō). 1997. *Asahi Shimbun* (25 May).

Samuels, Richard. 1987. *The Business of the Japanese State: Energy Markets in Comparative and Historical Perspective*. Ithaca: Cornell University Press.

Satō Seizaburō and Matsuzaki Tetsuhisa. 1986. *Jimintō seiken* (LDP administrations). Tokyo: Chūō Kōron-sha.

Political Realignment and Policy Conflict

Ōtake Hideo

PARTY realignment in the classic sense was not a characteristic of the period of political transformation in Japan that began with the collapse of the Liberal Democratic Party's (LDP's) one-party dominance in the summer of 1993. Party realignment commonly refers to a shift of voting behavior on a massive scale caused by social or economic crisis. Other types of transformations in party systems such as from the cadre party to the mass party are not necessarily accompanied by a policy reorientation among the mass public (Duverger 1951, chap. 2). In political theory party realignment is regarded as the result of a change in voters' attitudes toward critical issues. It occurs either swiftly in a serious crisis such as the Great Depression (Burnham 1970), or gradually through accumulating crises such as racial conflict in the United States since the mid-1960s (Carmines and Stimson 1989). In either case, the emergence of a new issue strongly felt by the masses is supposed to play a crucial role. The political realignment, or party system change, in Japan after 1993 lacked these characteristics.

One-party dominance by the LDP lasted for 38 years from 1955, institutionalizing a pattern of voting behavior among the mass public and a very stable party system comparable to the two-party systems in the United States and Great Britain. Although the 1993 Lower House election brought change to the party system, the change was not a result of voters' critical assessment of where parties stood on issues, a precondition of party realignment. Rather, political change in Japan was initiated basically by two groups of Diet members in 1993 and led to the breakup of existing parties and the creation of new ones. Unlike party realignment in other countries, it did not start with a substantial shift in voter support induced by calamitous events such as economic collapse or defeat in war.

A series of scandals from the mid-1970s generated widespread mistrust of party politicians. Exploiting this opportunity, some party leaders intended to induce party realignment from the top by a new policy package that would force voters to realign along issues. Some politicians attempted to sustain anti-establishment and anti-party sentiment, which had evaporated quickly in previous scandals, and consolidate the temporal shift of support for a new party into permanent allegiance. Other leaders intended to build and consolidate a new party on neoliberal ideologies. Another group tried to align voters along the axis of new social and political issues by advocating women's rights, privacy, environment, decentralization, and participatory democracy, an agenda roughly similar to that of liberals in the United States in the 1960s. To turn temporal discontents into electoral support, realign along policy issues, and institutionalize a new party system proved to be a daunting task.

This chapter traces these attempts and analyzes why they ultimately failed and one-party dominance by the LDP, albeit in a modified style, seemed to reemerge after the 1996 House of Representatives (Lower House) election through the hectic reshuffling of Diet members. Before examining the attempts at top-down party realignment since the mid-1970s, however, I will offer a theoretical framework and then examine the structure of party conflict by which LDP dominance was sustained for almost four decades.

ANALYTICAL FRAMEWORK AND HISTORICAL BACKGROUND

The political ideologies of parties and voters are usually conceptualized along a left-right unidimensional scale. Political parties have attempted to attract voters by identifying themselves along this left-right dichotomy; voters have also been found to identify their political positions along a similar scale (Inglehart and Klingemann 1976; Ysmal 1990, chap. 3). Reflecting distinctive historical and social milieus, the specific issues that draw the line between left and right have differed significantly across nations, ranging from the political regime itself to economic policies, religious controversies, and foreign policy questions.

Within a single nation, a variety of political issues may arise that resist a simple left-right taxonomy. However, most often the lines of cleavage are drawn across issues deemed the most important; thus, the political system can still be viewed as revolving around a single issue dimension. The benefit to voters of interpreting the polity in such a simplified manner is that it significantly reduces the cost of gathering information on and evaluating the platforms and capabilities of political parties, the prerequisites for shaping party identification and voting decisions. Political parties often present a deliberately simplified image to the electorate in hopes of stabilizing voter support. That the mass media often depict political parties and policies as if they could be placed along a left-right scale further contributes to the persistence of such unidimensional interpretations of the polity.

Japan has been no exception. For historical reasons, the left and right have been identified as "progressive" and "conservative," respectively (Miyake 1985). Despite the emergence of issues since the late 1960s that cannot be classified along the standard progressive-conservative cleavage, such as the environment and the violation of human rights in China, studies have shown that the majority of Japanese voters still identify their political ideologies along a left-right axis (Kabashima and Takenaka 1996, chap. 5). Most voters also identify political parties along a unidimensional scale that has the Liberal Democratic Party at the far right and moves leftward with the Democratic Socialist Party (DSP), the Kōmeitō (Clean Government Party), the Japan Socialist Party (JSP), and the Japan Communist Party (JCP). Survey results indicate that voters have interpreted the policy changes of the two parties with considerable accuracy. During the 1970s, the Kōmeitō sought to position itself as a centrist-progressive party, whereas the DSP began to lean to the right, particularly on national security. By the 1980s, the Kōmeitō, which was considered the more conservative in the 1960s, had reversed places with the DSP. The voters correctly perceived these shifts.

From the early 1950s to the 1980s, the main line of cleavage between the conservatives and the progressives ran through issues of defense, the status of the emperor, labor's right to strike, and revision of the Constitution.[1] Numerous opinion surveys have confirmed this division. Unlike many other countries, including the United States, economic policy has not been a significant issue between the left and the right. For example, according to a survey conducted in 1967 (the so-called Michigan survey), while the Japanese electorate was divided over tax cuts or expanded welfare benefits, voter attitudes on welfare policy had no correlation with their positions on defense and the emperor (Kabashima and Takenaka 1996, 271–272). Among the major political parties as well, welfare policy has been virtually a non-issue; both progressive and conservative political parties have endorsed expanded welfare services. This is also true of government intervention in the economy. In addition, although Japanese voters are wary of inflation, they have never been explicitly forced to choose between it and unemployment.

In sum, throughout the LDP era, party support was structured around two closely interrelated issues—the U.S.-Japan Security Treaty and the status of the Self-Defense Forces—that separated LDP and JSP supporters, with other political parties, except the JCP, considered to lie between the two. The defense issue emerged in the early 1950s, and the pattern of conservative-progressive confrontation was institutionalized by the 1960 political crisis over the renewal of the Security Treaty, shaping Japanese politics for the next 30 years.

Defense was not only debated in terms of the usual rhetoric of war, peace, and security, but was also closely linked to such issues as prewar militarism and the resurgence of fascism. Underlying this progressive-conservative cleavage was a social cleavage at the deeper level of political culture and the value system. Supporters of pacifism were well-educated, young, white-collar workers hostile to prewar Japanese political culture. On the other hand, the middle-aged, less-educated, elderly, and self-employed (including the agricultural sector) tended to support rearmament. The former group is characterized by a modern political culture, whereas the latter is more traditional. Both the conservatives and the progressives sought to capitalize upon this social cleavage, which Watanuki Jōji has labeled "cultural politics" or "value politics" (Watanuki 1967).

The nature of the defense question substantially changed from the 1960s to the 1970s. The LDP abandoned its hope of amending the Constitution and the link between defense and the political regime weakened significantly. As more information on political and economic circumstances in the Eastern bloc countries became available in the 1970s, the credibility diminished of socialist and nonaligned countries that had commanded widespread respect in Japan during the 1950s as defenders of peace. As a result, the appeal of socialist ideology, which had indirectly inspired pacifism, waned and pacifism became disconnected from a political and economic system. Japanese voters gradually lost interest in the defense issue.

Meanwhile, a clientelistic pattern of distribution, both to local constituencies and vested interest groups, gained importance in electoral competition. The LDP represented the interests of local constituencies, or of the agricultural and the self-employed sector, and the functional interests of industries, and the JSP represented the functional interests of public servants in nationalized fields like railroads, post and telecommunications, as well as education and local government. Two major parties competed not on the basis of policies or principles but on which could win a greater share of the pie. Various studies have confirmed the displacement of "high politics" by patronage as the primary factor in the voters' decision-making process (e.g. Miyake 1995, chap. 1).

Concurrent with the rise of patronage in voter mobilization, distributive politics became increasingly important in both intra- and interparty politics. JSP Diet members are known to have acted as intermediaries for labor unions seeking parochial, short-term interests from as early as the late 1950s (Matsushita 1960; Taguchi 1958). While JSP Diet members sought to win the support of mass movements and the general electorate by harshly attacking LDP policies, they also acted as de facto interest groups and lobbied for the distribution of particularistic benefits, in a manner similar to LDP *zoku* Diet members. The term *zoku* (literally "tribe") refers to Diet members who specialize in a certain policy area, represent a particular interest such as agriculture or the construction industry, and wield influence within the party and in the Diet. The most prominent example of rent-seeking behavior was in public transportation, where certain Diet members spoke for management and others for the Japanese National Railways' (JNR) unions. Both lobbied for higher railroad fares and subsidies to cover JNR's swelling deficits. Beneath the rhetoric of class struggle and pacifism/anticommunism, both managers and union leaders tacitly colluded for the same benefits.

Patronage politics was not an explicit ideological cleavage, but developed parasitically alongside it, within the framework of left-right division.

On the other hand, the expansion of distributive politics alienated groups that could not be reached through distributive channels. The white-collar middle class, youth, and urban housewives—the left wing of value politics in the ideological conflict over defense—found themselves without a party to defend their occupational and local interests. Distributive policies simultaneously bred an increasingly large group of voters who were potentially opposed to such policies and laid the groundwork for conflict between defenders of the status quo and vested interests versus groups demanding reform of the distributive apparatus as consumers or taxpayers.

This new pattern of conflict appeared intermittently, often in response to major political scandals, and profoundly affected electoral results and short-term partisan realignments. The founding of the New Liberal Club (NLC) shortly after the Lockheed scandal and its popularity in the 1976 general election of the Lower House, the anti–consumption tax movement that swept many female candidates into office —the "Madonna boom"—and gave the JSP a major victory in the 1989 election of the House of Councillors (Upper House), and the Japan New Party's success in the 1993 general election can all be accounted for as revolts by consumers and taxpayers. More recently, the personal popularity of Kan Naoto and Hatoyama Yukio, cofounders of the Democratic Party of Japan (DPJ) in 1996, can be seen as a similar phenomenon.

The brief approval enjoyed by the NLC, which was also supported by young urban women and university students, closely paralleled the rapid decline in the fortunes of the JSP and the JCP from 1973 to 1978 (Mita 1980, 83). A number of new political parties had short-lived expansions thereafter, but all drew their support from essentially the same social strata.

Many new political parties owe their brief success to the hostility of the new urban middle class toward vested interests. At the core of this hostility lies a strong distrust of political parties (including the JSP), party politics, the bureaucracy, and the government; in short, toward professionals in politics and administration as a whole.

This pattern of conflict is between professionals and amateurs, or the government and citizens, and is independent of the traditional conservative-progressive cleavage.

However, political parties have been incapable of exploiting this clash and organizing it into a stable base of support. Because of this failure, this cleavage has not determined the partisan realignment in the early 1990s, remaining merely an occasional irritant to the established party system. That the new political parties, without exception, have failed to sustain their momentum further illustrates this point.

Unlike other political parties that appeared prior to the 1993 Lower House election, the Japan New Party (JNP), the New Party Sakigake (*sakigake* means "pioneer"), and the Japan Renewal Party (JRP) all advocated policies that departed fundamentally from the old cleavage over defense that had shaped the pattern of party competition throughout the postwar era. Like the other new political parties, these three all came out strongly in favor of reform and of cleaning up Japan's money-ridden political system. However, what was singular about this trio was that they made no pretense about being conservative. They never claimed to be middle-of-the-road or attempted to distinguish themselves from the LDP by staking out a position to its left. Instead they urged a reinvigoration of the conservatives. The JNP and the JRP were particularly eager to propose policies in issue areas that cross-cut the old conservative-progressive cleavage over defense policy.[2]

The platforms of the JNP and the JRP, which signified a major break with the past in the nature of political competition in Japan, can be seen as the culmination of an evolving process. It is important to note that at the level of elites, conflict between economic (laissez-faire) liberalism and social democracy had significantly influenced Japanese politics and administration throughout the postwar era. There are many illustrations of this. First, ministries and the *zoku* Diet members who champion their objectives have consistently favored budget expansion. The demands of the Ministry of Health and Welfare and the Ministry of Labor to expand the welfare budget represent a social democratic stream of thought among Japanese political elites. The ministries of agriculture and construction have also championed "big government," albeit from a more conservative perspective than health and labor.

In contrast, the Ministry of Finance has been the champion of "small government," staunchly defending the principle of a balanced budget. Senior big business executives active in politics, known collectively as the *zaikai*, particularly the top leadership of Keidanren (Japan Federation of Economic Organizations), represent the interests of large corporations, and have been the prime advocates of "small government" in the private sector (except for their support for counter-cyclical budget outlays in recessionary periods) and have opposed budget expansion, especially agricultural subsidies and welfare benefits. Moreover, in hopes of defending private initiative, the *zaikai* has favored a "weak government" rather than the "strong government" espoused by the economic ministries (notably the Ministry of International Trade and Industry, MITI), and has strongly resisted attempts to reinforce government intervention in the economy. The *zaikai* often subverted MITI's attempts to gain greater control over corporate investments during the 1960s, for example. However, the conflicts between "big" and "small" government or "strong" versus "weak" government never became partisan issues. The major political parties were united in favor of welfare expansion and greater state intervention in the economy, particularly when scandals surfaced (Hiwatari 1995).

The emergence of neoconservatism among political elites in the late 1970s propelled this cleavage over broad economic issues—welfare, industrial, and fiscal policy—to the popular and partisan levels. Domestic policy (neoliberalism) and foreign policy are the two pillars of neoconservative thought in Japan. On the domestic side, neoconservatism expresses doubt over the social democratic "postwar settlement" or the Keynesian welfare state. Although the mass media, intellectuals, and citizens' groups had argued for curtailed distribution of particularistic benefits to local and functional interests on moral grounds, neoconservatism was the first set of ideas to provide a coherent policy prescription. The typical neoconservative policy program includes privatization, deregulation, and retrenchment, all policies that the Second Provisional Commission on Administrative Reform (Second Rinchō) proposed in the early 1980s. At the level of party competition, neoconservatism stimulated the rise of political parties that sought to represent the interests of the new urban middle class—consumers, salaried employees, and taxpayers—all of whom the established political parties had neglected in their mobilization strategies. This challenge also prompted the old parties to attempt to shift their support base to the new urban middle class.

Regarding foreign policy, from the mid-1970s neoconservatives argued for a greater Japanese contribution to the defense of the West, in the face of the arms buildup by the former Soviet Union; after the cold war, they favored a more activist role for Japan in the settlement of regional disputes. The neoconservatives simultaneously marginalized the right-wing and attacked LDP doves and JSP pacifists.

The seeds of neoconservative policies were in the New Liberal Club's platform, and the first fruits were in the Nakasone Yasuhiro administration's (1982–1987) more full-fledged neoliberal agenda. In the following section, I will examine the NLC's intentions and political outcomes and Nakasone's policy proposals as the forerunners of neo-liberal efforts to realign parties after 1993.

NEOCONSERVATIVE ATTEMPTS TO MOBILIZE NEW CLEAVAGES IN THE 1970S AND 1980S

The New Liberal Club and the Nakasone Administration

After a great leap forward in the 1976 general election, the NLC, led by Secretary-General Nishioka Takeo, focused primarily upon the new urban middle class. The economic policy prescriptions in the NLC platform included education, land-use regulation, and tax reform (especially ending preferential treatment for doctors). Although the platform was by no means a coherent or comprehensive neoconservative doctrine, many NLC policies were taken up by neoconservatives in the 1980s and 1990s. A prime example was the NLC's innovative proposals on agriculture, which included plans to reduce drastically the number of farm households by encouraging large-scale, professional farming (Hagiwara 1976, 146). While other opposition parties urged expanded pension outlays and welfare benefits during the deliberations on the budget for fiscal year 1979, the NLC advocated "small government," calling for a reduction of the budget deficit by curtailment of preferential tax treatment for doctors and a salary freeze for public employees. In a similar vein, the NLC approached Ushio Jirō, the president of Ushio Electronic Co. and a prominent member of the younger generation of the *zaikai*, to run as its candidate in the 1979 Tokyo gubernatorial election. The party said the capital's fiscal crisis "called for managerial talent" (Kawamura 1980, chap. 4). It is significant that Ushio's brain trust included the likes of Kōyama Ken'ichi, a professor at Gakushuin University, and the famous drama director Asari Keita. Both eventually played major roles in the administrative reforms of the Nakasone administration.

The NLC never went so far as to label itself explicitly as neoconservative. A major reason was that Kōno Yōhei, in hopes of forging an alliance among middle-of-the-road parties (including the Shaminren, or United Social Democratic Party), adopted a dovish stance on defense issues akin to the Kōmeitō and the JSP. Kōno sought unity by focusing on foreign policy and defense issues and attacking the Fukuda Takeo administration as dangerously right-wing. To this end, Kōno deliberately situated the NLC as middle of the road in the conservative-progressive cleavage. Nishioka agreed with Kōno on defense and foreign policy, but not on the strategy of emphasizing those issues. Looking back today, this clash between Nishioka and Kōno can be viewed as one between neoliberals seeking to reinvigorate conservatism and dovish conservatives who are also sympathetic to the JSP.[3] However, the dispute led to the breakup of the NLC and its subsequent demise. The first attempt to reset the political agenda along neoconservative lines was not explicit and ended in abrupt failure.

Regarding foreign and defense policy, neoconservative thought first manifested itself in the Ōhira Masayoshi administration (1978–1980) when proposals for Japan to contribute more to defense of the West began to win popular approval, and was stated more coherently during the Nakasone administration. Neoliberal thought also came into full bloom under Nakasone, yielding the Second Rinchō and its programs. I have traced the evolution of neoconservatism in Japan elsewhere (Ōtake 1994; Ōtake 1997). Here I will merely state briefly that Nakasone's neoconservative policies were at least partly rooted in partisan motives.

Nakasone sought to spark a political realignment through a multifaceted strategy of "expanding the LDP to the left." First, Nakasone wanted to reset the political agenda on defense by emphasizing close cooperation with Ronald Reagan, Margaret Thatcher, and other Western leaders. Defining Japan's international role as a champion of liberty and democracy justified stronger military forces. This signified abandonment of the nationalistic, right-wing elements of Japanese conservatism or, seen another way, the liberalization and Americanization of Japanese conservatism. Nakasone was reaching out to the new urban middle class and young voters who were attracted to the LDP, primarily because of its reliable management of the macro-economy.

Second, by attacking public-sector labor unions for clinging to narrow self-interests, Nakasone sought to drive a wedge between them and private-sector unions, simultaneously striking a blow at the JSP's support base and marginalizing the peace movement.

Third, Nakasone hoped to reduce the LDP's dependence upon less competitive sectors of the economy, such as retail shop owners and agriculture, and attract the urban new middle class and blue-collar workers in the private sector. He advocated consumers' interests, pushing for lower food and distribution costs, and appealed to taxpayers by proposing a cut in agricultural subsidies and outlays for retail shop owners.

Nakasone personally took the initiative on defense and the Second Rinchō was the engine driving the other two. The LDP's landslide victory in the 1986 Upper and Lower House elections shows that the prime minister scored at least a partial success.

The two opposition parties were also eager to ride this wave of partisan realignment. The DSP, which was backed by private-sector labor unions, strongly endorsed the Second Rinchō's policies on the grounds that they promoted taxpayer interests. Kōmeitō support of administrative reforms stemmed from its preference for "small government," partly because its membership embraced the value of self-help and partly because of its critique of the political system as heavily skewed in favor of special interests. (Cooperation between the DSP and the Kōmeitō on administrative reforms in the 1980s was an important factor leading to formation of the New Frontier Party in 1994.)

As mentioned earlier, Nakasone's strategy undermined the JSP's electoral support and led to the LDP's landslide victory in 1986; however, his policies never sparked a major political realignment. The immediate reason for this failure lay in massive protests against his bid to introduce a consumption tax after the election.[4] Although the policies enhanced Nakasone's personal luster, they did not translate into greater support for the LDP (Kawato 1988). In Carmines and Stimson's terms, Nakasone's policies, which were modeled after American neo-conservatism, were too "hard," i.e., difficult to understand, to exert a significant impact on the Japanese mass belief system (Carmines and Stimson 1982).

The issue of whether Japan should play a more activist role in world politics did not arise from a major international crisis, and it could not drastically alter the conservative-progressive cleavage, at least in the short term. The division over foreign policy and national security was not only a relatively easy issue for voters to comprehend, being closely related to the experience of World War II, but four decades of strife over the Constitution, especially Article 9, had made it readily identifiable to the electorate. Educated in the prewar era, Nakasone could not always conceal his traditionalist sentiments, limiting his capability to be the spokesman for a new ideology. His popularity stemmed more from skillful use of the media, especially televised coverage of summit conferences that showcased an equal partnership between the United

States and Japan, and his personal friendship with Ronald Reagan than the elucidation of foreign policy. Nakasone's diplomatic endeavors enhanced his standing in the polls but failed to stimulate a major political realignment.

Nakasone's emphasis on foreign policy and defense was rare for a Japanese prime minister, but neoconservatism in Japan was essentially a matter of economics. When it initially surfaced in Japan, neoconservative thought was not widely accepted. For instance, a 1983 survey asked voters if they agreed with these statements: (1) Small government is desirable, even if it brings a decline in the quality of government services, and (2) Pensions and medical care for the elderly should be expanded. The largest proportion of responses was, "Don't know." The pattern was almost the same among supporters of conservative and progressive parties (Miyake 1995, 106; Kabashima and Takenaka 1996, 255–256). More surprisingly, many voters answered affirmatively to both questions. The responses to question 2 were virtually the same in 1976 and 1983.

The average Japanese voter believed that liberalizing policies were necessary mostly because he or she distrusted bureaucrats. Administrative reform in Japan meant not just streamlining the government, but included policies ranging from deregulation, which was expected to reduce cartel-like behavior in the private sector, to revision of welfare policies. Neoliberalism was not an effective ideological symbol for far-reaching reforms.

Even Nakasone was not prepared to abandon completely the agricultural sector and retail shop owners, staunch LDP supporters; the rest of the LDP Diet members were even less willing. As long as "expanding the LDP to the left" stopped short of offending farmers and retail shop owners, Nakasone's attempts to reach the urban new middle class remained at best halfhearted.

The JSP had evolved by this time into a rural-based party. As support for the JSP steadily declined in the cities, it relied primarily for votes upon the network of unionized workers in the postal system, national railways, Nippon Telegraph and Telephone Public Corporation, and local governments. Thus, the JSP opposed liberalization of the rice market and relaxation of the Large-Scale Retail Stores Regulation Law, changes beneficial to urban voters. For the LDP to adopt policies attractive to urban salaried voters would have pushed dissatisfied rural votes and the traditional urban middle class into the JSP camp. In fact, this was precisely the reaction to the consumption tax and LDP agricultural policies, leading to the JSP's short-lived surge in popularity during the 1989 Upper House election (Mizusaki 1992; Yomiuri Shimbun-sha 1990).

It should be noted that for neoliberalism to influence voting behavior, the interests of consumers and taxpayers must be activated— voters must perceive their interests. Compared with American and European consumers, however, Japanese consumers are not particularly price conscious. It is often said they accord higher priority to courteous, obliging treatment such as prompt delivery and follow-up service. Symbolic elements such as brand name and packaging are also important. Consumers have not felt disadvantaged by the inefficient distribution system that raises prices. By the same token, because of the withholding tax system, most salaried workers do not grasp how much they are actually paying. On the whole, Japan's socioeconomic culture and institutions are relatively unconducive to neoliberal economic reforms.

This was a major reason why the consumption tax, which was accompanied by a cut in income taxes, met such severe opposition. The consumption tax was felt directly by the individual voter, whereas the income tax reduction was indirect and less visible.

Conversely, the practice of life-long employment coupled with inadequate unemployment benefits has made workers very averse to layoffs and fearful of bankruptcies. Voters readily support policies that promote the interests of producers over those of consumers and taxpayers.

In addition, administrative reforms coincided with a period when the Japanese economy was performing much better than those of the other major industrialized countries. Drastic changes in the agricultural and distribution sectors, with the danger of unemployment and bankruptcies, did not seem critical to the average voter. With some successes in deregulation and privatization and a dynamic economy—the "bubble" years from 1987 to 1990—the fiscal picture improved and the need for reform subsided. A fiscal crisis had put economic reforms on the political agenda in the early 1980s; the eased fiscal deficit doused the enthusiasm of political elites for economic changes.

As noted, the consumption tax issue in 1987 threw the debate on neoconservatism into utter confusion, both at the level of intellectuals and voters. After 1988, a wave of scandals over political funds revived the cleavage between parochial/professional interest group politics versus "clean politics," which became the prime determinant of party support until political reforms in 1994. After a ten-year hiatus, the debate over neoconservatism had reemerged, and the Japan New Party and the Japan Renewal Party were formed.

NEOCONSERVATIVE ATTEMPTS TO MOBILIZE NEW CLEAVAGES IN THE 1990S

Ozawa Ichirō and the Japan Renewal Party

Ozawa Ichirō rose to power within the LDP as a young leader in the Tanaka Kakuei faction and as Kanemaru Shin's protégé. Ozawa was a key political figure in the Takeshita administration as deputy chief cabinet secretary and in the Kaifu administration as LDP secretary-general. During this period, he had chief responsibility for managing trade friction with the United States and Japan's response to the Gulf War, experiences that shaped his views on a fundamental reappraisal of the political system in the 1990s. The late 1980s and the early 1990s were a time of highly optimistic forecasts for Japan's economy and polity. The fiscal and welfare crises that haunted the Nakasone administration had eased, at least for the time being. A major reform of the health care system integrated fragmented health insurance programs and resolved the welfare funding crisis. The Ministry of Health and Welfare, on the assumption that a consumption tax would be introduced sooner or later, was preparing the "Gold Plan," an ambitious welfare scheme for the elderly. It was widely assumed that strong economic growth would enable Japan to continue current levels of expenditures and undertake new obligations. Based on these assumptions, Ozawa argued for a more activist role in the international community.

Ozawa apparently decided that to push sweeping changes in the absence of the electorate's explicit consent required reform of the entire party system. His goal was to replace, through electoral reform, one-party dominance by the LDP with a two-party system, comprised of the LDP and a new, neoconservative party. Ozawa's *Blueprint for a New Japan* is the prime expression of his neoconservative thinking (Ozawa 1993). Ozawa's strategy was threefold. First, strike a fatal blow at the Social Democratic Party of Japan (SDPJ, the new name of the JSP from 1991), which had been reduced to defending the interests of public-sector labor unions and had barely managed to win seats in many electoral districts, by creating a single-seat electoral system. Second, eliminate the competition for pork-barrel funding of parochial and functional interests. Single-seat constituencies would encourage campaigning on issues and allow voters to choose between policy options, change or the status quo. The new system would also alleviate overrepresentation of the farming and self-employed sectors, centralize the political parties, and strengthen party leaders. Third, reapportion Diet seats to reduce the number of agricultural districts.

Ozawa's objectives were to abolish, through electoral reforms, the system of functional and parochial representation that had developed behind the conservative-progressive cleavage, and to realign the party system along the issue of neoliberalism versus big government.

The political scandals that surfaced from 1988 brought Ozawa's reform proposals widespread support from the mass media, intellectuals, big business, and private-sector union leaders. Ozawa wanted British-type party politics where the party leadership would be insulated from the rank-and-file Diet members, who single-mindedly sought funds for pet local projects, and have a stronger hand in policy making. Although Ozawa and leftist intellectuals wanted a two-party system, most intellectuals envisioned it as the LDP and the SDPJ, not a conservative and neoconservative party. The British party system was a model for historical reasons. Intellectuals had long advocated a coalition of the JSP, Kōmeitō, and the DSP to replace the LDP. The JSP's landslide victory in 1989 renewed hopes that it could attain power. The SDPJ suffered a major defeat, however, in the 1993 general election, while the new JNP gained substantial seats. Political realignment seemed to be unfolding according to Ozawa's blueprint. The SDPJ had suffered a fatal setback, and the chances of a second LDP breakup and the end of its dominance seemed quite good.[5]

However, the New Frontier Party, which Ozawa pieced together out of the JRP, the JNP, Kōmeitō, and the DSP at the end of 1994, failed to convert previous electoral support, which was primarily motivated by hopes for political reform, into support for neoliberal reforms. Ozawa triggered a reshuffling of Diet members among political parties, but accomplished little in realigning the electorate. The LDP's return to power in 1994 brought back business-as-usual pork barreling. And the NFP had no choice but to rely on the support organizations of individual

Diet members, the Sōkagakkai (an exclusionary religious sect), and labor unions formerly affiliated with Dōmei (Japan Confederation of Labor) in subsequent elections.

The NFP failed to project a clear image to the voters, who saw it as simply a coalition of parties, which it was. The NFP alienated urban voters who regarded the former Kōmeitō as the political wing of the Sōkagakkai. Having positioned itself to the left of the LDP by advocating welfare, as the party of the weak and poor, and peace, the Kōmeitō's abrupt reversal of these policies through joining the NFP perplexed both former Kōmeitō voters and Sōkagakkai activists. Neoliberalism lacked the symbolic power to expunge the Kōmeitō's image as a middle-of-the-road party.

The DSP had long represented a complex hybrid of interests—moderate labor unions and small and medium-sized enterprises. Within the party, support for administrative reforms had strengthened the position of the former; however, in many election districts the latter were still the core of its electoral support. Rengō (Japanese Trade Union Confederation) was in disarray during this period; the collapse of the "bubble" economy from 1990 left private-sector labor unions no time for politics or elections. The long recession in the 1990s forced them and public employee unions alike to protect jobs and abandon neoliberal economic reforms. Former DSP members were in no position to champion the interests of taxpayers and consumers in the NFP, as they had a decade earlier.

As I will discuss below, Hosokawa's personal image was tarnished by scandals, and the JNP lacked leaders who could take his place. No former JNP Diet members could fill the vacuum.

Many former Diet members of the JRP were dependent upon support groups and local interests; a significant proportion were from rural, agricultural districts.[6] They had joined the JRP not from sympathy with Ozawa's policies nor because of the nature of their election districts, but because of personal and factional ties with Ozawa (Ōtake 1996, 289). Many could not risk running on a neoliberal platform.

Ozawa was often seen as an old-fashioned party boss, reminiscent of the organizational culture of the Takeshita faction, a reputation reinforced by his penchant for maneuvering behind the scenes. In the eyes of the voters, Ozawa and other NFP leaders lacked Nakasone's charisma.

One reason the NFP failed to win support for its neoconservative goals was that Ozawa was unwilling to present his policies directly to the electorate. He chose to change voting behavior through institutional reform, a new electoral system, and realignment of the political parties. By contrast, Nakasone recognized the mass media's power to generate momentum for administrative reform; toured the country with Dokō Toshiwo, chairman of the Second Rinchō, to gain grass-roots support; and closely watched the opinion polls. Ozawa's leadership style was rooted in his personality. His ultimate goal was a centralized political party whose leaders would be free of particularistic groups; he had little interest in mobilizing voters for the "high politics" to be practiced in the new system.

In sum, no NFP politicians were prepared to campaign on a neo-conservative platform. Even if they had, it is doubtful the party would have gained many more votes.

The Hosokawa and Hata administrations accomplished substantial neoconservative policy outcomes. The Hosokawa cabinet approved partial liberalization of the rice market, a major issue of the Uruguay Round of the General Agreement on Tariffs and Trade. Toward the end, the administration expressed its intention to launch a second attempt at administrative reform; the targets included ineffective quasi-public corporations. The Hata cabinet announced Japan's candidacy for a permanent seat on the UN Security Council, demonstrating a willingness to assume a greater international role. There is no evidence that voters were impressed by these policy initiatives. The neoconservative agenda remained "hard" issues, as they had been under Nakasone, and did not affect party competition. Hosokawa's ambitious tax reform proposal also elicited little response from the public.

The majority of Japanese voters remained skeptical about promoting the interests of consumers and taxpayers over those of producers, and politicians lacked both the will and the capability to change this attitude.

Hosokawa Morihiro and the Japan New Party

It is important to note that there was a huge gap between voter expectations and the reforms Hosokawa Morihiro hoped to accomplish. The JNP was launched in May 1992, and Hosokawa quickly became the darling of the media and enjoyed nationwide popularity. In March 1993, the JNP's popularity rating rose to nearly 10 percent, putting it in third place behind the LDP and the SDPJ. Despite severe difficulties in recruiting candidates,[7] the JNP won 35 seats in the 1993 Lower House election (including 17 first-place winners) in its initial bid for the Lower House, doing particularly well in urban districts. In these respects, the JNP's early history closely resembled that of the NLC. The JNP benefited from voter distrust of the existing parties and professional politicians. Although Hosokawa adeptly projected an amateurish image through his urban lifestyle—affluence, fashionable casual attire, playing the piano—and relaxed informal manner, this appeal quickly faded. The JNP's popularity deteriorated within six months after Hosokawa became prime minister—the fall was accelerated by a scandal involving Hosokawa himself—leaving the party with no choice but to join the newly formed NFP if its Diet members were to survive.

The JNP rode the wave of political reform, but Hosokawa himself was not especially enthusiastic about the issues. He was reluctant to introduce electoral reforms or the single-seat constituency system, preferring neoliberal administrative and economic reforms (Nakai 1997, 54–58).

Although Hosokawa had espoused decentralization as governor of Kumamoto Prefecture, service on the Third Provisional Council for Promotion of Administrative Reform made him a convert to neoconservative thought. According to Hosokawa, the commission deliberations allowed him to see firsthand the symbioses ("iron triangles") among the ministries, *zoku* Diet members, and interest groups, and he understood the need for reforms from outside the system.

Many neoliberal intellectuals from Nakasone's brain trust helped draft the JNP's policy platform. It included decentralization to vent the collusive relationship between the central ministries and industries, deregulation to promote consumer interests, and opening Japanese markets to foreign enterprises. Particularly significant was the fact that during the 1993 election campaign Hosokawa called for the opening of the Japanese rice market, hitherto regarded as a taboo by political parties. Hosokawa was also explicitly neoconservative in foreign and defense policies, advocating Japan's participation in a standing UN military force as well as greater involvement in peacekeeping operations, although he was committed to Article 9.[8]

That Hosokawa chose to join forces with Ozawa, the Kōmeitō, and the DSP indicated he could not garner much voter support solely from his policies. Hosokawa recognized that neoconservatism by itself would not trigger a major voter realignment, his personal appeal and amateurish image aside. Unlike the NLC, the JNP did not waver between middle-of-the-road policies and neoconservatism, but in the end its policy platform also failed to maintain support. The most contentious issue during the Hosokawa cabinet was political reforms. When electoral changes were finally accomplished, Hosokawa's scandal forced his resignation in April 1994. The attempts by both Hosokawa and Ozawa to realign Japanese political parties and voters ultimately ended in failure. Although the two leaders launched a much more conscious effort than the NLC to reframe the political agenda along a new political cleavage, they accomplished little more than it had. These setbacks illustrate the difficulty of transforming a historically rooted political cleavage.

For the average voter to perceive that a new political party stands for a new political cleavage is no simple task. Accurate interpretation of a new platform requires voters be knowledgeable about the issues in question and the party's ability to accomplish its policies (Miyake 1985, 204). Had the new political parties identified themselves along the existing conservative-progressive cleavage over defense policy, voters might have more easily comprehended their policy stances. However, both the JNP and the JRP sought to introduce a completely new issue dimension into Japanese politics—administrative and economic reforms. National elites, perceiving Japan's position from an international perspective, saw administrative and economic reforms as crucial for the country's future, an understanding not necessarily shared by the population at large.

The party realignment in the United States since the 1960s unfolded along an issue—race—that is relatively easy for voters to comprehend (Carmines and Stimson 1989) and only involved the realignment of existing political parties. For a new party to spark a major party realignment along a completely new issue dimension, as the JNP and the JRP attempted to do, is a far more difficult task. It was an almost hopeless endeavor given that they had to enlist the support of the urban new middle class, certainly not known for their loyalty to political parties. What percentage of the population actually recognized that the JRP, the JNP, and the NFP stood for neoconservatism is uncertain (Kabashima 1998, 173–177); even if the voters had correctly perceived the three parties as neoconservative, it is doubtful what percentage would actually have cast their ballots for them because of their ideology.

The same can be said of the New Party Sakigake and the Democratic Party of Japan, considered next, which championed themselves as the "third force" or "liberal."

THE LIBERALS AS A THIRD FORCE

Within the LDP, conflict began early on between the so-called reform groups led by Takemura Masayoshi and Ozawa (Suzuki 1995, chap. 1). One area of contention was the new electoral system. Whereas Ozawa advocated a two-party system with centralized parties, Takemura's followers favored arrangements more accommodative of smaller parties that would preserve the characteristic decentralized structure under the single, nontransferable vote system in multiseat districts. These differences repeatedly surfaced in disputes over whether the Hosokawa cabinet's political reform bill should allow candidates to stand for both the proportional representation and single-seat constituency districts, how to decide the winner among several co-ranked candidates on the proportional representation list, and adoption of a one-ballot or a two-ballot system.

Ozawa and Takemura also clashed over security and foreign policy. Takemura's catch phrase and the title of his popular political manifesto, "Japan, a small resplendent country," symbolized a modest exemplary role and was an implicit criticism of Ozawa, who allegedly advocated great power status for Japan similar to its prewar standing (Takemura 1994).

Hostility toward Ozawa motivated young Diet members to found the New Party Sakigake and it is questionable that they seriously sought an original policy program. Passage of the political reform bill left Sakigake without a raison-d'être, a strange irony for a party that had called for elections based upon political parties and issues.

Sakigake was thus reduced to identifying itself along the existing conservative-progressive cleavage and advocating primarily backward-looking policies. These included a June 1995 Diet resolution on the 50th anniversary of the end of World War II to renounce Japan's aggression and wartime crimes and opposition to Japan becoming a permanent member of the UN Security Council. Party leaders attacked the idea of a greater Japanese contribution in international affairs as a disguised bid to make the country a military power, treating neoconservatism as if it were traditional, nationalistic conservatism to spark opposition to Ozawa and his allies. This strategy worked because the old conservative-progressive cleavage still wielded substantial symbolic power over politicians and party activists, if not over the electorate in general. Sakigake formed an alliance with the SDPJ, then on the ideological defensive, and cooperated with the LDP in the LDP-SDPJ-Sakigake coalition government against Ozawa's NFP.

However, in terms of distinguishing Sakigake's policy platform from other parties, participation in the new coalition backfired. After formation of the Murayama cabinet in June 1994, the SDPJ promptly reversed itself on the U.S.-Japan Security Treaty and the Self-Defense Forces, and the LDP, under Kōno Yōhei's leadership, subtly shifted to a dovish position on national security to accommodate the Murayama cabinet.

One of the few areas where Sakigake could distinguish itself from other parties was Japan's responsibility for the Pacific War (Ōtake 1995). However, this was not a topic that could garner widespread support. On the one hand, the elderly generation tends to deny Japan's responsibility for war crimes and aggression, if only to avoid guilt over their own past. On the other hand, the more cosmopolitan younger generation, which has never experienced war, does not deny Japan's responsibility per se, but finds Sakigake's policies are remote from their own experiences. Because the appeal of nationalism has almost disappeared in contemporary Japan, Sakigake's proposals often did not address the daily concerns of the average voter, who is also indifferent to many of the nationalistic proposals of prewar-generation LDP Diet members. Although the Diet resolution passed with little open opposition, the debate over Japan's responsibility for the conflict faded away.

Sakigake's next opportunity to take a bold policy initiative came at the founding of the Democratic Party of Japan (DPJ) in 1996. Most Sakigake members joined the new party, recruiting many SDPJ Diet members as well, and they tried to establish themselves as a third force, ideological equals with the LDP and the NFP, implicitly rejecting a middle-of-the-road position on the old conservative-progressive scale. However, this endeavor by former Sakigake Diet members to give substance to their liberalism again ended in failure. Rather than presenting a specific policy program, DPJ leaders criticized Murayama and Takemura and tried to project a "young" amateurish image through the party's two leaders, Hatoyama Yukio, scion of a distinguished political family (as were Kōno and Hosokawa) and Kan Naoto, who personified antibureaucratic sentiment for his forthright handling of a Ministry of Health and Welfare scandal involving the use of HIV-contaminated blood plasma products.

Although the specific meaning of "liberalism" does not seem to have been clear even to those who advocated it, here is a summary of what they theoretically stood for. Foremost was personal freedom and tolerance on social and moral issues, in other words acceptance of diverse lifestyles. Specifically, they would champion the rights of gays, women, and youth. Multiculturalism, or the encouragement of minorities—the Ainu and Japanese citizens of Korean descent—to preserve their ethnic identities, would be another example. This sense of liberalism is similar to that of the liberal wing of the Democratic Party in the United States or the Green Party in Germany.

Since the Hosokawa cabinet, numerous "liberal" issues of personal freedom and autonomy have emerged. Organ transplants relate to how society and the individual define death. Revision of the civil code permitting married couples to use different surnames and allowing illegitimate children to inherit their parents' property relates to individuality. Care for the elderly revolves around the question of whether the family or society at large should assume chief responsibility. Whether the Japanese army's forced prostitution of non-Japanese women during World War II should be taught in junior high schools, a contentious matter, can also be viewed as a liberal issue.

As noted earlier, it is doubtful that the DPJ leadership understood these questions to be the crucial litmus test of their self-proclaimed liberalism. Even if they did, these subjects are unlikely to replace defense as the primary cleavage between political parties.

These issues do not shape the fundamental pattern of political competition. Japanese political parties have chosen not to enforce strict party discipline on bills concerning brain death, elderly care insurance, and the use of birth names by married women, not because the correspondence between parties and issues has yet to be reestablished, but because these particular issues are not definitive. It is impossible for Diet members to decide their positions according to the view of their constituencies. They have little choice but to vote according to their own personal beliefs. In any case, these separate (or loosely related) "single issues" are not likely to determine the direction of political realignment in Japan.

The new liberalism was possibly the offspring of modernism in postwar Japan. As noted above, the modern value system lay deeply below progressive political beliefs, and constituted, together with the traditional value system, the fundamental cultural conflict in Japanese society and politics. However, as rapid economic growth modernized Japanese society and democracy appeared increasingly stable, making antifascist and pacifist positions irrelevant, the linkage between social conflict evolving around modern and traditional attitudes and political conflict over national security issues and revision of the Constitution was lost. Liberal issues became insulated from other political issues. Without renewed linkages with other agendas, such as social democratic policies, it is extremely difficult, if not impossible, for left-wing liberals to become a significant political force in Japan, at least for the moment.[9] The greater success of liberals in Germany and France seemed due not to the inherent appeal of liberalism, but to their focus upon environmental causes, widely regarded as urgent questions at the time. There is no reason to believe that liberalism will, by itself, enjoy greater popularity in Japan.

The other components of liberalism were decentralization and participation. Whether they are really liberal principles deserves closer scrutiny, yet for Diet members of Sakigake and the DPJ (and also of the JNP), these were an important policy agenda that accounts for their emphasis upon the "citizen."[10] However, in the 1990s interest in private (personal) life as opposed to interest in public activities was increasingly important in Japan and the desire to participate was on the decline, rendering a participatory policy platform somewhat unrealistic. Rather than the voluntaristic forms of participation liberals hoped for, the support groups of individual Diet members continued to be the common form of political participation (Ōtake 1998, Overview). Personal trust and a sense of camaraderie between the candidate and the kōenkai (personal support group) member were the primary motivation in voting. Although the antithesis of pork-barreling, it was far from the issue-oriented voting behavior that many liberals hoped for.

CONCLUSION

Political realignment in Japan began not with a change of voters' policy orientation nor with a massive shift in party support but with splits and mergers of the parties at the level of Diet member groupings. The ideology of individual politicians undeniably played a certain role in this reshuffling. In addition, because when politicians decided to leave or join a party, they assessed voter preferences based on media reports of popular support for the cabinet and parties, the voters' shifting policy choices may have substantially affected realignment. More importantly, however, the new parties tried to attract voters by espousing a policy package and consolidate their support by making a clear axis of policy conflicts vis-à-vis other parties.

This chapter analyzed the ideological policy packages and their efficacy. The parties all clearly failed to gain and stabilize support through policy packages. The traditional left-right scale was not replaced by a new stable left-right scale, leaving interparty conflicts over issues quite confused. The result seems to have been the reemergence of the previous form of voter mobilization—the distribution of patronage to and preferential treatment for particular occupational and regional groups. Although in a different form, one-party dominance by the LDP apparently has been revived and seems likely to continue for the foreseeable future, although the fact that nearly 50 percent of the electorate do not support any party or vote in elections poses a potential threat to LDP dominance, as was clearly shown in the July 1998 Upper House election.

NOTES

1. Japanese labor unions, particularly mainstream ones, often struck over such politically divisive issues as revision of the U.S.-Japan Security Treaty. Article 9 of the Constitution, which renounces war and prohibits full-fledged rearmament, has always been the focal point of controversy about revision of the Constitution.

2. As will be explored in detail subsequently, the New Party Sakigake gradually espoused traditional leftist positions on foreign policy issues because it suffered an ideological vacuum after political reforms were achieved.

3. Kōno later returned to the LDP, became its president in 1993, and was the driving force behind the alliance with the JSP and formation of the Murayama administration. Nishioka allied with Ozawa Ichirō and became secretary-general of the NFP. The conflict between Kōno and Nishioka within the NLC foreshadowed competition between the two conservative parties in the 1990s.

4. The emergence of taxes as a major issue in Japanese politics threw the debate over neoliberal reforms into utter confusion. As Prime Minister Nakasone stated, the consumption tax was initially designed to relieve the burden

on salaried employees, who were treated unfairly under a system that favored the agricultural and self-employed sectors. In other words, lawmakers sought to aid the new middle class and urban housewives, but ran into unexpected resistance from the very groups that were supposed to benefit. One reason was that the Finance Ministry failed to conceal its long-term ambition of increasing the overall tax base; a greater reason was the skepticism of the urban salaried class and housewives toward the government. Thus the consumption levy, like public outrage at political scandals, enabled voters to articulate their distrust of government and professional politicians. Scandals and the cleavage between amateurs and professionals became the primary determining factors of party support.

5. Many Sakigake Diet members, who played major roles in forging the LDP-SDPJ-Sakigake coalition, confessed to this writer that this was their fatal error. They overestimated Ozawa's power and underestimated the LDP's.

6. Survey research found that the largest groups of JRP supporters were in rural areas, while the bulk of JNP backers came from metropolitan areas.

7. Like the NLC years earlier, the JNP could not recruit attractive, talented candidates and drew from the usual pool of aspiring politicians, many of whom had failed to win LDP endorsement or had already lost several campaigns. This proved disastrous when Hosokawa was forced to step down—there was no successor.

8. The premise behind Hosokawa's proposals on the environment is elusive. The policy can be categorized as "liberal" and similar to that advocated by the New Party Sakigake, whose leader Takemura Masayoshi began his political career by cleaning up Lake Biwa.

9. Since the NFP's collapse at the end of 1997, the DPJ seems to be attempting to make itself the "second pole" through an alliance with social democratic forces and "liberal" forces, whatever the latter may mean.

10. Kan Naoto, one of the founders of the Socialist Citizens' League in 1977, had strong ties to citizens' movements and epitomized this form of activism. The Socialist Citizens' League reorganized as Shaminren in 1978. Established around the same time in the mid-1970s, the NLC also often used the word "citizen." Hatoyama Yukio, too, employed it frequently ("Citizens' Party") when he and Kan created the DPJ in 1996.

BIBLIOGRAPHY

Burnham, Walter D. 1970. *Critical Elections and the Mainsprings of American Politics.* New York: W. W. Norton & Company.

Carmines, Edward G., and James A. Stimson. 1982. "Racial Issues and the Structure of Mass Belief Systems." *Journal of Politics* 44: 2–20

———. 1989. *Issue Evolution: Race and the Transformation of American Politics.* Princeton: Princeton University Press.

Duverger, Maurice. 1951. *Les partis politiques* (Political parties). Paris: Armand Colin.

Hagiwara Michihiko. 1976. *Kōno shintō no subete* (All about Kōno Yōhei's new political party). Tokyo: Chibun-sha

Hiwatari Nobuhiro. 1995. "Gojū-gonen taisei no 'shūen' to sengo kokka" (The end of Liberal Democratic Party dominance and the postwar state). *Leviathan*, no. 16: 121–144.

Inglehart, Ronald, and Hans D. Klingemann. 1976. "Party Identification, Ideological Preference and the Left-Right Dimension among Western Publics." In Ian Budges, Ivor Crewe, and Dennis Farlie, eds. *Party Identification and Beyond*. New York: Wiley.

Kabashima Ikuo. 1998. *Seiken kōtai to yūkensha no taido hen'yō* (New administrations and the transformation of voter attitudes). Tokyo: Bokutaku-sha.

Kabashima Ikuo and Takenaka Yoshihiko. 1996. *Gendai Nihonjin no ideorogī* (Ideology among contemporary Japanese). Tokyo: Tokyo Daigaku Shuppan-kai.

Kawamura Yuzuru. 1980. *Seitō no hōkai: Shinjiyū-kurabu zasetsu no kiseki* (The collapse of the New Liberal Club). Tokyo: Ōesu Shuppan-sha.

Kawato Sadashi. 1988. "Shūsan dōjitu senkyo to Nakasone ninki" (Nakasone's charisma: The 1986 elections). *Hokudai Hōgaku Ronshū* 39 (2): 238.

King, David. 1997. "The Polarization of American Politics and Mistrust of Government." In Joseph S. Nye et. al., *Why People Don't Trust Government*. Cambridge: Harvard University Press.

Matsushita Keiichi. 1960. "Rōdōkumiai no Nihongata seiji katsudō" (Union politics, Japanese style). In Nippon Seiji Gakkai, ed. *Nempō Seijigaku: Nihon no atsuryoku dantai* (Annuals of the Japanese Political Science Association 1960: Japanese pressure groups). Tokyo: Iwanami Shoten.

Mita Sōsuke. 1980. "Nanajūnendai ni okeru seinenzō no hembō" (Japanese youth: Changing values in the 1970s). In Nippon Hōsō Kyōkai Hōsō Yoron Chōsasho, eds. *Daini Nihonjin no ishiki* (Second attitudinal survey on the Japanese). Tokyo: Shiseidō.

Miyake Ichirō. 1985. *Seitō shiji no bunseki* (A study of party identification). Tokyo: Sōbun-sha.

———. 1994. "Shintō no shutsugen to shijisha shūdan no hensei" (New parties and their supporters). *Senkyo Kenkyū*, no. 9: 2–15.

———. 1995. *Nihon no seiji to senkyo* (Japanese electoral politics in disarray). Tokyo: Tokyo Daigaku Shuppan-kai.

Mizusaki Tokifumi. 1992. "Ichinin-ku ni okeru Jimintō no kampai: Hachijūkunen Sangiin senkyo shūkei dēta no kaiseki kara" (The complete defeat of the LDP in single-member constituencies). *Leviathan*, no. 10: 82–103.

Nakai Ayumu. 1997. "'Sotokara kita' kaikakuha-Nihon Shintō to Hosokawa Morihiro" (Reformers outside of politics: Hosokawa Morihiro and the

Japan New Party). In Ōtake Hideo, ed. *Seikai saihen no kenkyū* (Studies of political realignment). Tokyo: Yūhikaku.

Ōtake Hideo. 1994. *Jiyū shugiteki kaikaku no jidai* (The era of neoliberal reform). Tokyo: Chūō Kōron-sha.

———. 1995. "Accounting for the War: An Overview of the Debate." *Japanese Book News*, no. 11: 1.

———. 1996. *Sengo Nihon no ideorogī tairitsu* (Ideological confrontation in postwar Japan). Tokyo: San'ichi Shobō.

———. 1997. *'Gyōkaku' no hassō* (The ideology of administrative reform). Tokyo: TBS Buritanika.

———, ed. 1998. *How Electoral Reform Boomeranged: Continuity in Japanese Campaigning Style*. Tokyo: Japan Center for International Exchange.

Ozawa Ichirō. 1993. *Nippon kaizō keikaku* (Blueprint for a new Japan: The rethinking of a nation). Tokyo: Kōdan-sha.

Suzuki Touichi. 1995. *Nagatachō tairan 2: Seiji kenryoku no hōkai* (Chaotic politics II: The collapse of political power). Tokyo: Kōdan-sha.

Taguchi Fukuji. 1958. "Nippon Shakaitō ron" (The Japan Socialist Party). *Chūō Kōron* 73 (9): 124–143.

Takemura Masayoshi. 1994. *Chīsakutomo kirari to hikaru kuni, Nippon* (Japan: A small resplendent country). Tokyo: Kōbun-sha.

Watanuki Jōji. 1967. "Patterns of Politics in Present-Day Japan." In Seymor M. Lipset and Stein Rokkan, eds. *Party Systems and Voter Alignments: Cross-national Perspectives*. New York: The Free Press.

Ysmal, Colette. 1990. *Le comportment electoral des Français* (Electoral behavior in France). Paris: La Decouverte.

Yomiuri Shimbun-sha, ed. 1990. *Gekihen no seiji sentaku: Hachijūkyū san'insen, kyūjū shūinsen tettei bunseki* (Voters' fluctuating choices: The 1989 Upper House election and the 1990 Lower House election). Tokyo: Yomiuri Shimbun-sha.

Failed Reform and Policy Changes of the SDPJ

Shinkawa Toshimitsu

F OR the first time since the Katayama cabinet in the late 1940s, the Social Democratic Party of Japan (SDPJ)[1] entered office as part of a non–Liberal Democratic Party (LDP) coalition government in 1993. Only one year later, the SDPJ formed a government with its old nemesis, the LDP, and a small centrist party called the New Party Sakigake (*sakigake* means "pioneer") founded by LDP defectors. At this time the SDPJ, which critics formerly labeled as a "party that opposed everything," or "the perpetual opposition," abandoned its dogmatic leftist policies and transformed itself into what those same critics regarded as "a responsible party with realistic policies."

Indicative of this transformation was the party's about-face on defense and foreign affairs issues. At the time the SDPJ joined the non-LDP coalition government, party leaders signed an agreement indicating acceptance of the fundamental policies of the LDP government, which meant in effect that as long as it was part of the ruling coalition, the SDPJ would neither challenge the U.S.-Japan Security Treaty nor call into question the legality of the Self-Defense Forces as it had done in the past. With the establishment of an LDP-SDPJ-Sakigake government, the Socialist leader Murayama Tomiichi became prime minister and the SDPJ officially relinquished its basic stance of "constitutional pacifism."[2]

The SDPJ, formerly called the Japan Socialist Party (JSP), had long clung to its dogmatic leftist positions, despite a widespread perception that they had caused the party's appeal to stagnate. Even after the then-JSP began reviewing its leftist policies in the mid-1980s, resistance by deeply rooted leftist forces within the party blocked any attempts to modify the philosophy of constitutional pacifism. Within a year after the start of the non-LDP coalition government, however, the SDPJ was able to breach its long-standing ideological framework of constitutional pacifism. How did it accomplish this feat? The question is intellectually challenging because the theme in the literature on the JSP/SDPJ to date has focused exclusively on why the JSP/SDPJ repeatedly failed to transform itself into a more "realistic" party.

It is equally significant to consider the consequence of the sudden about-face of the JSP/SDPJ: the plunge in public popularity subsequently experienced by the party. After changing its name to the Social Democratic Party (SDP) in January 1996, the party fissured, with many Diet members defecting to other parties, and the remaining SDP forces barely survived the general election of the House of Representatives (Lower House) in October 1996, retaining only 15 seats. If the party's leftist policies had been the cause of its stagnation, why didn't their revision restore the party's popularity? Instead, the JSP/SDPJ experienced an even worse fate than stagnation as the largest opposition party: becoming a minor (albeit, ruling) party.

I would argue that the most important factor in explaining the transformative process of the JSP/SDPJ is its major constituency, organized labor, as suggested by the model of power resource mobilization presented by Korpi (1978). This model posits that organized labor serves as the underpinning of many Socialist or pro–labor union parties, and the degree to which the links between parties and labor unions have been institutionalized is the key to understanding the parties' strategy or behavior. This model can be applied to the JSP and its affiliated union group, Sōhyō (General Council of Trade Unions of Japan). Therefore, it is essential that we examine interactions between the JSP and Sōhyō to understand the policy changes of the JSP.

The institutional settings of power resource mobilization are critical factors, as well. The theory of historical institutionalism suggests that institutions define political struggles. Institutions can include both formal organizations and informal rules and procedures that structure conduct (Thelen and Steinmo 1992, 2). As resilient and solidly established as they are by definition, institutions are subject to drastic change when an emergency arises that cannot be dealt with according to routines or conventions (see Gourevitch 1986).

Labor's degree of penetration into the JSP/SDPJ was dependent on the party's institutions. The JSP/SDPJ's organizational dependence on labor and the primacy of the party convention as the main decision-making body allowed leftist labor elements to predominate in the party. Moreover, the electoral system, a much broader institution, determined the JSP/SDPJ's strategy and conduct. Before the 1996 Lower House election, Japan's multiseat district system allowed candidates to secure seats with a relatively low proportion of the vote. (Under the multiseat district system, each district had from two to six seats. Thus, a candidate needed to secure 33.4 percent of the vote to win in a two-seat district, and only 16.7 percent of the vote in a six-seat district.) The system allowed the JSP/SDPJ to retain its second-place status (following the LDP) by relying mainly on labor unions' ability to mobilize their members in elections. The JSP/SDPJ neglected to try to expand its support among the electorate.

Concurrent with the JSP's policy shift and subsequent decline, all of the above-mentioned factors changed dramatically. The declining influence of the leftist-oriented labor movement, combined with the party abandoning the primacy in decision making it had formerly placed on the national convention under the pressure of joining the ruling coalition, led to the review of former leftist policies. Under the newly introduced single-seat district system combined with proportional representation, the SDPJ/SDP attempted to overcome its organizational dependence on labor and forge a new path for power resource mobilization, but it was unsuccessful. The fissure and decline of the SDPJ/SDP was thus caused by the party's strategic inability to respond effectively to the new electoral system.

In the first two sections of this chapter, I will explain the earlier leftist principles of the JSP/SDPJ. Then, in the third section, I will explain why the party's review of its leftist policies in the 1980s succeeded in eliminating Marxist principles from the party discipline but failed to alter the party's fundamental stance of constitutionally based pacifism. The fourth section outlines the background behind the party's institutional changes and its sudden abandonment of constitutional pacifism. The fifth and sixth sections deal with why the Socialists suffered sharp electoral setbacks despite their swing to the right. Two factors are especially noteworthy in this respect: the SDPJ/SDP's strategic failure to mobilize new power resources and the effects of the new electoral system.[3]

TWO BASIC PARTY PRINCIPLES CAUSE CONTROVERSY

The Japan Socialist Party was notorious for its internal division between leftist and rightist forces. Although the internal tensions arose from a complicated variety of causes, two issues can be identified as the major sources of confrontation throughout the party's history. The first issue concerned whether the JSP should be class-oriented or mass-oriented. Leftists argued that the JSP must be class-oriented, whereas the right wing insisted that the JSP be based on much broader constituencies, including not only wage earners but farmers, the self-employed, small and medium-sized business owners, and others.

While this first issue provides a universal criterion by which to distinguish the right wing from the left wing in leftist politics, the second issue concerning defense and national security is historically specific to postwar Japan. In the face of heightened tensions between the West and the East, the General Headquarters of the Supreme Commander for Allied Powers (SCAP) modified its policy of permanently disarming Japan and supporting the growth of liberal and leftist forces as part of a democracy. Communists were oppressed and purged from the workplace, and at the outbreak of the Korean War the government instituted the Police Reserves, which evolved into the Self-Defense Forces in 1954.

From that period on, in opposition to Japan's involvement in the cold war, the JSP leftists insisted on the maintenance of pacifism as expressed in the Constitution, which, ironically, had been drafted by SCAP officials. They proposed the philosophy of unarmed neutralism as the best way to adhere to the spirit of the Peace Constitution. Right-wing factions in the JSP were not necessarily opposed to the Peace Constitution or neutralism as an ideal, but they contended that the JSP must accept the reality of the worldwide cold war and present a concrete plan indicating clearly how to achieve their ideal. The rightists criticized the leftists by stating that hoisting the flag of neutrality without a realistic alternative is not what a "responsible party" (meaning a party responsible to the people) should do. In retrospect, the rightist arguments appear to have been reasonable. At the time, however, due to increased tension between idealistic pacifism and conservative realism, those in the Socialist right espousing "realistic policies" appeared to many to be in sympathy with the conservatives.

This schism is illustrated in figure 1. The vertical axis shows constitutional pacifism and international realism, and the horizontal axis shows Marxism and social democracy. Leftists and rightists in the party in the 1950s are largely represented by (B) and (D), respectively. In other words, the leftists advocated Marxism and constitutional pacifism, while the rightists favored social democracy and international realism. The nature of this confrontation changed abruptly after 1960, when the rightists who advocated international realism split from the JSP and formed the Democratic Socialist Party (DSP). The remaining JSP members reached a consensus that enabled the party from then on to identify itself as the party of constitutional pacifism. Henceforth, the party's internal tensions primarily centered on conflicts between those espousing social democracy and the Marxists, that is, between (A) and (B).

Figure 1. Division within the JSP

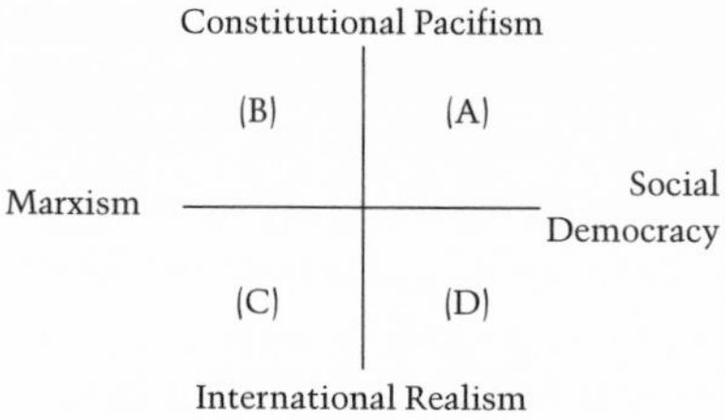

```
            Constitutional Pacifism
                    |
         (B)        |      (A)
                    |
  Marxism  ─────────┼─────────  Social
                    |           Democracy
         (C)        |      (D)
                    |
            International Realism
```

Curiously, in the confrontation between (A) and (B), those advocating social democracy were not exclusively right-wing members who had remained in the JSP. The views of some leftist members, who advocated "structural reform" of Japanese society, came into conflict with the orthodox Marxist assumptions of Socialist revolution. The philosophy of structural reform resembled that of social democracy, in that it proposed modifying the negative effects of capitalism through democratic procedures. Structural reformers, however, reproached social democrats for their "piecemeal reforms" (kairyō shugi). Structural reformers presumably wanted to avoid being identified with social democrats, because the latter were often criticized as having acquiesced to fascism and totalitarianism during World War II. Strategically, however, they made a wrong choice. Since both branches of the party subscribed to constitutional pacifism, the only clear-cut position from which they could credibly attack the Marxists (B) was that of social democracy (A). Structural reformers were unable to secure a place of their own in this scheme, thereby making their position too vague and obscure to appeal to potential allies.

The structural reformists' approach failed in 1964 when the JSP adopted a document called "The Road to Socialism in Japan" as an official supplement to its platform. This document calls for a Socialist revolution based on the Marxist-Leninist assumption that wage earners pauperized through capitalist exploitation would be unified as a revolutionary class. The idea of peaceful revolution presented in "Road to Socialism" certainly deviated from Marxist-Leninist orthodoxy. However, the document did not suggest that the JSP follow the rules of parliamentary democracy after it acquired power. "Road to Socialism" contended that gaining a majority in the Diet is useful for the revolution only when the Diet is surrounded by a national front against monopolistic capitalists. Once obtaining power, the Socialists would monopolize it in order to carry out their destiny to build a Socialist society. The adoption of "Road to Socialism" thus determined the JSP's character from the late 1960s onward as an explicitly Marxist party hostile to social democracy.

LEFTISTS AND THE JSP

Although it managed to become the largest opposition party, the JSP remained out of power throughout its history, and it continued to lose popularity after the late 1950s. The 166 seats gained in the 1958 Lower House election proved to be the party's best showing, to its members' great disappointment. After hitting bottom with 90 seats in 1969, the JSP recovered to claim 118 seats in 1972 and 123 in 1976. In 1979, however, it suffered another reversal and its seat count plunged to 107. Meanwhile, the JSP's share of the total vote in the Lower House election declined from 32.9 percent in the 1958 election to 19.3 percent in the 1979 election (Masumi 1985, 621).

In spite of the broadly shared view that the JSP's prolonged stagnation and decline was caused by its unrealistic, leftist policies, the JSP held to the tenets of Marxism and constitutional pacifism during this period. In trying to explain the JSP's continuing leftist orientation, we must examine its links to organized labor. As a pro-labor party, the JSP's actions and policies were greatly shaped by the positions taken by organized labor. The preference of the JSP's major constituency, the leftist-oriented Sōhyō, was reflected in every critical decision made by the JSP. A temporary split of the JSP in 1949 was caused by an attempt by left-wing unionists (who later organized Sōhyō) to steer the party leftward. When a confrontation between the right and left intensified over the ratification of the San Francisco Peace Treaty in the fall of 1951, Sōhyō led the left-wing factions in defecting from the party.[4] The reunification of the JSP in 1955 would have not been successful without the support of Takano Minoru, chairman of Sōhyō.

Over time, the JSP became organizationally dependent upon Sōhyō or unions affiliated with Sōhyō, allowing labor forces to strongly influence JSP policy making. According to Stockwin, "this was expressed at the electoral level, where a high proportion of endorsed party candidates were former trade unionists from unions attached to the Federation [Sōhyō], and derived much of their electoral organization and funds from their former unions rather than from the Party itself. This continued dependence upon trade unions both for its supply of electoral candidates and for much of the logistics of local organization remains the Achilles heel of the JSP, and has inhibited the growth of a broader and more independent organizational base" (1982, 176; see also Taguchi 1969; Watanabe 1991; Ōtake 1996).

Sōhyō affiliates accounted for 42.4 percent of the JSP Lower House members on average from 1958 to 1979. In the case of elections for the House of Councillors (Upper House), the ratio reached 66 percent (Masumi 1985, 561–562). It is therefore no exaggeration to refer to the JSP as the political arm of Sōhyō.

Sōhyō's own stance was driven leftward by a leadership dominated by the members of an ultraleft faction, the Socialist Association. The Socialist Association was established in 1951 by anticommunist left-wing Socialists as a Marxist study organization, not for the purpose of engaging in political activity. Within the JSP, its members belonged to the largest leftist group, the Sasaki faction. By engaging in debates with rightist factions, the Socialist Association established ideological hegemony within the party. Its dominance was confirmed with the adoption of "Road to Socialism" in 1964.

Throughout the 1960s, the Socialist Association had grown to be a de facto political faction. It increased its members and sympathizers in local chapters and secretariats through such activities as producing its own daily newspaper and organizing Marxist study groups. By the late 1960s, the association came to be identified as a cohesive political group, the source of the largest number of delegates to the JSP's party convention. It could no longer hide in the shade of the Sasaki faction.

The JSP adopted rules and procedures that would promote both organized labor and the Socialist Association. Despite its assertion that it was a class-based party with a broad grass-roots membership, the poorly organized JSP was actually no more than a parliamentary party. The JSP's annual national convention was supposed to serve as its supreme decision-making body, but in practice in the 1950s the party was managed and controlled by its Diet members. To strengthen the party organization and curtail the power of Diet members, the JSP conducted a major reform in 1958 by depriving its Diet members of the privilege of qualifying automatically as delegates to the convention, rearranging the secretariat to increase its power and authority, and introducing a system that would expand and strengthen local organizations.

The principle of making the national convention paramount failed to allow the JSP to curb its dependence on organized labor but certainly succeeded in reducing the influence of Diet members. Leftist union members, and particularly Socialist Association adherents, were most enthusiastically involved in increasing the number of party members and expanding local organizations. They became predominant in local branches, allowing their delegates to overwhelm right-wing delegates at the convention.

Thus the views of Diet members did not automatically hold sway over party policy making. In the 1970 convention, for instance, the Socialist Association proved to be the dominant force; in rivalry with the Sasaki faction, it accounted for more than 70 of the 385 delegates, with few Diet members included. The centrist Katsumata faction, in contrast, could only claim about 20 delegates, despite the fact that it accounted for the largest number of Lower House members, 22, of any of the factions (Fukunaga 1996, 272–274).

In conclusion, the JSP adopted mechanisms that favored left-wing unions and radical activists. Its emphasis on the national convention as its main decision-making body and the decision to deny automatic representation privileges to Diet members allowed left-wing activists to determine party policies through their overrepresentation at the convention.

STEERING TOWARD THE RIGHT

The JSP's "1986 Manifesto" marked a watershed in its shift from being a party of resistance to being a more realistic party. The manifesto was a product of the movement for political realism that began back in the early 1970s. As early as 1970, JSP Secretary-General Eda Saburō, who led the largest moderate faction, started to look for a way to collaborate with Kōmeitō (Clean Government Party) and the DSP. With the idea of a JSP-Kōmeitō-DSP coalition, Eda ran for party head and challenged the left-biased Narita leadership in the convention of November 1970, but he was defeated by a substantial margin. Eda's second challenge was also unsuccessful. He attempted to pass a reso-lution concerning the establishment of a JSP-Kōmeitō-DSP coalition government in the convention of January 1972, but the convention-managing committee rejected his proposal before the convention.

During the election campaign of December 1972, the Narita leader-ship publicized as a counterproposal the idea of a coalition government formed by all the opposition parties. Given the antagonism between Kōmeitō and the DSP on one hand and Kōmeitō and the Japan Com-munist Party on the other, it was most unlikely that all the opposition parties would form a coalition. The Narita leadership presented the idea only for the purpose of containing Eda's moves toward collaborat-ing with Kōmeitō and the DSP. Eda's efforts over the years yielded little but criticism from other party members and verbal abuse at the na-tional convention held in 1977. A defeated Eda subsequently left the JSP to establish a new party. Unfortunately, however, poor health left him little time to accomplish his goals; he passed away in May 1977.

Eda's attempt over nearly two decades to make JSP policies more flexible and realistic finally bore fruit after his death, when the party of-ficially approved the JSP-Kōmeitō-DSP coalition strategy. The JSP con-cluded an agreement on eventually forming a coalition government with Kōmeitō in 1980, in which the JSP admitted that joining a coali-tion would necessitate reconsideration of its basic stance on such is-sues as opposition to the Self-Defense Forces, the U.S.-Japan Security Treaty, recognition of the South Korean polity, and nuclear energy.

Revision of the positions stated in "Road to Socialism" had been under way since 1978. The Ishibashi leadership, formed in 1983 with the slogan of making the JSP a "responsible party," precipitated the review process and finally abandoned "Road to Socialism" philoso-phy with the adoption of the 1986 Manifesto at the January 1986 con-vention. The 1986 Manifesto brought an end to the interminable debates in prior years over whether the JSP was a class-based party or had a broader orientation, by defining the JSP as a national party. It also implicitly supported Western European-style social democracy by proclaiming as its goal the pursuit of an alternative to traditional, Soviet-style socialism (communism). The JSP explicitly announced its intention to adhere to European-style social democracy at the 1990 convention; accordingly, at the next convention the party decided to announce its official English name as the Social Democratic Party of Japan.

An internal struggle in the party served as a trigger for change and helps to explain why the party departed from its earlier Marxist principles. As it gradually amassed power, to the extent that it appeared to be a "party within a party," the Socialist Association began to cause tension and conflict with other established factions. The Sasaki faction, which was once the patron of the Socialist Association, most seriously suffered from the group's unilateral political activity. Consequently, in the 1970s, the Sasaki faction approached an old enemy, the Eda faction, to form an anti–Socialist Association front. Sasaki's rejection of the Eda group's JSP-Kōmeitō-DSP coalition overture made it impossible to consummate their union, but anti–Socialist Association sentiments peaked with Eda's death, just after he left the party in despair.

The unified front against the Socialist Association included both leftist and rightist factions. During party reform initiatives conducted between 1977 and 1978, they urged the Socialist Association to promise to confine itself to theoretical activities. The party then reintroduced the privilege that allowed Diet members to automatically qualify as delegates to the convention, since it was commonly felt that granting greater power to local activists tended to favor the Socialist Association. Entering the 1980s, the cohesion and integrity of the Socialist Association weakened. An internal schism formed between hard-core Marxists and social democratic converts, which brought about the defection of several leading scholars from the association in 1984. In the following year, charismatic leader Sakisaka Itsurō passed away, and in 1987 about 40 of 50 central secretaries left the association. Accordingly, the Socialist Association lost its hegemony in the 1980s, although it retained substantial influence over decision making mainly through the local chapters.

Behind the decline of the Socialist Association was the waning strength of the leftist labor movement, which experienced a turning point in the year 1975. In that year's spring wage offensive, the leftist Sōhyō, which called for higher wage raises, was overwhelmed by a unified front formed by the LDP government, employers' associations, and moderate unions, which had forged a consensus to restrain wage increases. Another fatal blow to Sōhyō was the failure of its "strike to regain the right to strike" in the autumn. The Council of Public Workers' Unions, the group at the core of Sōhyō, called a large-scale illegal work stoppage for eight days demanding their right to strike, but they were unable to wrest any concessions from the government. This strike, held during a time of economic stagnation, was sharply criticized by both the mass media and private-sector unions. The strike's poor reception enabled the government to maintain an unyielding stance on the issue; the government later sued the unions involved for compensation.

The decline of the leftist Sōhyō enabled moderate labor groups, such as Dōmei (Japan Confederation of Labor) and the IMF-JC (International Metal Workers' Federation–Japan Council) to initiate a movement toward greater union confederation. Sōhyō-affiliated unions individually joined forces with the moderate labor movement. In 1989, private- and public-sector unions jointly established a new confederation, Rengō (Japanese Trade Union Confederation), which brought together the former national federations in a moderate unified front.

Indicative of the power shift within Sōhyō was the decline of Kokurō (National Railway Workers' Union) and the rise of Zendentsū (All- Japan Telecommunications Workers' Union). Kokurō was fatally injured when it fought an all-out battle against the privatization of the Japanese National Railways (JNR). The ensuing inequitable deployment of Kokurō members and anticipated unfairness in their reemployment at the newly privatized railway companies caused Kokurō membership to plunge sharply. Kokurō, which once boasted 250,000 members, had lost almost three-quarters of its members by the time JNR was broken up and privatized in 1987. Two years later, Kokurō held only 30,000 members.

Like Kokurō, Zendentsū initially opposed plans to privatize its employer, the Nippon Telegraph and Telephone Public Corporation (Denden-kōsha). As soon as union leaders realized that it would be nearly impossible to reverse the trend of privatization, however, Zendentsū shifted its strategy from resisting privatization to opposing a breakup of Denden-kōsha lest its organization be divided along company lines. This strategy enabled Zendentsū to collaborate with management and thereby to successfully reverse the government's plan to dismantle the monopoly. This achievement enhanced Zendentsū's prestige and influence within Sōhyō. The chairman of Zendentsū, Yamagishi

Akira, was thus able to take the initiative among Sōhyō-affiliated union leaders in steering the group toward merging its national organization with Dōmei and bringing about a transformation of the JSP.

Pressure from the moderating Sōhyō defined the subsequent course of the JSP. The adoption of a noncommunist coalition strategy, the review of "Road to Socialism" and the adoption of the 1986 Manifesto were all requested by union leaders. Asukata Ichio, JSP chairman between 1978 and 1983, later recollected that against his own wishes he directed the party to take a moderate line, in accordance with Sōhyō's demands (Asukata 1987).

After the ratification of the 1986 Manifesto, the JSP's next task was to modify its traditional stance of constitutional pacifism. Labor's influence was again obvious here. In January 1987, prior to the annual convention, Yamagishi and his associates from major unions organized a gathering to promote a new path for the JSP, requesting that the JSP and the DSP reach an historical reconciliation to establish an anti-LDP, noncommunist coalition government. To this end, Yamagishi called for a review of the JSP's basic policies, constitutional pacifism in particular. Despite labor union pressure, however, the review of constitutional pacifism made little progress until a non-LDP coalition government was formed in 1993. If, as was often claimed, the JSP/SDPJ was nothing more than labor's political arm, such a delay would not have occurred. The JSP/SDPJ resisted labor's requests and continued to hold to constitutional pacifism, in spite of the fact that moderate labor increased its influence with the birth of Rengō in 1989. How best can we explain such autonomy?

For one thing, it should be noted that constitutional pacifism was much more deeply rooted than Marxist philosophy in the JSP. Even while "Road to Socialism" functioned in practice as the JSP's platform, Marxist principles were occasionally challenged by party moderates. But party members had reached consensus on backing constitutional pacifism by the 1960s, and the philosophy became the backbone of the JSP, providing the party with cohesion and unity. Naturally, it was more difficult for the party to relinquish constitutional pacifism than Marxist principles.

Doi Takako, who succeeded Ishibashi Masashi as head of the JSP in September 1986, played a decisive role in delaying the review of constitutional pacifism. She rejected it by repeatedly emphasizing at party conventions the importance of preserving the Peace Constitution–based status quo and maintaining the principle of unarmed neutrality. When Doi was chosen as chair, she was famous as a champion of constitutional pacifism. She was nonetheless selected as a compromise candidate by competing factions, which did not expect her to become a strong leader because she neither had her own faction nor belonged to a major faction. Contrary to such expectations, however, she gained popularity as the first female JSP head and a leader able to give straightforward messages, such as strongly opposing the introduction of the 3 percent consumption tax.

Doi's popularity led the JSP to an historic victory in the 1989 Upper House election. The JSP gained 46 of the 126 contested seats, leaving the LDP, with 36 seats, far behind. The LDP retained its status as the largest party by securing 109 seats in the Upper House, though the number of seats was far less than the 127 needed for a majority. The JSP was still on an upward trend in the 1990 Lower House election. It gained 136 seats, increasing its share of the vote from 17.2 percent in the previous election to 24.4 percent. The JSP's impressive performance in two consecutive elections enhanced Doi's authority and prestige. Doi's weak power base within the party was offset by her popularity outside the party, enabling her to decline labor's request to review the party's stance on constitutional pacifism. It was ironic that Doi took advantage of her popularity to forestall adoption of more "realistic" policies, considering that Doi's supporters were concerned mainly with lifestyle issues, including taxes (see Kobayashi 1991).

The remaining strength of party leftists played a decisive role in the party's decision to cling to constitutional pacifism. Given Doi's strong support among leftists, her effective leadership can be easily understood. Dogmatic leftists who had not joined Rengō had consistently resisted Sōhyō's rightward swing. The most influential leader of this group was Iwai Akira, who steered Sōhyō toward the left as its secretary-general from 1955 until 1970. Iwai and two other former Sōhyō leaders established the Labor Research Center in 1982 to mobilize leftist unions to oppose Sōhyō's rightward move. In 1989, in an effort to counter the emergence of the moderate Rengō, Iwai and his associates organized Zenrōkyō (National Liaison Conference of Trade Unions). Iwadare Sukio, who worked as Doi's right-hand man, acted as Zenrōkyō's representative within the party.

Zenrōkyō, with a membership of 500,000 workers, was no match for Rengō, whose affiliated union members totaled eight million. Nevertheless, Zenrōkyō maintained substantial influence within the JSP. It was estimated that by the early 1990s about a third of the party membership belonged to or sympathized with Zenrōkyō. Its strength was demonstrated during the election for party head held in July 1991, after Doi stepped down to take responsibility for a poor showing in the unified local elections held in April. Tanabe Makoto, then-secretary-general and the leading figure among the moderates, was expected to win a sweeping victory with the support of Rengō, but he won by a much smaller margin than predicted. Ueda Tetsu, who was backed by Zenrōkyō and who advocated maintaining the constitutional pacifism plank, gained 30 percent of the total vote, only nine points behind Tanabe.

The vote reflected the continuing bias toward Zenrōkyō owing to the party's emphasis on the national convention as its primary decision-making organ. Since local branches were guaranteed a strong say in the institutional pattern of decision making, especially at the convention, local leftist stalwarts were able to resist the policies and will of the central leadership. Consequently, at the convention where Tanabe was chosen as the new leader, a proposal for the review of constitutional pacifism drafted by a Tanabe-led committee was rejected.

Debates over the peacekeeping operations triggered by the outbreak of the Persian Gulf crisis in the summer of 1990 sparked antiwar sentiment by the still leftist-leaning party. Ironically, Tanabe, a champion of the right wing, had no choice but to accede to this antiwar opinion. He eventually found himself in a difficult position, as the party leadership adopted a stance of unyielding opposition to dispatching Self-Defense Forces overseas under any conditions. That decision scotched the prospect of further negotiations on forming a coalition with Kōmeitō and the DSP, as those two parties favored collaborating with the LDP to support Japanese peacekeeping operations.

Lastly, it is important to note that Rengō's enormous power resources were not mobilized effectively to exert influence over the JSP/SDPJ. As basically an amalgam of unions with different ideological and policy orientations, Rengō was neither capable of having a unified political view nor capable of undertaking political activity. Ex-Sōhyō affiliates and ex-Dōmei affiliates were in confrontation over political issues, including national security, social security, and nuclear energy policies. Rengō head Yamagishi's actions therefore were not based on

a Rengō consensus. He received his greatest support from ex-Sōhyō affiliates, but ex-Dōmei affiliates were also in agreement on the necessity
of reconciliation between the DSP and the JSP.

IMF-JC leaders, on the other hand, were skeptical about Yamagishi's commitment to the JSP. Miyata Yoshiji, then chair of the IMF-JC
as well as president of Tekkō Rōren (Japan Federation of Steel Workers'
Unions), and his successors, including Washio Etsuya, head of Tekkō
Rōren, and Tokumoto Teruo, chairman of the Confederation of Japan
Automobile Workers' Unions, insisted that organized labor should keep
political parties at arm's length and should mobilize its power when
labor-related policies are placed on the political agenda. To this end,
the most effective step, they believed, would be to establish a two-
party system by introducing single-seat electoral districts. Whether or
not the Socialists would be able to be one of these two parties mattered
little to them (Watanabe 1994, 434–442). Washio says: "A conventional
way for labor to influence politics is by establishing an affiliation with
a political party, but by doing so organized labor has weakened its
power. This is why the new Rengō was organized. Although President
Yamagishi's activities give the wrong impression that Rengō is committed to a specific party, Rengō's basic policy is to collaborate with
various political forces on a case-by-case basis, after examining individual policies" (Honzawa 1997, 245).

To sum up, an assumption that the JSP/SDPJ was dominated by the
policy preferences of organized labor fails to account for the party's adherence to constitutional pacifism despite pressure from labor. Constitutional pacifism was so deeply imbedded in the JSP platform as its
most widely shared philosophy that leftist members at the party's local branches were able to effectively shelve its review by taking advantage of the primacy of the party convention in JSP decision making.

THE SUDDEN DEATH OF
CONSTITUTIONAL PACIFISM

In order to complete the JSP/SDPJ's transformation to becoming a
"realistic" party, it was essential that reformers breach the party's institutional barrier, by modifying the "convention-first" rule of decision
making in such a way as to enhance the power of the Diet members.
In the early 1990s, the JSP/SDPJ carried out a series of revisions of party
rules to this end, deciding that the national convention would be held

every second year instead of every year, the Diet committee system would be introduced as a shadow cabinet, the appointment of organizers would be abolished, and the party rules would be appended with an explicit statement that the general meeting of both the Upper and Lower House members would be their supreme decision making body. These revisions, however, made no substantial changes in the actual management of the party.

The institutional pattern of party convention dominance in decision making finally dissolved with the start of the coalition era. The LDP's seemingly unending grip on political power abruptly ended with its split in 1993 after a string of political scandals. In the Lower House election of July 1993, the LDP gained only 223 seats, short of a majority of 256 of the 511 seats, and the idea long-cherished by the SDPJ of a non-LDP government suddenly looked plausible. The SDPJ itself, however, with only 70 seats secured in the election, having lost almost half of its preelection seats, lacked the wherewithal to take the lead among the opposition parties.

Instead, the initiative for forming a coalition was taken by newly created conservative/centrist parties, including the New Party Sakigake and the Japan New Party. They proposed that party support for a single-seat district system combined with proportional representation be a prerequisite for joining a non-LDP coalition. The SDPJ accepted the proposal immediately because party leaders were convinced that participating in a non-LDP coalition government was in the best interests of the electorate.[5]

The decision was noteworthy not only because it meant that the SDPJ had changed its long-standing opposition to the single-seat district system, but also because the party's central leadership exercised unusual discretion in deciding such an important issue. They obtained only ex post facto consent from ranking members, including a gathering of Lower House members and an extrordinary meeting of the Central Executive Committee. In a national meeting of local secretariats on July 27, 1993, the leadership succeeded in authorizing the Central Executive Committee to decide coalition government–related matters.

Henceforth, the leadership was able to act relatively independently of the party's leftist forces. The SDPJ leadership signed an agreement forming the non-LDP Hosokawa coalition government on July 29, 1993, that included the suggestion of continuity between the previous

LDP government and the new government as concerned basic policies. The agreement implied that established policies concerning national security, defense, external affairs, and nuclear energy would remain unchanged. All these decisions were endorsed at the national convention of September 1993.

The SDPJ, however, while a part of the Hosokawa government, had yet to amend its pacifist principles. Socialist ministers in the Hosokawa cabinet professed that they considered the Self-Defense Forces unconstitutional as SDPJ members, but as cabinet members they of course respected the coalition agreement. In the LDP-SDPJ-Sakigake coalition government formed on June 30, 1994, the Socialists were no longer able to use that argument, since their leader Murayama was selected to preside over the cabinet as prime minister.

In order to make the party's stance consistent with established government policy and to assume responsibility for leading the government, Murayama decided to relinquish the party position on constitutional pacifism. In his first speech to the Diet as prime minister, on July 18, 1994, Murayama expressed his intention to maintain the U.S.-Japan Security Treaty and to accept as necessary a minimal number of defense forces. The Central Executive Committee of the SDPJ subsequently endorsed Murayama's statement.[6]

Murayama recollected his historical decision to transform party policies as follows: "It would have been better if the decision had resulted from open debate within the party. In that case, the policy change would have been more warmly accepted. There was no time for that, however, since I was elected as prime minister by chance, with no preparation whatsoever. At that time, I firmly resolved that I would resign as prime minister if my decision was rejected at the convention" (Murayama 1996, 63).

In the convention held in September following this about-face, dissatisfied leftists were furious, as expected. Secretary-General Kubo Wataru weathered the storm of dismay by asserting that as prime minister Murayama could not have expressed views that differed from government policy. The SDPJ, therefore, must adjust its stance to conform to government policy to fulfill its obligations as the prime minister's party. Kubo later confessed that "the decision received ex post facto approval only because Murayama was prime minister. If he had been just another Socialist leader, he would have been ostracized immediately after his statement."[7]

In conclusion, strong leadership was needed to overcome institutional resistance to abandoning the stance of constitutional pacifism. Strong leadership, however, was all but impossible given the party's institutionalized pattern of decision making in which basic policies had to be endorsed at a convention where leftists still maintained substantial power. The SDPJ's conventional pattern of decision making left the party little room to make drastic changes.

This rigidified pattern was weakened, however, when the party leadership gained discretionary power in the turmoil following the 1993 election. Their authority was strengthened by Murayama's appointment as prime minister to the extent that the leader was able to discard a fundamental party position without the prior consent of party members.

FAILURE TO MOBILIZE
NEW POWER RESOURCES

Soon after Murayama's resignation as prime minister in January 1996, the SDPJ changed its name to the Social Democratic Party (SDP) and revised its rules and platform at its convention as a first step toward becoming a new nonconservative party. A small number of hard-core leftists defected before the convention to form the New Socialist Party. According to the predominant view that the SDPJ's stagnation had been caused by its leftist policies, its turnabout should have opened the door to a new, golden era for the SDP. Contrary to these expectations, however, the majority of SDP members moved to the newly formed Democratic Party of Japan (DPJ) and the SDP survived the Lower House election of October 1996 as a minor party holding only 15 seats out of 500.

How best can we explain the gap between expectations of restored party glory and the reality? The JSP/SDPJ's rightward swing was an attempt to expand its constituency, to mobilize new power resources. The party's fall, therefore, meant that its attempt had failed, basically because of two major factors: party strategy and fundamental changes in the electoral system. This fifth section deals with the first factor, and the sixth section discusses the latter.

Social Democracy

The JSP/SDPJ's decision to reposition itself as a social democratic party raises questions about how useful social democracy is for mobilizing power resources in Japan. Social democracy has achieved full-fledged development in places where organized labor is powerful enough (that is, the unionization rate is reasonably high and centralized labor organizations span varied enterprises and localities) to counterbalance market-oriented forces. Japan obviously lacked such conditions. The nation's unionization rate remained at about a third of its total labor population from the 1950s to the mid-1970s. The rate has declined consistently since then, and currently hovers close to the 20 percent mark. Centralization is weak as an effect of enterprise-based unions, as these unions operate independently from higher-level umbrella organizations.

Whereas in most social democracies confederated labor unions tend to request income redistribution and welfare provisions through government policy, Japanese enterprise-specific unions typically call for wage raises, improved working conditions, and welfare provisions within their individual enterprises. Wage earners try to improve their living standards by enhancing business performance in cooperation with company management. The Japanese style of labor-management relations, therefore, discourages wage earners from organizing themselves across enterprise lines. The common strategy of social democratic parties of mobilizing support by improving working conditions and national welfare through government policy is unlikely to appeal to workers, at least to employees in large firms, who constitute the majority of organized labor.

It should be noted furthermore that Western social democratic parties, which had promoted the welfare policy since the 1960s, lost their popularity by 1980, as many industrialized countries faced huge financial deficits caused by the oil crises in the 1970s. The Keynesian effects of social democratic policies on domestic demand were negated to a considerable extent by the impact of economic globalization. Neoconservatism asserts that the aggrandized state deprives the private sector of financial resources, thereby causing economic stagnation. The social democratic welfare state is also criticized on moral grounds, in that excessive welfare services make people lazy and dependent upon the state. Regardless of the validity of these criticisms, the conventional style of social democracy certainly lost its attractiveness to many in the 1980s.

Had the SDPJ taken a serious approach toward introducing social democracy in Japan, it would have discussed the problems and limitations faced by Western social democracies and it would have presented a new version of social democracy tailored to Japan's specific circumstances. What the JSP actually did was to condemn Marxist-Leninist ideologies and blindly applaud Western-style social democracies (see Ōuchi 1989; Fukuda and Tanaka 1988). This may have been a necessary strategy to take to emerge victorious from intraparty conflict, but to defend Western-style social democracy against Marxism in the 1980s was a questionable approach as far as voters were concerned. Nobody cared about Soviet-style socialism by that time except for hard-core ideologues. The claim of being "better than Russian socialism" did not appeal much to the general public.

An old Socialist made an insightful comment on the strategy of unifying social democratic forces just before he passed away: "Rengō president Yamagishi has referred to social democracy for years. But what he has said merely means 'non-LDP and anti-JCP [Japan Communist Party],' as if everyone but LDP and JCP supporters were the supporters of social democracy. Social democracy is presented as something left after rejecting the LDP and the JCP, without a clear vision of what social democracy is or its basic policies. It is, therefore, easy [for him] to move on to something else" (Shimizu 1995, 388).

A Lost Identity

Another strategic failure was in policy development by the Murayama cabinet. Since the SDPJ had tried to appeal to voters in the previous election by participating in a non-LDP government, it was critical for the SDPJ to legitimize forming a coalition with the LDP and thus overcome the relative unpopularity of the Murayama cabinet by introducing policies that demonstrated a strong new identity. The Murayama cabinet, however, failed to present policies that were distinguishable from those of previous LDP governments, although it was able to resolve some old issues with statements apologizing for former government actions, such as a statement of remorse for the nation's behavior during World War II and a statement expressing regret to those who suffered from Minamata disease, an illness of the nervous system caused by mercury dumped by a chemical company in Minamata Bay in Kumamoto Prefecture in the 1950s.

I would like to cite two specific examples of the Murayama cabinet's policy failures, in the areas of social security and new postindustrial policies. The first has been known as the province of social democrats and the second as an area where social democrats can potentially take a leading role.

SOCIAL SECURITY   To what extent were the social security policies of the Murayama cabinet different from those of previous LDP governments? The SDPJ released an interim report entitled "The Welfare Program from the Welfare Society in Post–World War II to Welfare Policy in the 21st Century" in May 1994, one month before the start of the Murayama government. It was noteworthy because it contained arguments directly opposed to LDP-led retrenchment on welfare programs. Its essence can be summarized as follows:

> A society that guarantees the elderly freedom of choice and independence is a system in which individuals can lead independent lives with the help of universal social services when necessary. The central pillar of this system is public services, complemented by self-help programs and voluntary organizations. Shifting the burden from the public sector to the individual will increase social costs tremendously, due to the enormous expenditure of energy and time required of caretakers in the home and the cost of excluding them from the labor market.
>
> It is misleading to assume incompatibility between social security and economic growth. Pensions and family assistance increase the purchasing power of the elderly. Social security expenditures promote business expansion in the fields of medical care, care for the elderly, and child care, thereby creating jobs. Improvements in social security, moreover, create an environment in which workers can work with peace of mind. Social security pays for itself by facilitating economic growth with new benefits. (Nippon Shakaitō 1994a, 4–22)

This report was undoubtedly targeted at the neoconservative backlash against welfare at the time. It is unclear, however, to what extent the ideas expressed in the report were reflected in social policy development during the Murayama era. The Murayama cabinet's most significant achievement in this field was the adoption of the New Gold Plan, aimed at increasing manpower and facilities for care for the elderly. However, this was basically an upgraded version of the Gold Plan that had been formulated by the Ministry of Health and Welfare in 1989; it simply expanded the established policy, displaying little sign of Socialist initiative.

The government's revision of the pension scheme appeared to contradict the original stance of the JSP/SDPJ. The party had been opposed to a raise in the pensionable age from 60 to 65 for company employees, as proposed by the LDP government since the late 1970s. The JSP/SDPJ agreed to the proposal, however, once it joined the government. The pension reform bill passed the Diet during the Murayama administration.

The SDPJ made its case in a commentary on the pension reform bill, asserting that increases in social expenditures under the current pension scheme would become too burdensome for future generations (Nippon Shakaitō 1994b, 21). This argument, however, is far from persuasive because the party had criticized this very line of reasoning for so long. The commentary caused raised eyebrows about other assertions as well, such as its claim that increased employment should be a prerequisite for raising the pensionable age, even though this is unlikely in the current economic recession. The SDPJ's reasoning seemed to make little sense in terms of policy rationale. Its acceptance of raising the pensionable age appeared above all to be a concession to the LDP in order to stay in power.

NEW POLITICS   Whereas social welfare is an area in which social democrats have traditionally had the upper hand, "new politics," concerning postindustrial values, or issues that arise in a maturing, postindustrial society, are often considered to be a field in which social democrats may gain an edge over neoconservatives. Often included under the "new politics" rubric are such issues as environmental protection, feminism, minority rights, consumer rights, and participatory democracy. To what extent did the JSP/SDPJ exercise its leadership in this field?

The passage of the Promotion of Local Autonomy Law, designed to promote local autonomy, during the Murayama administration can be seen as a result of continuing efforts by the SDPJ. The law closely resembled a report that the party's shadow cabinet had drafted in the autumn of 1992, in collaboration with scholars and younger elite bureaucrats. The SDPJ widely distributed copies of the report, with the

aim of encouraging local assemblies to call for greater decentralization. In June 1993, the SDPJ proposed a resolution on promoting local
autonomy, which unanimously passed the Diet.

As visibly active as the SDPJ was, however, the fact that all parties
except the JCP supported the idea of decentralization made it difficult
to assess the importance of the role the SDPJ played. According to Ishihara Nobuo, then deputy chief cabinet secretary, the promotion of local autonomy was authorized in a cabinet meeting because of strong
support for it voiced not only by SDPJ ministers but by LDP and Sakigake ministers as well, although it was not included in the day's agenda.[8]

The party's promotion of nonprofit organizations (NPOs) was noteworthy in terms of citizen involvement in politics. Voluntary relief
activities in the Kobe area after the Great Hanshin-Awaji Earthquake
of 1995 helped increase public awareness of a bill that would facilitate
NPO activities by making it easier for the organizations to incorporate.
The Murayama government submitted its NPO bill in late 1996. In
the meantime, the New Frontier Party, which had been established in
late 1994 by the merger of the DSP, the Japan New Party, the Japan Renewal Party, and the Kōmeitō, had already submitted its own NPO bill
three times. As was the case with decentralization, no major parties
voiced opposition to the idea of an NPO bill.

Among the ruling parties, Sakigake, not the SDPJ, was most active
in this issue. The party publicized a research report on the activities of
nonprofit groups in December 1994, before the Kobe earthquake, in response to requests from a citizens' group. When the LDP attempted to
revise a bill in such a way as to strengthen bureaucratic supervision
and control over NPOs, it was Sakigake that pushed for the draft to be
rewritten in its original form.

In the field of environmental protection, the SDPJ's moves were
disastrous in terms of power resource mobilization. The SDPJ had
long been supported by environmentalists and environmental citizens'
groups owing to its consistent opposition to nuclear energy and industrial pollution. Along with relinquishing constitutional pacifism, however, the SDPJ altered its pro-environmental stance by accepting the
use of nuclear energy as a transitional energy source.

Soon after this policy switch, the occurrence of some accidents at
nuclear power stations during which accurate information was sup-
pressed by the nuclear energy authorities greatly increased public anxiety about nuclear power. Against this backdrop, a pivotal event took

place on August 4, 1996, when a majority of the residents of the small town of Makimachi in Niigata Prefecture rejected, via a plebiscite, construction of a nuclear power station. Taking these events into account, it can be said that the SDPJ abandoned its antinuclear energy stance just when it had become attractive and possibly useful for mobilizing popular support.

More awkward and damaging were the SDPJ's dealings regarding the construction of an estuary dam in Nagara River in Mie Prefecture. The dam issue had already become politically sensitive by the time the Hosokawa government was formed. Understanding the political risks involved, the Socialist minister of construction, Igarashi Kōzō, took a prudent stance: He let the dam be constructed on the condition that its operations be suspended. Nosaka Kōken, another Socialist minister of construction in the Murayama cabinet, was neither as sensitive nor cautious as Igarashi. He declared on May 22, 1995, in accordance with advice from bureaucrats, that the government would start full-scale operations of the Nagara River dam. His decision met with nationwide criticism. The party's image was severely damaged by extensive mass media coverage of a hunger strike protesting the Nagara River dam. Igarashi recollected, "When we relinquished constitutional pacifism, we didn't receive a single protest call at headquarters. But the telephone bell did not stop ringing for a while after Nosaka's decision. It was said that the mishandling of the Nagara River dam issue resulted in cutting the SDPJ's votes in half. We in the SDPJ paid scant consideration to what today's citizens take seriously."[9]

It must be concluded from the above cases that the SDPJ failed to find a way to mobilize new power resources during the Murayama administration.

EFFECTS OF THE NEW ELECTORAL SYSTEM

Another important influence on the party's ability to mobilize power resources was the new electoral system of the Lower House. The relatively low proportion of the vote required to gain a seat under the prior multiseat district system had enabled the SDPJ to remain the largest opposition force by depending on labor and appealing to the leftist electorate.

The party's failure to broaden its constituency was not a serious drawback under the multiseat district system, because it could count on labor to secure the second largest bloc of seats in the Lower House. This conventional wisdom, however, could not be applied to the new electoral system, which featured 300 single-seat districts. Without gaining substantial new power resources, the SDPJ was expected to suffer a disastrous setback, losing in most single-seat districts and unlikely to gain anywhere close to half of the 200 proportional representation seats, given its highest share of the vote to date, 20 percent (the 24.4 percent share the party recorded in the 1990 election was considered exceptional and attributable to then–Chairperson Doi's popularity).

This argument was often cited during moves to create a new party within the SDPJ starting in 1994. Former party head Yamahana Sadao and his associates organized an intraparty group, the New Democratic Coalition, to pursue possibilities for forming a new non-LDP government in the near future. Secretary-General Kubo sympathized with the Yamahana group and voiced his intentions to form a new party by mobilizing social democratic and liberal forces. Chair Murayama counterbalanced that idea with his proposal of integrating the SDPJ and Sakigake into a single party. When all these attempts failed, the SDPJ lost the chance to form a new party under its initiative. As a result, each Diet member was later presented with the need to decide whether or not to join the non-Socialist DPJ.

It remains a puzzle as to why the SDPJ accepted the electoral system reforms despite its perception that the introduction of a single-seat district system would be to its disadvantage. The SDPJ formerly voiced opposition to this kind of electoral reform whenever it was proposed by the LDP. Why not in 1993? Given the political circumstances of the time, in which the multiseat district system was criticized as a main cause of political scandals and corruption and all other parties except for the Communists supported revising the electoral system, a Socialist leader recalled, the SDPJ was unable to take a strong, unilateral stand against the change.[10]

By regarding a non-LDP government as the supreme objective, the SDPJ acquiesced to the single-seat district system without much deliberation. This stance received strong backing from Yamagishi Akira, the president of Rengō. By early 1993, however, shortly after conflict surfaced between the SDPJ and Kōmeitō-DSP about the issue of peacekeeping operations, thwarting efforts to realize a joint social democratic strategy, Yamagishi had shifted his stance from establishing a social democratic unified front to creating a non-LDP coalition. To this end, he now collaborated with a champion of neoconservatism, Ozawa Ichirō, secretary-general of the Japan Renewal Party, which had been formed by LDP defectors.

Similar as it might appear, the idea of a non-LDP coalition is quite different from a merger of social democratic forces. Both proposals posit that the unification of non-LDP (and anti-JCP) forces is necessary to promote a shift of power in Japan that will lead to a more mature democracy. The non-LDP coalition proposed by Ozawa, however, implied a system of two conservative-leaning parties; his alternative to the LDP was not social democratic but conservative in its basic stance. Yamagishi's original concept of an SDPJ-Kōmeitō-DSP coalition was apparently incompatible with Ozawa's vision. The thinking of the IMF-JC union leaders echoed Ozawa's perspective, and they actually tried to collaborate behind the scenes. Yamagishi thus jumped on the bandwagon for forming a non-LDP coalition as a preemptive move, to contain his potential rivals and reconfirm his leadership.

Yamagishi felt forced to accede to the introduction of single-seat districts, even though he likened the process to being served a "poisoned sweet," implying that its slow-working poison would fatally injure the SDPJ later on. To neutralize the poison, he asserted, the parties joining the coalition government should help each other and form a unified front against the LDP in single-seat districts (Yamagishi 1995a; 1995b). He did not hide his distrust in Ozawa, however, and doubted that they could cooperate for long. And with the coalition government looking unlikely to last, it was questionable whether Yamagishi's antidote would be attainable.

The "Murayama initiative" adopted at the convention of January 1994 demonstrated the inability of the SDPJ to think outside the traditional paradigm of a multiseat district system. It stated that the SDPJ would work to forge a pluralistic party system, in which the party would take the initiative in forming a coalition government with the goals of social justice and solidarity. The plurality referred to by the SDPJ is most likely to emerge from proportional representation voting. In order to form a government, however, the SDPJ and its potential allies would also have to win a majority in single-seat districts, which account for 300 of the total 500 seats. If the SDPJ seriously hopes to win among single-seat districts, its proposed pluralistic party system is unlikely to be maintained, because, without unifying themselves, the SDPJ and its allies have no chance to command a majority.

In short, the SDPJ's conventional electoral approach was totally inapplicable to the new electoral system that the party had accepted, but it lacked a clear vision about how to proceed or a strategy for its own survival.

CONCLUSION

The JSP/SDPJ, once known as a "perpetual opposition party," finalized its rightward shift with the surrender of constitutional pacifism in 1994. Two major changes lay behind the SDPJ's transformation to being what was regarded as a "realistic" party. The first concerned organized labor. Leftist union forces suffered setbacks in the 1975 spring offensive as well as in the "strike to regain the right to strike" that shifted the balance of power in favor of the moderates. Rivals of Sōhyō, such as Dōmei and the IMF-JC, came to play leading roles in the spring offensive and the unification of labor organizations in the late 1970s. A power shift took place within Sōhyō as well, as moderates gradually overwhelmed the influence of left-wing unions. Decisive was the fall of Kokurō, the leading left-wing union, in the mid-1980s. By the late 1980s, the weakened leftists had few means by which to challenge the moderate-led forces for labor affiliation.

The changes in organized labor were naturally reflected in the policies of the heavily labor-dependent JSP. In parallel with Sōhyō's rightward shift, the JSP started a review of its party platform, expressed in the 1964 report "The Road to Socialism in Japan." It is misleading, however, to assume that leftist elements in the JSP were neutralized with the party's adoption of the 1986 Manifesto. Leftist influences remained strong enough to prevent the party from modifying its basic advocacy of constitutional pacifism.

Although the leftists became a weakened, minor force in the labor movement, they retained substantial power within the JSP thanks to the primacy placed upon the national convention as the party's principle decision-making body. This approach brought about an institutional pattern of decision making that increased the power of local chapters and rank-and-file members and limited the leadership potential of Diet members. Through their dominance at the local-chapter level, leftists were able to achieve overrepresentation in decision making at party conventions.

The second major change had to do with the political disorder that arose when the LDP's long-term dominance came to an end. The SDPJ leadership was able to increase its discretionary authority in order to deal with the rapidly changing political situation in the coalition era. With the appointment of party head Murayama as prime minister, the leadership's range of discretion expanded to such an extent that it was able to overthrow the basic party stance of constitutional pacifism.

The swing to the right was based on the assumption that the SDPJ would prosper as a ruling party if it reversed its leftist orientation. When the SDPJ finally did so, however, the party split and weakened to become a minor party. How had it erred? First of all, social democracy was ill-suited to the Japan of the 1980s as a strategy for mobilizing popular support. Social democracy was losing its luster in most advanced capitalistic nations at that time, as neoconservatism gained wide acceptance as a fundamental policy. The idea of social democracy proposed by the JSP, after all, implied achieving reconciliation between the JSP and the DSP as part of a unification of "anticommunist, non-LDP" forces. The party was unable to present any forward-looking policies that would recast it as a party of the future.

During the coalition era from 1993 to 1998, the SDPJ finally abandoned constitutional pacifism, but it was unable to find an alternative for its dependence on labor that would allow it to mobilize new power resources. Even in an administration led by a Socialist leader prime minister, the SDPJ was unable to forge a new identity, thereby causing it to appear to be little more than a "second LDP."

The party's failure to mobilize new power resources would not have been so serious had the multiseat district system remained unchanged. The new single-seat district system with proportional representation, however, did not allow the SDPJ to enjoy a comfortable second-place position by depending upon organized labor, as it always had. When the SDPJ failed in an attempt to form a new party, the bulk of the party's membership fled to the centrist DPJ.

NOTES

1. Since the 1940s, the official name in English of the Nippon Shakaitō had been the Social Democratic Party of Japan. However, the English name Japan Socialist Party (JSP) was commonly used. At its party convention in February 1991, the JSP announced that its official English name was the Social Democratic Party of Japan (SDPJ). The SDPJ changed its English name to the Social

Democratic Party (SDP) in January 1996. Following custom, we use the JSP in referring to the party in this chapter. When the party is referred to from an historical perspective, it is called the JSP/SDPJ.

2. Constitutional pacifism means to advocate unarmed neutrality based on the pacifistic stance expressed in the Japanese Constitution. The Constitution's Article 9, also known as the "peace clause," renounces "war as a sovereign right of the nation and the threat or use of force as a means of settling international disputes" and bans the maintenance of "land, sea and air forces, as well as other war potential."

3. Throughout this chapter, descriptions of the JSP rely mainly on the following three books: Nippon Shakaitō (1986; 1996) and Iizuka, Uji, and Habara (1985).

4. The left-wing factions in the early 1950s based their pacifist stance on what was called the "four peace principles": a "total peace" (that is, a peace pact with all the former Allied Powers), refusal to allow foreign troops to be stationed in Japan, permanent neutrality, and no rearmament. The leftists were opposed accordingly to the San Francisco Peace Treaty and the U.S.-Japan Security Treaty of 1951, and the introduction and expansion of the Self-Defense Forces. The right-wing factions in the party favored the Peace Treaty as a first step in Japan's reentry to the international community, but they opposed the Security Treaty.

5. As stated to the author in an interview with former Prime Minister Murayama Tomiichi on February 14, 1997.

6. The meeting proceeded as if the SDPJ was trying to deny its past; party leaders unhesitatingly accepted Japan's commitment to peacekeeping operations within constitutional limitations and nuclear energy as a transitional energy source. Furthermore, they recognized the sun flag and the traditional anthem "Kimigayo," which the JSP formerly criticized as symbols of Japan's prewar militarism, as the national flag and national anthem, respectively.

7. Interview with Kubo Wataru on May 27, 1997.

8. Interview with Ishihara Nobuo on February 15, 1997.

9. Interview with Igarashi Kōzō on February 17, 1997.

10. Interview with Kubo Wataru on February 15, 1997.

BIBLIOGRAPHY

Asukata Ichio. 1987. *Asukata Ichio kaisōroku* (Memoirs of Asukata Ichio). Tokyo: Asahi Shimbun-sha.

Fukuda Yutaka and Tanaka Shin'ichirō. 1988. *Shakai minshushugi no sentaku* (The choice of social democracy). Tokyo: Ariesu Shobō.

Fukunaga Fumio. 1996. "Nippon Shakaitō no habatsu" (Factions in the Japan Socialist Party). In Nishikawa Tomokazu and Kawata Jun'ichi, eds. *Seitō habatsu* (Factions in political parties). Kyoto: Mineruva Shobō.

Gourevitch, Peter. 1986. *Politics in Hard Times*. Ithaca: Cornell University Press.

Honzawa Jirō. 1997. *Rengō no tsumi to batsu* (Rengō's sin and penalty). Tokyo: Piipuru-sha.

Iizuka Shigetarō, Uji Toshihiko, and Habara Kiyomasa. 1985. *Kettō yon'jū–nen: Nippon Shakaitō* (Forty years of the Japan Socialist Party). Tokyo: Gyōken Shuppan-kyoku.

Ishihara Nobuo. 1995. *Kantei 2668-nichi* (2,668 days in the Prime Minister's Office). Tokyo: Nippon Hōsō Shuppan-Kyōkai.

Kōno Masaru. 1997. "Electoral Origins of Japanese Socialists' Stagnation." *Comparative Political Studies* 30 (1): 55–77.

Kobayashi Yoshiaki. 1991. *Gendai Nippon no senkyo* (Elections in contemporary Japan). Tokyo: Tokyo Daigaku Shuppan-kai.

Korpi, Walter. 1978. *The Working Class in Welfare Capitalism*. London: Routledge and Kegan Paul.

Masumi Jun'nosuke. 1985. *Gendai seiji, gekan* (Contemporary politics in Japan, vol. 2). Tokyo: Tokyo Daigaku Shuppan-kai.

Murayama Tomiichi. 1996. *Murayama Tomiichi ga kataru "tenmei" no 561-nichi* (Murayama Tomiichi talks about his 561 days in office). Tokyo: KK Besto Serāzu.

Nippon Shakaitō, ed. 1986. *Shiryō Nippon Shakai-tō 40-nen shi* (Historical documents: Forty years of the Japan Socialist Party). Tokyo: Nippon Shakaitō.

———, ed. 1994a. "Kōrei shakai fukushi puroguramu—chūkan hōkoku" (The welfare program in the aged society—interim report). *Seisaku shiryō*, no. 334: 4–40.

———, ed. 1994b. "Renritsu yotō nenkin kaisei hōkoku—an no kaisetsu" (A commentary on the pension reform plan by the ruling parties). *Seisaku shiryō*, no. 329: 15–19.

———, ed. 1996. *Nippon Shakaitō shi* (The history of the Japan Socialist Party). Tokyo: Nippon Shakaitō.

Ōuchi Shūmei et al. 1989. *Doi Shakaitō* (The Doi socialist party). Tokyo: Akashi Shoten.

Ōtake Hideo. 1986. "Nippon Shakaitō higeki no kigen" (Roots of the tragedy befalling the Japan Socialist Party). *Chūō Kōron* (October): 146–161.

———. 1996. *Sengo Nihon no ideorogī tairitsu* (Ideological confrontations in postwar Japan). Tokyo: San'ichi Shobō.

Sakamoto Yoshikazu 1962. "Nippon ni okeru kokusai reisen to kokunai reisen" (The international cold war and the domestic cold war in Japan). Reprinted in Sakamoto Yoshikazu. 1982. *Shinban kakujidai no kokusai seiji* (International politics in the nuclear age, revised edition). Tokyo: Iwanami Shoten.

Shimizu Shinzō. 1995. *Sengo kakushin no han-hikage* (The half-shade of the postwar progressives). Tokyo: Nippon Keizai Hyōron-sha.

Stockwin, J. A. A. 1982. *Japan: Divided Politics in a Growth Economy.* 2nd ed. London: Weidenfeld and Nicolson.

Taguchi Fukuji, ed. 1969. *Nippon Shakaitō ron* (A study of the Japan Socialist Party). Tokyo: Shinnihon Shuppan.

Thelen, C., and S. Steinmo. 1992. "Historical Institutionalism in Comparative Politics." In C. Thelen et al., eds. *Structuring Politics.* Cambridge: Cambridge University Press.

Watanabe Osamu. 1991. "Gendai Nippon shakai to shakai minshu-shugi." (Contemporary Japanese society and social democracy). In Tokyo Daigaku Shakai Kagaku Kenkyūsho, ed. *Gendai Nippon shakai 5* (Contemporary Japanese society, Vol. 5). Tokyo: Tokyo Daigaku Shuppan-kai.

———. 1994. *Seiji kaikaku to kempō kaisei* (Political reform and the revision of the Constitution). Tokyo: Aoki Shoten.

Yamagishi Akira. 1995a. *"Renritsu" shikake-nin* (Mastermind behind the coalition governments). Tokyo: Kōdan-sha.

———. 1995b. *Renritsu seiken jidai o kiru* (Review of the coalition government era) Tokyo: Yomiuri Shimbun-sha.

Generational Change and Political Upheaval

Wada Shūichi

WHEN the Liberal Democratic Party (LDP) lost its Diet majority as a result of the House of Representatives (Lower House) election of 1993, it was forced to relinquish its monopoly on ruling power for the first time since its establishment in 1955. Eight opposition parties subsequently formed a ruling coalition under Hosokawa Morihiro, head of the Japan New Party (JNP). The LDP, however, retrieved power within one year by forming a coalition government with the Social Democratic Party of Japan (SDPJ) and the New Party Sakigake (*sakigake* means "pioneer") under Prime Minister Murayama Tomiichi, leader of the SDPJ. The SDPJ held the prime ministership for the first time in 46 years, but its brief stint at the helm of government ended with a crushing defeat in national-level elections after 1995.

Many books and articles have been written explaining changes in Japan's political party system in the 1990s. Some analysts point to the structural erosion of the "1955 system"[1] during the LDP's 38-year tenure as the main cause of change. Others argue that the end of the LDP-dominant system was linked with global systemic shifts, specifically

During the writing and editing of this chapter, I received many thoughtful and constructive comments. I would like to thank L. William Heinrich, Jr., Kurusu Kaoru, Paul Midford, Pamela Noda, Ōtake Hideo, Jane Singer, Wada Jun, and Yamamoto Tadashi. The views expressed herein are mine alone and do not reflect the views or policy of the Japan Center for International Exchange (JCIE). An earlier version of this chapter was submitted to the study project "Japan's Pluralization and New Actors," organized at JCIE with the financial support of the Nippon Foundation.

the end of the cold war in 1989. Yet another argument emphasizes the importance of disputes over political reform between conservatives and reform advocates, especially in the LDP (Narita 1997; Inoguchi 1993; Sakamoto 1994; Morita 1993; Yomiuri Shimbun-sha Seiji-bu 1993).

In this chapter, I will show that the political realignment, or party system changes, of the 1990s can be explained by the emergence of two new types of actors in Japanese politics since the late 1980s. Traditionally, the major actors in the political arena were political parties and factions, not individual politicians. Unlike United States congressmen under the presidential system, Diet members in Japan's cabinet-parliamentary system are kept on short reins by political parties. When a party decides on its position regarding a bill after accounting for intraparty considerations, it is almost impossible for an individual member to take a position different from that of the party to which he or she belongs. If a member does not respect the party position in the Diet, he will be punished as a "rebel," which often leads the member to later abandon the party.[2]

The first group of newly significant actors I will focus on is the younger generation of politicians, especially those LDP Lower House members first elected in the general elections of 1986 and 1990 and those Japan Socialist Party (JSP; the party changed its name in English to the SDPJ in 1991) members first elected in the 1990 general election. The decade from 1986 to 1995 could be characterized as a period during which the system that had dominated post–World War II Japan was remodeled. During that time, many basic policy premises were reconsidered and revised—the introduction of the value-added tax system (1986–1988); U.S.-Japan trade friction (1985–1994), including Tōshiba Machine company's violation of the COCOM (Coordinating Committee for Multilateral Export Control) agreement, the semiconductor export issue, and the Strategic Impediments Initiatives talks; opening the rice market (1989–1993); the dispute over international contributions during the Persian Gulf crisis and war (1990–1991); legislation of international cooperation for peacekeeping operations activities (1990–1992); and discussion over political reform, especially electoral reform in the Lower House (1990–1994). The young generation of politicians both in the LDP and the JSP were exposed to these issues immediately after being elected to the Diet. Although it was very hard for these young politicians to exert leadership, their junior role in the political world meant that in the early 1990s many of them were in-dependent of traditional ties binding them to parties or factions and they were therefore able to encourage a tide of political change by sup-porting younger more senior leaders.

The second type of actors were those outside the political establish-ment. I will discuss four groups: the JNP, formed by Hosokawa in 1992; Rengō (Japanese Trade Union Confederation), formed by the merger of two national centers of trade unions in the late 1980s; the "Reform of Heisei" group led by Ōmae Ken'ichi; and a nongovernmental ad hoc council for political reform. These outside forces benefited from the electorate's growing distrust of the political establishment fed by two major political scandals—the Recruit Company's stock-for-favors scandal in 1988 and the Tokyo Sagawa Kyūbin scandal in 1992. The JNP presented itself as a new party with a clean image, while the other three groups pushed political reform by appealing to the existing po-litical parties, especially to their younger members.

A NEW GENERATION ARISES IN THE 1980S
New Characteristics of LDP Factions

The LDP factions, or *habatsu*, were fully institutionalized in the 1956 LDP presidential election, when eight newly formed groups competed against each other for the LDP presidency (Uchida 1983, chap. 2). Dur-ing the LDP's long years of government dominance, the politician who was able to be elected president of the LDP became the prime minister of Japan. In order to gain the prime ministership, LDP leaders formed their own factions to run in the LDP presidential election. When a leader finished his term as LDP president, his faction would be reorganized by a younger leader or leaders who would then seek to become prime minister. Leadership succession within a faction was often accompa-nied by conflict among the younger leaders, frequently causing the faction to split apart.

By the mid-1970s, however, the traditional character of LDP fac-tions had changed. There were at least two major reasons for this trans-formation. The first was the establishment of a seniority rule regarding promotions within the LDP, which then–Prime Minister Satō Eisaku established with his initial ministerial appointment in the late 1960s. Under this rule, all LDP Lower House members elected more than six or seven times had at least one chance to be appointed to a cabinet post (Satō and Matsuzaki 1986, chap. 2 in part 1, especially 42–44). As a result, the share of ministerial posts reflected the power balance among the factions.

The second reason was the Lockheed scandal of the mid-1970s. Although Tanaka Kakuei was forced to resign as prime minister in 1974, he expanded membership in his own faction after he was prosecuted in the Lockheed affair in the summer of 1976. As part of his strategy of "politics is power, power is numbers (of Diet members)," Tanaka thought that a strengthened faction would bolster his ability to uphold his innocence in court. He was to retain his strong influence over the LDP leadership as a "shadow shogun," or kingmaker, until the mid-1980s (Schlesinger 1997), and the manner in which he maintained his hard-won faction came to be emulated by other faction leaders.

Given these new circumstances, LDP factions had "scale merit," in that by the early 1980s the larger factions were more advantageous at least concerning the following four functions. The first was to provide support for elections. This support included providing election expertise, arranging campaign appearances by ministerial-level politicians, and introducing candidates to local politicians and local business organizations. The second function was to provide political funding. Candidates needed an enormous war chest because they found it necessary to campaign for two or three years before an election was actually held.[3]

The third function was to secure cabinet posts and other important positions for faction members. Under the seniority rule and the norm of factional power-sharing, a member of a large faction had a better chance to be appointed to a ministerial or powerful party position during his second nomination.[4] The final function was to provide services to constituents. A Diet member needs to respond to petitions or requests from his constituents concerning the allocation of public funds. He is more likely to be able to satisfy their requests if his faction members hold important ministerial positions (see Serizawa 1998, chap. 2).

Even after the Lower House election in 1983, three of the five major LDP factions, those of Tanaka, Fukuda Takeo, and Suzuki Zenkō, were headed by former prime ministers (see fig. 1 and table 1). Nakasone Yasuhiro also retained control of his faction in order to maintain his clout in the LDP. Seniority remained the dominant feature among

Figure 1. Reorganization of the LDP's Five Major Factions: 1970s—1990s

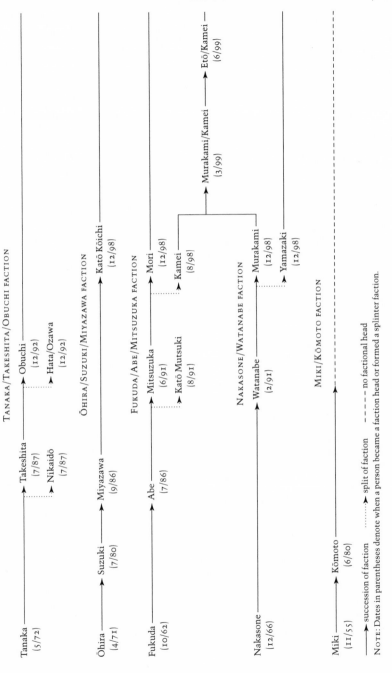

TANAKA/TAKESHITA/OBUCHI FACTION

Tanaka (5/72) ──▶ Takeshita (7/87) ──▶ Obuchi (12/92)
Nikaidō (7/87)
Hata/Ozawa (12/92)

ŌHIRA/SUZUKI/MIYAZAWA FACTION

Ōhira (4/71) ──▶ Suzuki (7/80) ──▶ Miyazawa (9/86) ──▶ Katō Kōichi (12/98)

FUKUDA/ABE/MITSUZUKA FACTION

Fukuda (10/62) ──▶ Abe (7/86) ──▶ Mitsuzuka (6/91) ──▶ Mori (12/98)
Katō Mutsuki (8/91)
Kamei (8/98) ──▶ Murakami/Kamei (3/99) ──▶ Etō/Kamei (6/99)

NAKASONE/WATANABE FACTION

Nakasone (12/66) ──▶ Watanabe (2/91) ──▶ Murakami (12/98)
Yamazaki (12/98)

MIKI/KŌMOTO FACTION

Miki (11/55) ──▶ Kōmoto (6/80)

──▶ succession of faction ········▶ split of faction ----- no factional head
NOTE: Dates in parentheses denote when a person became a faction head or formed a splinter faction.

Table 1. LDP Faction Leaders Holding the Party Presidency

TANAKA/TAKESHITA/OBUCHI FACTION

Tanaka Kakuei (July 1972–December 1974)
Takeshita Noboru (November 1987–June 1989)
Obuchi Keizō (July 1998–)

ŌHIRA/SUZUKI/MIYAZAWA FACTION

Ōhira Masayoshi (December 1978–May 1980)
Suzuki Zenkō (July 1980–Njovember 1982)
Miyazawa Kiichi (November 1991–July 1993)

FUKUDA/ABE/MITSUZUKA FACTION

Fukuda Takeo (December 1976–December 1978)

NAKASONE/WATANABE FACTION

Nakasone Yasuhiro (November 1982–November 1987)

MIKI/KŌMOTO FACTION

Miki Takeo (December 1974–December 1976)

LDP PRESIDENTS WHO WERE NOT FACTION HEADS

Uno Sōsuke (June 1989–August 1989)	Nakasone faction
Kaifu Toshiki (August 1989–November 1991)	Kōmoto faction
Kōno Yōhei (July 1993–September 1995)	Miyazawa faction
Hashimoto Ryūtarō (September 1995–July 1998)	Obuchi faction

NOTE: Dates in parentheses denote a person's term as LDP president, which is the same as that person's term as prime minister. The exceptions are Hashimoto, who became prime minister in January 1996, and Kōno, who was not prime minister.

LDP factions, reflecting their stable structure, and little generational change could occur.

This began to change with the LDP presidential election held in the fall of 1984, when Prime Minister Nakasone was at the end of his first term as LDP president. In early September 1984, Nakasone was believed to be in a comfortable position, bolstered by support from the Tanaka faction, the largest in the LDP. It was therefore assumed that he would be reelected for a second term. However, former prime ministers Suzuki and Fukuda decided to back Nikaidō Susumu, a senior politician in the Tanaka faction, to run against Nakasone. The leaders of both the Kōmeitō (Clean Government Party) and the Democratic Socialist Party (DSP) were also said to be involved in this effort (Yano 1994, chap. 1).

Although this effort did not succeed, it contributed tremendously to spurring generational change in the LDP factions. In this process, younger leaders took positions independent of their factional leaders.

Abe Shintarō of the Fukuda faction and Miyazawa Kiichi of the Suzuki faction, both promising new leaders in their respective factions,
were reluctant to support Nikaidō. Takeshita Noboru, who was then
considered the most promising potential successor to lead the Tanaka
faction, knew that if Nikaidō was elected LDP president he would also
try to wrest control of the Tanaka faction, so he and his ally Kanemaru
Shin moved to block Nikaidō's candidacy. Takeshita soon decided to
break from the Tanaka faction and form his own faction in February
1985, centered on supporters from the Tanaka faction. Takeshita's move
infuriated Tanaka, who subsequently suffered a stroke from which he
never completely recovered. The era of Tanaka as "shadow shogun"
was ended.

The 1986 Double Election and
New LDP Diet Members

The 1986 general election was a rare double election, in which balloting for the House of Councillors (Upper House) and the Lower House
was held on the same day. This proved especially significant for Nakasone and the "new leaders" of each faction, including Watanabe Michio
of the Nakasone faction. Nakasone, who was completing his second
term as LDP president, sought to extend his term by leading the LDP
to victory in the general election. There is no legal limit on the number of terms a prime minister may serve, but LDP rules prohibit any
member from holding the position of party president for more than two
terms. With this in mind, the new leaders of each faction worked hard
to enlarge their factions by recruiting and supporting younger factional candidates in preparation for the LDP presidential race in the
fall of 1986.

The LDP was able to use the double election to its advantage because the proportional representation system of the Upper House
forced opposition parties to compete, thereby preventing them from
cooperating in fielding joint candidates for the Lower House. As a result, the LDP won by a landslide, securing 300 of 512 seats in the Lower
House and 72 of the 126 contested seats in the Upper House. Based on
these results, the LDP agreed to provide Nakasone with special consideration, extending his term as LDP president for another year.
Nevertheless, although the contest among new leaders for the party
presidency was delayed until the fall of 1987 as a result of the double
election, the poll did help to advance generational change among LDP

members. Of 66 newly elected Lower House members in the 1986 election, 46 belonged to the LDP. Younger leaders took control of two LDP factions after the election: Abe replaced Fukuda in July, and Miyazawa took over from Suzuki in September 1986.

In the fall of 1986, LDP first-term members faced their first challenge. Although Prime Minister Nakasone had promised during the election campaign not to introduce any "large-scale indirect tax schemes," he raised the possibility of a new type of value-added tax—a sales tax—after the election. As Nakasone prepared to introduce sales tax legislation in late 1986 he faced rising criticism, not only from opposition parties but also from within the LDP.

Newly elected LDP members regarded the sales tax issue as a major threat to their chances for reelection. In general, younger LDP members are more sensitive to the prevailing views of their electorate, because they have not yet secured a stable support base. Thus they were unnerved when they encountered strong criticism by their constituents for allowing the LDP to break its campaign promise. About 40 young LDP Lower House members who had been elected in the 1980 or subsequent elections joined an interfactional group of younger members that was formed to study the proposed tax system in October 1986. Momentum for passing sales tax legislation further weakened after the LDP candidate was defeated in an Upper House by-election in Iwate held in February 1987, presumably partly due to public opposition to the tax. After a nearly three-day filibuster on the Lower House floor by opposition members, marked by a slow-motion "cattle-walk" voting procedure, the sponsoring LDP government decided in April 1987 to shelve the bill to introduce the sales tax.

Takeshita, who had persuaded former Tanaka faction members to join him in creating the largest faction in July 1987, was selected LDP president that fall by the endorsement of Nakasone. To avoid any further factional friction, all the faction leaders were allotted key positions in the cabinet or in the party after the presidential race. Adoption of this "all mainstream faction system" served to stabilize intraparty factional politics, as positions were assigned according to seniority and factional considerations.

The LDP first-term Diet members had to overcome another hurdle in the fall of 1988, with the disclosure of the Recruit Company stock-for-favors scandal. Several LDP leaders, as well as some opposition members, including those in the JSP, Kōmeitō, and the DSP, were accused of accepting shares of Recruit stock in return for future political favors. The Recruit scandal, along with deliberations on a bill to impose a "consumption tax," a revised version of the sales tax, became the object of severe public censure. In an effort to deal with the electorate's growing distrust of politics, ten of the 1986 LDP newcomers formed an interfactional group, the Utopian Politics Study Group, in September 1988 to discuss political reform. Five of them later left the LDP to form the core of the New Party Sakigake, which was conceived in June 1993.

In the spring of 1989, younger LDP members organized two other interfactional groups that also called for greater attention to be paid to political ethics. One was the Liberal Reform Federation with 36 members, headed by Kamei Shizuka and Shirakawa Katsuhiko, both mid-ranking members of the Miyazawa faction. The other group, called Diet Members for Political Reform, consisted of 14 members. This group activity by younger LDP members can be regarded as a response to public criticism of politicians, and as an expression of their discontent with the faction-based seniority system. Faced with tepid public support for his cabinet[5] and intraparty criticism by younger LDP members, Prime Minister Takeshita, who succeeded Nakasone in November 1987, was forced to announce his resignation in late April 1989, when the 3 percent consumption tax went into effect. Foreign Minister Uno Sōsuke became the new prime minister in June, but public anger deepened with revelations of yet another scandal, this time involving allegations concerning Uno's long-term involvement with a mistress, forcing Uno to resign after only two months in office.

The LDP suffered the worst defeat in its history in the Upper House general election held in the summer of 1989, winning only 36 of 126 contested seats. (Half of the seats are up for election every three years, and members hold office for six years.) The most serious damage came in the single-seat districts, where the LDP presumably enjoyed an advantage as the largest party. This time it won only three of 26 contested seats. Even with the addition of the 72 members who had been elected in 1986, the LDP was for the first time unable to maintain its majority in the Upper House (Kabashima 1992; Mizusaki 1992). Prime Minister Uno resigned after the election, and was replaced by Kaifu Toshiki in early August 1989; both Uno and Kaifu were relatively weak leaders, as neither headed a faction or could boast of a personal power base in the LDP. Meanwhile, however, Takeshita and Kanemaru were gaining greater political clout as the new kingmakers.

A New Generation in the Socialist Party after the 1989 and 1990 Elections

Members of the JSP faced a number of difficulties in the late 1980s. Under the 1955 system, the JSP stood staunchly opposed to the conservative LDP. However, the party wasted its energy on intraparty debate between its right wing, which favored Western European-style social democracy, and its left wing, which persisted in its support for Marxism-Leninism, and the JSP remained the "perennial major opposition party" after the 1958 Lower House general election. In the fall of 1959, the Nishio faction, a right-wing group led by Nishio Suehiro, former secretary-general of the JSP and chief cabinet secretary in the Katayama cabinet, split from the JSP over the renewal of the U.S.-Japan Security Treaty. After he and his followers formed the DSP in early 1960, the 1955 system, characterized by two major parties, began to undergo structural transformation, eventually becoming the LDP-dominant system of the 1970s and 1980s. In mid-1970, Eda Saburō, a former secretary-general, left the JSP and formed the Socialist Citizens' League, which was later reorganized as the Shaminren (United Social Democratic Party) in 1978.

From the late 1960s to the mid-1980s, the JSP suffered a long-term decline in popularity. Its share of popular votes in Lower House elections fell from 29.0 percent in 1963 to 17.2 percent in 1986 (Asahi Shimbun Senkyo-hombu 1990, 318–319). The JSP's popularity revived in the second half of the 1980s, but this reflected factors exogenous to the JSP. The party failed to implement structural reform and had lost almost all its popular support by the mid-1990s.

The first of the JSP's major dilemmas came with the party's January 1986 adoption of the 1986 Manifesto. The manifesto resulted from an initiative by party president Ishibashi Masashi to make the JSP into a more responsible opposition party. After four months of intraparty debate, the party announced a shift from Marxism-Leninism to social democracy, but this change did little to enhance the party's popular support. In the double election of July 1986, held less than six months later, the party was badly defeated. Ishibashi subsequently announced his resignation, and he was replaced by Doi Takako, the first woman to head a political party in Japan.

Under Doi's leadership, the JSP at last made progress. In unified local elections held in April 1987, the party garnered strong public support from voters, who vehemently opposed introduction of the sales tax. Doi then initiated an effort to mobilize women voters by endorsing a greater number of women candidates and in the run-up to the 1989 election she focused party efforts on campaigning against the consumption tax. The JSP prevailed during the 1989 Upper House election, securing 46 of 126 contested seats. Added to the seats it had won in the 1986 election, the JSP increased its seats from 42 to 66 in the Upper House, while the number of its women Upper House members increased from three to 14.

These victories created a second dilemma for the JSP, however. The JSP's success, both in the 1987 unified local elections and in the 1989 Upper House election, was due to the mistakes of the ruling LDP. The JSP had functioned more as a "responsive" rather than a responsible party, benefiting from negative votes cast by an electorate dissatisfied with the LDP. Doi maintained a no-compromise principle against the LDP with her well-known slogan, "No means no!" (*Damena mono wa dame!*). In the fall of 1989, the JSP introduced a bill to scrap the consumption tax, in keeping with Doi's promises during the Upper House election campaign, but the party leadership neglected to offer any alternative sources for national revenue.

It was perhaps unrealistic to expect ideological JSP to alter its basic policies to prepare for taking over the government. Doi's positions on defense and foreign policy issues reflected those of the party's dogmatic left wing: protecting the Peace Constitution, denying the existence of the Self-Defense Forces (SDF), and ending security ties with the United States in favor of an "unarmed neutrality (*hibusō chūritsu*)" policy.[6]

Doi succeeded in maintaining her popularity and led the JSP to another victory in the Lower House general election in February 1990. The 1990 election not only featured party divisions over the controversial tax issue, but it also saw the revival of the 1955 system, with direct confrontation between two major parties, the LDP and the JSP. While the JSP campaigned largely on the demand that the consumption tax be scrapped, the LDP tried to rally voters by stressing the superiority of the liberal democratic system, alluding to the corruption of communist regimes in Eastern Europe. In the election, the LDP managed to retain a stable majority with 275 of 512 seats, while the JSP received 136 seats, its largest number since 1967.

This victory posed an additional challenge for the JSP. Nearly half of the JSP's seats, 60 of 136, were occupied by newcomers, including two former Upper House members. Their views and orientation differed greatly from those of traditional JSP members, and their involvement in intraparty reform had no ideological basis. These first-term members paid little heed to the JSP's traditional power structure. Instead, they acted to transform the party's structure from the bottom up, as I will discuss later. Ironically, however, although they effected dramatic, beneficial change, most of them were not active for long. Forty-six of the 60 newly elected members did not survive the two general elections held in 1993 and 1996. Of the 1990 first-term members, only two remained in the Social Democratic Party (SDP, the new name adopted by the SDPJ in January 1996) after the Lower House general election in 1996.

THE DIVIDED DIET AND A CALL FOR POLITICAL REFORM

More Generational Change in LDP Factions

The Kaifu cabinet of the early 1990s faced difficulties both at home and abroad. On the international front, Japan had to decide how to respond to the Persian Gulf crisis after Iraq's invasion of Kuwait in August 1990. The LDP administration was taken to task for what were seen as overly passive foreign and security policies, while the Kaifu cabinet's contributions to multinational efforts for the restoration of peace in the Middle East—US$4 billion by September 1990 and US$9 billion immediately after the breakout of the Gulf War in January 1991—were criticized as "checkbook diplomacy" by some countries.

The Kaifu cabinet, supported by Ozawa Ichirō, the powerful LDP secretary-general, belatedly offered to send SDF aircraft to the Middle East to transport refugees during the Gulf War in January 1991 (notwithstanding the fact that there had never been a request for such assistance from the International Committee for Migration, the main nongovernmental group involved). After the Gulf War, in April, four SDF minesweepers and a supply ship were dispatched to the Persian

Gulf (Research Institute for Peace and Security 1991, 29–34, 136–139). This was the first dispatch of the SDF outside Japan since 1952, when Japan regained its independence.[7]

On the domestic scene, the Kaifu administration had to deal with a "divided Diet" after the LDP lost its Upper House majority in the 1989 election. The party was forced to collaborate with opposition parties, such as Kōmeitō and the DSP, in order to obtain a majority. Although the United Nations Peace Cooperation Bill was tabled in the Lower House in November 1990, during its deliberations Ozawa succeeded in establishing a good relationship with his counterparts, Ichikawa Yūichi, Kōmeitō secretary-general, and Yonezawa Takashi, DSP secretary-general. The LDP government–sponsored International Peace Cooperation Bill, a revised version of the United Nations Peace Cooperation Bill, was passed through the Diet in June 1992, clearing the Upper House with the support of Kōmeitō and the DSP.

Prime Minister Kaifu also emphasized political reform in an effort to overcome public distrust of politicians. An advisory council to the prime minister on the electoral system, reactivated in June 1989 for the first time in 17 years, submitted a recommendation to Kaifu in April 1990, in which members proposed to introduce a system of single-seat districts combined with proportional representation for Lower House elections. Kaifu, who had a weak power base in the LDP, regarded political and electoral reform efforts as ideal means for him to maintain his popularity among the electorate. In response to recommendations by the advisory council, Nishioka Takeo, chairman of the LDP's General Council, Katō Mutsuki, chairman of the party's Policy Research Council, and Hata Tsutomu, chairman of the LDP Electoral Research Council, worked diligently to build a consensus within the LDP for electoral reform.

The party had adopted a slogan after the 1989 Upper House election calling for dissolution of LDP factions, and it was now regulating factional activities on a voluntary basis. However, the factions' enduring influence was readily apparent as the 1991 presidential race approached. Members of the Miyazawa, Mitsuzuka, and Watanabe factions formed an anti-Kaifu coalition to prevent Kaifu from winning another term as LDP president. The young leaders of these factions, Yamasaki Taku, Koizumi Shin'ichirō, and Katō Kōichi, criticized Kaifu's plan for political reform, preferring a less ambitious approach. These three, who were later referred to as the "YKK" group, combining the

initial letters of their last names, succeeded in tabling the electoral reform bill in the Lower House in September, forcing Kaifu to abandon his
presidential campaign. The split between pro-reform and antireform
elements in the party continued through the end of 1996. Many pro-
reform members left the LDP by the summer of 1994 and established
the New Frontier Party in December 1994, while many of the antireform group were influential in maintaining the LDP-SDPJ-Sakigake
coalition after June 1994.

Prime Minister Miyazawa, who succeeded Kaifu as party president
in the fall of 1991, was lukewarm on political reform. When Miyazawa
decided to shelve the electoral reform plan in November, 54 young LDP
members responded by forming a new interfactional group, the Group
of Junior Members for Political Reform, headed by Ishiba Shigeru, who
had first been elected in the 1986 poll, and Watase Noriaki, whose first
election victory had been in 1990. Members of this group were critical
of the LDP's indifference to political reform and they felt strongly that
such reform was needed. By early in the summer of 1993, they had become strong opponents to LDP conservatives who opposed or did little
to further the cause of political reform.[8]

Factional leaders faced another tide of generational change in 1991
and 1992. Both Watanabe Michio, who had taken over the Nakasone
faction in early 1990, and Abe suffered serious health problems. Ozawa
resigned as LDP secretary-general after the Tokyo gubernatorial election in April 1991 and became acting chairman of the Takeshita faction. Although Ozawa was the youngest of seven prominent Takeshita
faction members, including Hashimoto Ryūtarō, Obuchi Keizō, and
Hata, he was often accused by members of leading the Takeshita faction in a high-handed manner, with the support of Kanemaru.

Generational change in the early 1990s was a little different from
that of the mid-1980s, however, in that the later transitions in factional leadership were accompanied by intrafactional conflict. The
Abe faction split into the Mitsuzuka faction and a minor Katō Mutsuki group with 13 members in the fall of 1991. But the most drastic
change was the fissure of the Takeshita faction in 1992. The Takeshita
faction, with more than 110 Diet members, was divided into two sub-
groups, the Takeshita group, including the anti-Ozawa group, and the
Kanemaru-Ozawa group, in the early 1990s. At the end of August 1992,
Kanemaru was accused of receiving ¥500 million from Tokyo Sagawa
Kyūbin, a parcel delivery firm, far exceeding the ¥1.5 million annual

ceiling allowed by the Political Fund Control Law. On Ozawa's advice, Kanemaru called a press conference at the end of August to admit receiving the money. This strategy backfired, earning Kanemaru more criticism from the public. Other LDP leaders, notably including Kajiyama Seiroku, one of the more prominent members of the anti-Ozawa group in the Takeshita faction, blasted Ozawa's defense strategy for Kanemaru. Kanemaru was able to strike a deal with the Prosecutor's Office to pay only ¥200,000 in penalties, but this just sparked additional public anger, forcing Kanemaru to resign as a member of the Lower House in October.[9]

Obuchi and Hashimoto, senior members of the Takeshita group, failed to support Ozawa's effort to become chairman of the Takeshita faction, leading to heated factional wrangles over leadership that lasted nearly a month. In late October, Obuchi was finally appointed chairman of the Takeshita faction. The Ozawa group decided to form their own faction with Hata in December 1992 (Yomiuri Shimbun-sha Seiji-bu 1993, 22–38). Twelve of the 14 Takeshita faction members who had first been elected in 1986 joined the Hata-Ozawa faction, which seceded from the LDP and formed the Japan Renewal Party (JRP) in June 1993, ending 38 years of LDP ruling party dominance.

With the split of the Takeshita faction, the system of single-faction dominance in the LDP was transformed into a turbulent system in which six factions competed against each other. The double power structure, characterized by LDP presidents and kingmakers backed by the largest faction, was no more.

Rise of Younger Groups in the JSP

Soon after the 1990 Lower House election, newly elected JSP members took active roles in challenging the status quo. They were organized into two groups. One was the New Wave group formed in March 1990 with 30 members. Many of them had had professional careers prior to the election; they included lawyers, television reporters, a university professor, a medical doctor, and a nurse. Their ties with the JSP were relatively weak. The other was the Group of 1990, which was reorganized in November into the New Power group, with 32 members. Most of them had previously been local politicians and leaders of local trade unions or the JSP's local chapters.[10]

Members of the two groups presented quite different proposals in response to the electoral reform plan issued by Prime Minister Kaifu in April 1990. The New Wave proposed a mixed system of single-seat districts and proportional representation, modeled upon the West German electoral system. The Group of 1990 insisted on a plan based on the existing multiseat system. In February 1991, the JSP changed its name in English to the Social Democratic Party of Japan (SDPJ), but there were no substantial changes in the party's structures or policies.

Traditionally, JSP factions had been categorized into three ideological blocs: the right wing, the left wing (sometimes called "the middle group" between the right and the ultraleft), and the ultraleft wing. The 1990 cohort worked to effect structural change in the JSP factions. In January 1991, the left-wing members formed the Social Democratic Forum. JSP's factions were reorganized into three: the Governing Vision Study Group (the right wing), the Social Democratic Forum (the left wing), and the Group for a New Socialist Party (the ultraleft).

After the SDPJ suffered defeat in the 1991 unified local elections, the New Power and the New Wave groups requested a reshuffling of party leaders. A weakened Doi insisted on remaining chairperson to carry out party reform, but after being criticized by younger members she was forced to announce her resignation in May. By raising the issue of structural reform before she resigned, however, Doi refocused attention on the party's traditional division between right and left. In June, the right-wing group issued a scheme for party reform which recommended that the party recognize the SDF as constitutional, as long as the SDF focused on defensive operations. Ten members of the leftist bloc, on the other hand, formed a group insisting on defending the party's traditional position that the SDF had no constitutional legitimacy. Separately, 19 of the 1989 Upper House and 1990 Lower House first-term members formed the Action New Democracy group to review the SDPJ's traditional policy on the SDF and to propose new policies for the post–cold war period. The party held an election to select a new leader in July, at which Tanabe Makoto was selected as party chairman, the first right-wing candidate to claim the post in 26 years.

The SDF soon figured again in party activities, as legislation proposing that Japan participate in international peacekeeping operations became the most controversial issue in Diet sessions from September 1991 to June 1992. The International Peace Cooperation Bill, a revised version of the United Nations Peace Cooperation Bill that had been tabled in the Diet in November 1990, was introduced in the Diet in September 1991. The SDPJ resolutely opposed the bill, insisting that the dispatch of the SDF violated the Constitution, and the party tried to stymie passage with a "cattle-walk" filibuster when the bill came to a vote in the Upper House in June 1992. Despite the party's efforts, however, the bill was passed by the Diet with the support of the LDP, Kōmeitō, and the DSP.

In the Upper House general election in July 1992, the SDPJ won 22 of 127 contested seats, approximately the same number it had had before the election. However, this was less than half the number won by the SDPJ (JSP) in the 1989 Upper House election, suggesting that the SDPJ's aggressive moves to block passage of the International Peace Cooperation Bill legislation were not supported by the electorate. The average Japanese voter appeared to regard cynically the SDPJ's time-consuming tactics in the Upper House and the threat by SDPJ Lower House members to resign in protest following passage of the International Peace Cooperation Bill. Their letters of resignation were ultimately shelved in the Lower House administration committee, and the SDPJ members retained their seats.

During the Upper House election campaign, Tanabe, seeking to reassure voters of the party's basic stability, announced his intention to review the 1986 Manifesto of the SDPJ. With the onset of discussions of the new Manifesto in the late autumn of 1992, members began to organize new groupings within the party, and the second stage of the SDPJ's intraparty reorganization began. In November, 21 members of the SDPJ's 1989 cohort in the Upper House and the 1990 cohort in the Lower House organized a transpartisan group calling for political reform. The group, Sirius, also included two Shaminren members, Eda Satsuki and Kan Naoto, and four Upper House members of the Rengō group (a group formed by union-backed Diet members first elected in 1989 from single-seat districts), and it was headed by Eda Satsuki. Another newly formed group, Leadership 21, which consisted of 23 members first elected in 1990, appealed for changes in the SDPJ's dogmatic policies regarding the SDF, the U.S.-Japan Security Treaty, and nuclear power plants. Spurred by these groups' examples, many mid-ranking party members also formed interfactional study groups, such as the New Political Generation Forum, comprised of former student movement leaders from the late 1950s when renewal of the U.S.-Japan Security Treaty was controversial, and a group composed of members first elected in 1983. These groups were generally nonideological and policy-oriented (Richardson 1997, 81–82, table 3.4 on page 71), a further sign that the SDPJ's traditional factional balance based on ideological blocs had greatly weakened.

In December 1992, SDPJ Chairman Tanabe came under fire for being friends with Kanemaru of the LDP, who was then being charged by the Tokyo prosecutor's office. Kanemaru and Tanabe had established close relations in the 1980s when they had both headed up their respective parties' Diet Affairs Committee, the body that deliberates a party's strategy and tactics in the Diet.[11] Tanabe was pressured to resign as SDPJ chairman in December 1992, and Yamahana Sadao replaced him in January 1993. Yamahana tried to encourage younger party leaders by appointing Akamatsu Hirotaka, who had first been elected in 1990, as secretary-general of the SDPJ. Surprisingly, although Akamatsu had previously served as a prefectural assembly member in Aichi, he had been inactive in the SDPJ national organization before the 1990 election.

Tanabe remained a senior leader of the right wing after he resigned as SDPJ chairman. In the spring of 1993, based on his group's review of the party's basic policies, he drafted the 1993 Manifesto, which fomented another reorganization of factions and blocs within the SDPJ. In early March, three groups of younger members—Leadership 21, Action New Democracy, and Sirius—agreed to cooperate in discussing basic party policies. In mid-April, the Governing Vision Study Group, the SDPJ's largest right-wing group, was reorganized into the Party Reform Federation, with 87 members. They shared a consensus on basic security policies, such as recognition of the constitutionality of the SDF and the need to maintain the U.S.-Japan Security Treaty. The draft of the 1993 Manifesto was released in May, but the party did not have the time to adopt it officially before the drastic changes that occurred in Japanese politics after June.

New Political Forces in Japanese Politics

The late 1980s witnessed the emergence of new political forces from outside the traditional political arena. While these groups did not always directly lead political activities, they had an enormous impact on politicians, especially younger Diet members. The first was Rengō, formed by the unification of four major trade union national centers, including Sōhyō (General Council of Trade Unions of Japan) and Dōmei (Japan Confederation of Labor). Sōhyō and Dōmei had been rivals in the Japanese labor movement since the 1960s, with the former supporting the JSP in election campaigning and the latter backing the DSP. Private-sector trade unions were first unified under the Rengō umbrella in 1987, while trade unions in the public sector followed in November 1989.

However, those two blocs were not completely unified. When the JSP/SDPJ and the DSP took different positions on a controversial bill or in a local election, Rengō often divided into two blocs, the ex-Sōhyō and the ex-Dōmei. Rengō leaders, especially Yamagishi Akira, who served as president from 1989 to 1994, began to advocate structural reform of the JSP to facilitate the reorganization of opposition parties.

The Upper House general election in 1992 proved a turning point for Rengō's policy toward the political parties. Differences between the SDPJ and the DSP, both in backing candidates for the Tokyo gubernatorial election in April 1991 and in positions toward the International Peace Cooperation Bill legislation from 1991 to 1992, prevented Rengō from being able to carry out unified planning for the Upper House election campaign. Rengō endorsed 12 candidates in single-seat districts for the Upper House election, but even though Rengō-backed candidates had routed LDP candidates in these 12 districts in 1989, largely due to the group's lack of internal cooperation not a single Rengō-backed candidate was elected in 1992. After the 1992 Upper House election, Rengō leaders called for formation of a new opposition party as a powerful counterforce to the LDP ("Rōso ga aitsuide" 1992, 4).

Rengō was able to function as a very useful umbrella for anti-LDP cooperation. The opposition parties could campaign together under the Rengō banner for Upper House candidates in single-seat districts where opposition parties were relatively weak against the LDP. In this way, Rengō-backed candidates prevailed in two Upper House by-elections in early 1993, one in Nara in February and the other in Miyagi in March. By-elections are widely regarded as a litmus test of public opinion on important national issues, and their results can have national implications. For example, the LDP's defeat in the Iwate by-election in February 1987 led to the party shelving the sales tax bill. The LDP's victory in an Ibaraki by-election in October 1989 led the LDP government to believe that the headwinds blowing against it, which had resulted in the LDP's historical defeat in the 1989 Upper House election, were now abating. And the LDP's win by a narrow margin in the Aichi by-election of November 1990 wrought serious damage to prospects for passing the United Nations Peace Cooperation Bill. Consecutive

Rengō wins in early 1993 were seen as reflecting the electorate's distrust of politics in general.

The second active force outside of the political establishment was the Japan New Party, led by Hosokawa. Hosokawa once belonged to the Tanaka faction as an Upper House LDP member from 1971 to 1983, but he subsequently ran for governor of his native Kumamoto Prefecture in western Japan. After serving for eight years as the governor, he declared the formation of a new party in a monthly magazine in early May 1992 (Hosokawa 1992, 94–106). Only two months later, his new party (later named the JNP), won four seats in proportional representation balloting in the July 1992 Upper House election. The Kanemaru scandal in 1992 greatly boosted the JNP's popularity. Reflecting widely felt public distrust of the political establishment, the support rate for the JNP, as indicated in newspaper opinion polls, increased from 1.9 percent in November 1992 to 5.2 percent in March 1993, the third largest after the LDP and the SDPJ (Yomiuri Shimbun-sha Seiji-bu 1993, 48).

The third major force was the Reform of Heisei group, led by Ōmae Ken'ichi. Ōmae was the well-known head of the Japanese branch of a top management consulting firm and a prolific writer, notably of books such as *Heisei Reform: Zero-based Organization and Construction* (Ōmae 1989). As a management consultant, he stayed outside of the political arena, but his unique strategy allowed him to try to influence politicians by persuading the electorate to concur with his vision for the future. When he announced he was organizing the Reform of Heisei group in November 1992, many young Diet members, including those from the LDP and the SDPJ, reacted positively. Thirty-three younger members of the LDP formed a counterpart group in February 1993, and 25 from the SDPJ organized the Heisei Forum in May. When the Reform of Heisei group organized its first convention in April 1993, the leaders of both the LDP and the SDPJ responded nervously, seeing the group as functioning as a precursor to forming a new party. Despite clear LDP and SDPJ disapproval, 27 Diet members and staff representatives of 47 other members attended the convention.

The fourth actor was the Nongovernmental Ad Hoc Council for Political Reform, organized in April 1992 by opinion leaders in business, academia, and labor unions. These leaders were former members of an advisory council to the prime minister on the electoral system, which submitted a recommendation in April 1990 to introduce a system of single-seat districts combined with proportional representation for Lower House elections. Similar sentiment in the Diet was shown when 95 young Diet members organized a counterpart group to discuss political reform in April 1992, when the council was officially launched ("Seiji kaikaku" 1992, 4). This council issued recommendations for political reform, and in November 1992 adopted a declaration to abolish the existing multiseat district system in the Lower House. The council's declaration was signed by 188 Diet members.

In April 1993, the LDP was deadlocked with the SDPJ and Kōmeitō over electoral reform. The LDP insisted on a single-seat district system, while the other two parties wanted to introduce a German-type system combining single-seat districts and proportional representation. The ad hoc council proposed a compromise ("Shōsenkyoku hireidaihyō" 1993, 4). Although their efforts were not successful at the time, their moves prompted six major opposition parties to reach agreement on election reform in late May. These six parties formed a non-LDP coalition government in August with two groups that had split off from the LDP, the JRP, and Sakigake.

THE NON-LDP COALITION AND THE BREAKDOWN OF THE SDPJ
Power Struggles within the LDP and the End of LDP Dominance

From December 1992 to June 1993, the political world was rocked by two events: a power struggle within the LDP, initiated by the Takeshita faction, and the emergence of a nonpartisan movement calling for political reform. Aware that the Miyazawa cabinet was to be reshuffled in early December 1992, the Obuchi group took the initiative in seeking to assume control of the posts that would be allocated to the Takeshita faction. The Hata-Ozawa group in the Takeshita faction opposed the actions of the Obuchi group and decided to form their own faction. The Obuchi group, the fourth largest grouping within the LDP, received three ministerial posts, including the powerful post of construction minister. More importantly, Kajiyama, a leader of the anti-Ozawa forces, was appointed LDP secretary-general. Although two ministerial positions were awarded to the Hata-Ozawa group—directors-general of the Economic Planning Agency and the Science and Technology Agency—these posts were less influential. The Hata-Ozawa group announced one week later that it was leaving the Takeshita faction. By the end of

1992, the Hata-Ozawa faction was calling for political reform, deriding members of the LDP mainstream factions as antireform "conservatives."

Meanwhile, younger LDP politicians took further action. Members of the Utopian Politics Study Group, led by Takemura Masayoshi, organized the System Reform Study Group, a nonpartisan group, in December. At their first meeting in January 1993, the LDP members were joined by members from five opposition parties, including Eda Satsuki and Kan of Shaminren and Hosokawa of the JNP (Asahi Shimbun Seiji-bu 1993, 53). Of course, by organizing young LDP pro-reform members Takemura also intended to increase his own political influence. When Hosokawa asked Takemura and his allies in the LDP to join the JNP at the end of 1992, Takemura spurned the offer, preferring to form his own new party first and then join the JNP later on an equal footing with Hosokawa (Ōtake 1996, 274). The conservatives also formed interfactional groups. In February 1993, 75 mid-ranking and senior members, including YKK leaders, organized a group to oppose the LDP Heisei reform group. At the end of May, Group New Century, led by the YKK trio, was formed with 64 members.

Impetus for political reform increased dramatically in March, when Kanemaru was arrested in connection with the Sagawa scandal for violating the Income Tax Law. When prosecutors searched his office, they confiscated cash, gold bullion, and bank debentures totaling ¥4 billion. Shortly thereafter a new scandal came to light when several major construction companies were found guilty of providing illegal political donations to Kanemaru totaling nearly ¥1 billion a year. The LDP expeditiously drafted guidelines for political reform to counter public criticism, but it was unclear whether party leaders would fullheartedly promote legislation based on these guidelines.

At this point, reform groups within the LDP began to cooperate with their counterparts in opposition parties to bring about political reform. When the Miyazawa cabinet threatened the reformers with dissolution of the Lower House in May, the Group of Junior Members for Political Reform protested by collecting signatures of LDP Diet members who agreed that electoral reforms should be carried out before the dissolution of the Lower House. Two hundred and four LDP members signed in defiance of LDP efforts to control the actions of the young reformers ("Kanjichō ni nihyaku-yo-nin" 1993, 7).

Figure 2. Ruling-Opposition Relations in the 1980s

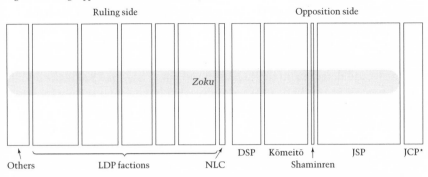

NOTE: The size of the boxes denotes party or faction strength after the 1983 Lower House election.
* The JCP has no *zoku* members.

The most impressive reform initiative at this time was the formation of the Solidarity of Transfactional Junior Members for Political Reform in June 1993. This group was organized with 55 members elected in 1990: ten from the LDP, 23 from the SDPJ, 11 from Kōmeitō, and one from the DSP. They agreed to cooperate in a push for passage of the electoral reform bill.

These cooperative moves within the LDP and between the ruling and opposition parties in the cause of political reform differed markedly from that of the 1980s. LDP factions and political parties in the 1980s had vertical power structures, based on members' seniority. Interfactional activities based on policy issues were horizontally structured, bringing together *zoku*—mid-ranking and senior Diet members with common knowledge, interests, and involvement in a specified policy area—in networks with bureaucrats and interest groups (Satō and Matsuzaki 1986, chap. 4, especially 92). Although the *zoku* members were relatively senior, their expertise and experience was the primary source of their influence. It should be noted that *zoku* relations extended to opposition party members (see fig. 2). *Zoku* members in the opposition usually belonged to Diet committees dealing with their special interests. Opposition *zoku* members often shared common interests with their counterparts in the LDP, and they played key roles when their parties decided positions and tactics on legislative matters.

In this context, the actions taken by the Hata-Ozawa faction could be categorized as traditional factional fragmentation. Although 12 members of the 1986 cohort and seven from the 1990 cohort defected from the LDP with Hata and Ozawa and joined the JRP, their decision was motivated primarily by considerations derived from a faction-based power struggle. Ozawa was said to have had no desire to leave the LDP prior to the June 19, 1993, announcement by the Sakigake group that it would defect from the LDP (Hirano 1996, 80). Had Sakigake decided to stay in the LDP, Ozawa might also have remained and continued to struggle against his opponents within the party.

Unlike the behavior of the Ozawa group, the actions taken by other young pro-reform Diet members, including newly elected members of the SDPJ, differed greatly from those that took place in accordance with the traditional power structure: Their actions were interfactional without consideration for seniority. These cooperative efforts between pro-reform members of both the LDP and the opposition parties weakened the once solid factional structure that had developed over the previous two decades. They thus lowered the barriers between factions and narrowed the gap between the ruling and opposition parties (see table 2 for a listing of transfactional and transpartisan groups).

The Four Coalition Governments and the Breakdown of the SDPJ

The Lower House was dissolved when a no-confidence motion against the Miyazawa cabinet was passed on June 18, 1993. After the general election in July, the LDP was unable to maintain its majority in the Lower House. But this was not a direct result of the election itself, since the LDP was able to secure 223 of the 511 seats in the Lower House, almost the same as its preelection strength of 227 seats. The reason the LDP lost its majority was not electoral defeat, but the decision of the Hata-Ozawa faction and the Sakigake group to leave the party before the election was held. The Hata-Ozawa group created the JRP with 36 members and the latter group of ten members organized Sakigake as a party, enabling both groups to campaign under their new party banners.

Only one party was truly vanquished in the general election—the SDPJ. The SDPJ lost considerable support, as it saw its seats decline by almost half from its preelection strength of 134 to 70. Although the SDPJ was still the second largest party after the LDP, it was no longer powerful enough to take the initiative in organizing non-LDP forces. SDPJ Chairman Yamahana was blamed by left-wing members for the

Table 2. Major Transfactional and Transpartisan Groups

	TRANSFACTIONAL GROUPS IN THE LDP
October 1986*	Study Group on a New Tax System (40 younger members)
September 1988	Utopian Politics Study Group (10 freshman members)
March 1989	Diet Members for Political Reform (14 younger members)
April 1989	Liberal Reform Federation (36 younger members)
September 1991	YKK group (three senior members)
December 1991	Group of Junior Members for Political Reform (54 young members)
February 1993	LDP Heisei reform group (33 younger members)
May 1993	Group New Century (64 antireform members)
June 1993	Transfactional Liaison Committee for Political Reform (middle-ranking members)
June 1993	Members League for Political Reform (159 members)
August 1993	Democratic Politics Study Group (some 50 antireform members)
August 1993	Group for Clean Politics (169 antireform members)

	TRANSFACTIONAL GROUPS IN THE JSP/SDPJ
March 1990	New Wave group (30 freshman members)
March 1990	Group of 1990 (32 freshman members)
November 1990	New Power (former Group of 1990)
January 1991	Social Democratic Forum (left-wing members)
May 1991	Action New Democracy (freshman members in both the Upper House and the Lower House)
November 1991	Leadership 21 (23 freshmen members)
November 1991	New Political Generation Forum (middle-ranking members)
April 1993	Party Reform Federation (87 right-wing members)
May 1993	Heisei Forum (25 members)
December 1993	The Democrats (40 reformers of eight SDPJ groups and 10 former Lower House members)

	TRANSPARTISAN GROUPS
October 1991	Strong Wind Group (23 freshman members from the LDP, SDPJ, Kōmeito, and DSP)
November 1991	Group of Comparative Political Studies (21 freshman members from the LDP, SDPJ, Kōmeitō, and DSP)
November 1992	Sirius (21 SDPJ freshman members from both the Upper House and the Lower House, two Shaminren members, and four Upper House Rengō members)
January 1993	System Reform Study Group (19 freshman members from the LDP, SDPJ, Kōmeitō, DSP, and JSP)
June 1993	Solidarity of Transfactional Junior Members for Political Reform (55 members from the LDP, SDPJ, Kōmeitō, and DSP)

NOTE: Younger members refers to Lower House members elected less than five times. Young members are those elected less than three times.
* Month and year of formation.

SDPJ's failure in the election, and he was replaced by left-wing leader Murayama in September.

An eight-party coalition government was established on July 29 under Ozawa's leadership, and Hosokawa was appointed as prime minister on August 6. The eight-party coalition, including the SDPJ, announced that it would adhere to the LDP's foreign and security policies, which implied that the SDPJ tacitly accepted the constitutionality of the SDF and its participation in overseas peacekeeping operations.

The most important task for this non-LDP coalition was political reform. At his first press conference in August, Hosokawa promised to push through legislation for political reform by the end of 1993, and in September he introduced a political reform bill to the Diet. This political reform initiative again fostered dissension within both the LDP and the SDPJ. In the LDP, proponents of reform numbered some 200 by the end of August. Antireform LDP members established their own groups, including the Democratic Politics Study Group with some 50 members and the Group for Clean Politics with 169 members (Uezumi 1995, 226–27; tables on 56–59, 109–112, 186–195). SDPJ infighting intensified between the right wing, led by former chairmen Yamahana and Tanabe, and the left wing, led by Murayama. Right-wing and centrist members joined with members of the Democratic Reform Party and Shaminren to establish a group they called The Democrats in December 1993 (Akamatsu 1994).

The vote on the political reform package tested the allegiance of both LDP and SDPJ members. In the vote in the Lower House chamber in November 1993, five SDPJ members stood against the government-sponsored bill and 13 LDP members supported it. Four LDP members, including three first elected in 1986 who supported the bill, defected from the LDP after the vote. In January 1994, the bill was narrowly approved in the Upper House Special Committee on Political Reform by a vote of 18 to 16, including one LDP vote in its favor. When it reached the Upper House chamber, however, the bill lost 118 to 130, mainly due to opposition by 17 SDPJ members. The Hosokawa cabinet was forced to yield to the LDP and accept its proposed legislative revisions.

After the watered-down political reform package finally cleared the Diet, the centripetal force binding the ruling coalition seemed to weaken. Differences between Ozawa, a key member of the ruling alliance, and Takemura, chief cabinet secretary of the Hosokawa cabinet, gradually came to the surface. LDP antireform "conservatives" approached Sakigake and the left wing of the SDPJ to propose collaboration. These groups shared anti-Ozawa feelings and a dovish position on security policy. Ozawa tried to encourage reform proponents in the LDP to leave the party and join the coalition.

In early April 1994, Hosokawa suddenly announced his resignation as prime minister, after he was questioned about a ¥100 million loan from Sagawa Kyūbin, the parent company of Tokyo Sagawa Kyūbin, which had been party to the Kanemaru scandal in 1992. About this time two more groups split from the LDP. One was a group of Watanabe faction members, who supported Watanabe Michio as successor to Hosokawa. Seven of these members formed the Liberal Party. The other group, comprising five members of the Miyazawa faction, formed Mirai (New Vision Party). These groups could be categorized as faction-based movements.

Two weeks later, the non-LDP coalition appointed Hata as Hosokawa's successor. On the same day he was appointed prime minister, the JRP, the JNP, and the DSP established a parliamentary group in the Lower House. The SDPJ strongly criticized this action, regarding it as a move designed to contain the party's influence, and in retaliation withdrew from the ruling coalition, which led Hata to form a minority cabinet.

After withdrawing from the coalition, the SDPJ divided into two blocs: the right wing, comprising those who continued to feel an affinity with the non-LDP Hata cabinet, and the left wing, whose members resented what they saw as Ozawa's high-handed ways and were thus willing to consider cooperating with the LDP's antireform conservatives. In late June, the LDP, the SDPJ, and Sakigake tried to introduce a no-confidence motion against the Hata cabinet, forcing Hata to resign as prime minister. While the right wing of the SDPJ sought to rejoin the non-LDP coalition, LDP conservatives tried to persuade the left wing of the SDPJ to join with them in a coalition, sweetening their argument by proposing that the SDPJ would be awarded the prime ministership. In June 1994, the LDP-SDPJ-Sakigake coalition government was established.

As a coalition partner, the SDPJ was forced to revise its traditional foreign and security policies. Replying to a question from an opposition leader, Prime Minister Murayama announced in the Lower House in late July that the SDPJ now accepted the existence of the SDF and the necessity to maintain security ties with the United States. The SDPJ ratified Murayama's position in September. The SDPJ's ultraleftists, not surprisingly, would not sanction the party's policy reversal. When Murayama resigned as prime minister in January 1996, this group split from the SDPJ and formed the New Socialist Party. The right wing, on the other hand, organized a new policy group, the New Democratic

Coalition, in August 1994. Most of these members later defected from the SDPJ and helped establish the Democratic Party of Japan (DPJ) in September 1996, just prior to the Lower House general election.

CONCLUSION

As I discussed above, younger members in both the LDP and the SDPJ played important roles in overthrowing the stagnating, often deadlocked political system that had developed in the 1970s and the 1980s. The LDP's seniority-based factional system seems to have reached its apex in the mid-1980s. Each LDP faction functioned almost like an independent political party, by offering support to electoral candidates, raising funds for its members, participating in the government by placing members as ministers and vice-ministers, and advocating its own policy positions, especially during the LDP presidential race. In other words, the LDP's structure was that of a coalition of party-like factions.

Many younger members in the LDP, however, began to adopt stances at variance with party policy in the late 1980s, when they confronted such controversial issues as introduction of a new tax system and political reform. About the same time, the SDPJ was joined by newly elected Diet members who were uninvolved in the traditional ideological disputes between the party's right and left wings. They organized nonideological, policy-oriented intraparty groups and debated structural reform of the party. Young members from both the LDP and the SDPJ even worked cooperatively to achieve political reform in 1993.

They were also the core of political realignment in the 1990s. Forty-one of the 46 LDP freshmen who were elected first in 1986 were reelected in the 1990 Lower House election. In June 1993, eight left the LDP to join the JRP and six left to form Sakigake. Another three split from the LDP when the political reform bill passed the Lower House in November 1993. In April 1994, after Prime Minister Hosokawa announced his resignation, another three quit the LDP. By the summer of 1994, only 23 of the 46 remained in the LDP. Meanwhile, 26 of the 60 JSP freshmen who were elected first in the 1990 Lower House election survived the 1993 Lower House election. They were banded into small groups, reflecting the SDPJ/SDP's disarray. In the 1996 general election, 35 of the 1990 cohort ran from five parties: six from the SDP, 22 from the DPJ, two from the Democratic Reform Party, two from the NFP, and three from the New Socialists. Only two of the 14 seats these candidates won went to members of the SDP.

Factional coherency weakened in both the LDP and the SDPJ during the Hosokawa and Hata governments in 1993 and 1994. Although strong LDP reform advocates such as the Sakigake group and the Hata-Ozawa group had already left the party, the LDP was still divided into pro-reform and antireform (conservative) blocs. Observers expected several more pro-reform members to defect from the LDP between the fall of 1993 and the winter of 1994. The SDPJ also contained two blocs, a conservative, left-wing group led by Chairman Murayama and a pro-reform group under Secretary-General Kubo Wataru. Despite this internal rift, the SDPJ finally succeeded in shifting to what most of the electorate considered to be more "realistic" policies in 1994, though this was largely a quid pro quo for being awarded the prime ministership for the first time since 1948.

In this sense, an alliance between LDP conservatives and SDPJ conservative (although ideologically left wing) members under Prime Minister Murayama in June 1994 was reasonable and understandable. Faced with the opposition of young reformist members, conservatives in both the LDP and the SDPJ cooperated with each other in order to survive. For many LDP members, the decision to support the SDPJ chairman for prime minister was a thunderbolt, a radical shift in allegiance that was difficult for them to accept. It is likely that, had Hata reconstructed his cabinet with SDPJ pro-reform members after his announcement to resign in late June 1994, more members would have defected from both the LDP and the SDPJ to join the ruling coalition.

In the first Lower House general election under the new electoral system, held on October 20, 1996, the LDP received 239 of 500 seats. Although the SDPJ had changed its name to the Social Democratic Party (SDP) in both Japanese and English in January, it found it difficult to make over its image among the electorate. The SDP had already lost its raison d'être as an anti-LDP party. The SDP and Sakigake were soundly defeated, with the SDP capturing only 15 seats and Sakigake only two, largely because many of their members left to join the newly established DPJ shortly before the election. As with the coalition government between the LDP and the New Liberal Club from 1983 to 1986, voters soon forgot the achievements of smaller coalition partners. After the 1996 general election, both the SDP and Sakigake agreed to stay in the coalition framework with the LDP, but they refrained from joining the cabinet. In September 1997, the LDP regained a majority in the Lower House for the first time since June 1993, as members defected from the opposition parties and rejoined the LDP.

In late May 1998, while preparing for the Upper House election, the SDP and Sakigake announced their intention to dissolve their coalition with the LDP. However, this strategy of emphasizing their independence from the LDP failed to impress voters in the Upper House election in July. The SDP won only five of 126 seats, while Sakigake was unable to claim a single seat.

The 1990s was a period of tumultuous change in Japan's party system. Under the system of LDP dominance that had prevailed until the summer of 1993, relations between the ruling and opposition parties were both stable and unvarying. The LDP president was automatically appointed to be prime minister, and the JSP/SDPJ could enjoy its status as the largest opposition party under the multiseat electoral system.

In the coalition era that has held sway since 1993, all of the political parties have had a chance to join the ruling government. The Hata-Ozawa faction and the Sakigake group split off from the LDP and established a non-LDP coalition with six opposition groups in 1993. The following year, the SDPJ and Sakigake left the non-LDP camp and formed a three-party coalition with the LDP. In this situation, a party's most critical decision was whether to stay on the ruling side or join the opposition. After a stint as part of the opposition, the LDP decided to return to the ruling side by whatever means necessary. The party thus opted to cede the prime minister's post in forming an alliance in June 1994 with the SDPJ, its rival for almost 40 years.

With the enactment of political reform laws, including introduction of the new electoral system, the political landscape has changed yet again. Contributions to factions of political parties were prohibited by the revised Political Fund Control Law of 1994, which has weakened the power of LDP factions, while the power of parties has been strengthened with the introduction of public subsidies for political parties. Under LDP Presidents Kōno Yōhei and Hashimoto, neither of whom were faction heads, LDP factions lost their traditional role as organizations backing their leaders in vying for the LDP presidency. With the rise of new leaders after the 1996 Lower House election, LDP factions have again entered a period of reorganization.

Unlike under the previous multiseat district system, what matters most under the single-seat district system is not which party or faction a candidate belongs to, but whether the candidate can draw enough votes to prevail in the election. The winning candidate in a single-seat district can represent his or her electoral district exclusively. This is why many former LDP members returned to the LDP, both before and after the 1996 election.

The period from the summer of 1993 to the fall of 1996 was a time of transition comparable in its volatility to the years from 1951 to 1955, when the chaotic postwar political system was transformed into a system characterized by LDP dominance. The widely held expectation that the political system would evolve to feature two competitive conservative parties suddenly collapsed with the dissolution of the NFP at the end of 1997. However, the LDP's defeat in the 1998 Upper House election prevented the revival of single-party dominance, and Japanese politics again entered a coalition period. It now looks unlikely that a new party system will be firmly established within the next few years.

NOTES

1. The term "1955 system" has at least four meanings: (1) the structure of the two-party system formed in 1955; (2) ideological confrontation between the LDP and the Japan Socialist Party (JSP; the name of the SDPJ in English until 1991); (3) major policy differences between the LDP and the JSP on the Constitution and security issues since the 1950s; (4) collaborative management of Diet affairs by the LDP and the JSP (Wada 1999, 29). In this chapter, I will use the term "system of LDP dominance," emphasizing the party system structure from 1955 to 1993, except when I specifically refer to the two-party system of the late 1950s as the "1955 system."

2. In the spring of 1987, LDP leaders succeeded in controlling "rebels" who opposed the introduction of a sales tax by threatening them with expulsion from the LDP ("Uriagezei zōhan-giin" 1987, 1). Ironically, many LDP Lower House members and SDPJ House of Councillors members who did not follow their parties' position on political reform later left their parties during deliberations on a political reform bill in 1993 and 1994.

3. Although it was commonly said in the 1980s that a candidate needs ¥500 million to win in the Lower House election, there is no available data that discloses the amount individual candidates spent on their campaigns except during the official campaign period. In the spring of 1989, some first-term LDP members of the Utopian Politics Study Group agreed to disclose their annual

political expenditures. Their average annual spending to maintain their offices, including paying staff salaries, came to more than ¥100 million per member. One can imagine how prohibitively expensive campaign costs are for younger Lower House members who lack the access to campaign funds enjoyed by senior members ("Shikin atsume anote konote" 1989, 2).

4. The most important power-sharing norm is associated with the LDP's four top positions: president, secretary-general, chairman of the General Council, and chairman of the Policy Research Council. After the Miki administration in 1974, these positions were typically divided among members of the four major factions (Curtis 1988, 86–87).

5. Takeshita maintained a 40 percent approval rating in public opinion surveys from November 1987 to October 1988. After the Recruit scandal came to light, however, his support rate dropped sharply to the 20 percent level by December 1989, and down into the teens by March 1989 ("Approval Rate of Takeshita Cabinet" 1989).

6. In an effort to resolve the contradiction since 1954 between the party's position on the SDF and the actual existence of the SDF, the JSP introduced a unique and somewhat contradictory interpretation of the SDF in the mid–1980s, which posited that although the SDF was established by the Diet in accordance with proper legal procedures, the SDF itself was in violation of the Constitution (iken gōhō-ron).

7. Under the U.S. occupation, 20 minesweepers from Japan's Coast Guard Agency (later reorganized as the Maritime Self-Defense Force) were dispatched to the Korean peninsula in 1950 during the Korean War (Yomiuri Shimbun Sengoshi-han 1981, chap. 2). Regarding the Japanese government's policy toward the Gulf, see also Tejima (1993).

8. In this chapter, I will use the term "conservatives" to refer to those who took a passive or negative stance toward political reform during deliberations from 1992 to 1994.

9. According to Hirano Sadao, an advisor to Ozawa, Kajiyama initiated the deal with the Prosecutor's' Office (Hirano 1996, 60–61).

10. Five of the newly elected members belonged to both groups, while three did not belong to either ("Shakaitō tōsen" 1990, 2).

11. The chairmen frequently met to resolve problems between ruling and opposition parties regarding management of Diet matters. These discussions at the party head level functioned as the most important channel of communications between the ruling and opposition parties in the Diet in the 1970s and 1980s.

BIBLIOGRAPHY

Akamatsu Hirotaka, ed. 1994. *Warera demokurattsu* (We, the Democrats). Tokyo: Ningen-sha.

"Approval Rate of Takeshita Cabinet Plunges to Mere 15%." 1989. *Asahi Evening News* (18 March).

Asahi Shimbun Seiji-bu. 1993. *Seikai saihen* (Political realignment). Tokyo: Asahi Shimbun-sha.

Asahi Shimbun Senkyo-hombu, ed. 1990. *Asahi senkyo taikan* (The Asahi election databook). Tokyo: Asahi Shimbun-sha.

Curtis, Gerald. 1988. *The Japanese Way of Politics.* New York: Columbia University Press.

Hirano Sadao. 1996. *Ozawa Ichirō tono nijū-nen* (Twenty years with Ozawa Ichirō). Tokyo: Purejidento-sha.

Hosokawa Morihiro. 1992. "'Jiyū shakai rengō' kettō sengen" (Declaration establishing the 'Liberal and Social Federation'). *Bungei Shunjū* 70 (6): June: 94–106.

Inoguchi Takashi. 1993. "Jimintō ittō yūi taisei no houkai" (Collapse of the system of LDP dominance). In Inoguchi Takashi, *Gendai Nihon gaikō* (Contemporary Japanese diplomacy). Tokyo: Chikuma Shobō (originally published as "Japanese Politics in Transition: A Theoretical Review." 1993. *Government and Opposition* 28 (4): 445–455).

Itō Masaya. 1982. *Jimintō sengoku-shi* (A history of LDP power struggles). Tokyo: Asahi Sonorama.

Kabashima Ikuo. 1992. "89-nen Sangiin Senkyo" (1989 House of Councillors election). *Leviathan*, no. 10: 7–31.

"Kanjichō ni nihyaku-yo-nin no shomei-bo" (Secretary-general receives petition signed by 204 LDP members). 1993. *Asahi Shimbun* (22 May): 7.

Kubo Wataru. 1998. *Renritsu seiken no shinjitsu* (The truth behind coalition governments). Tokyo: Yomiuri Shimbun-sha.

Mizusaki Tokifumi. 1992. "Ichi-nin-ku ni okeru Jimintō no kampai" (The complete defeat of the LDP in single-member constituencies). *Leviathan*, no. 10: 82–103.

Morita Minoru. 1993. *Seiken kōtai* (Change of government). Tokyo: Jiji Tsūshin-sha.

Narita Norihiko. 1997. "'Seiji kaikaku no katei-ron' no kokoromi: Dessan to shōgen" (On the process of political reform: Witness and analysis). *Leviathan*, no. 20: 7–57.

Nippon Seiji Gakkai, ed. 1995. *Nempō seijigaku 1996: 55-nen taisei no houkai* (Annuals of the Japanese Political Science Association 1996: The collapse of the 1955 system). Tokyo: Iwanami Shoten.

Nihon Keizai Shimbun-sha, ed. 1994. *Renritsu seiken no kenkyū* (Study of a coalition government). Tokyo: Nikkei Shimbun-sha.

Ōmae Ken'ichi. 1989. *Heisei ishin* (Heisei reform: Zero-based organization and construction). Tokyo: Kōdan-sha.

———. 1992. *Heisei ishin part 2: Kokka shuken kara seikatsu-sha shuken e* (Heisei reform part 2: From state sovereign to people's sovereign). Tokyo Kōdan-sha.

Ōtake Hideo. 1996. "Forces for Political Reform: The Liberal Democratic Party's Young Reformers and Ozawa Ichirō." *Journal of Japanese Studies* 22 (2): 269–294.

Research Institute for Peace and Security. 1991. *Asian Security 1991–92*. London: Brassey's.

Richardson, Bradley. 1997. *Japanese Democracy: Power, Coordination, and Preference*. New Haven and London: Yale University Press.

"Rōso ga aitsuide egaku shin-tō ezu" (The shape of new parties drawn by the labor unions). 1992. *Asahi Shimbun* (18 September): 4.

Sakamoto Yoshikazu. 1994. "Heiwa-shugi no gyakusetsu to kōsō" (Paradox of pacifism and its initiatives). *Sekai*, no. 603: 22–40.

Satō Seizaburō. 1997. "Shin ittō yūisei no kaimaku" (Beginning of a new system of one-party dominance). *Chūō Kōron* 112 (5): 170–183.

Satō Seizaburō and Matsuzaki Tetsuhisa. 1986. *Jimintō seiken* (LDP administrations). Tokyo: Chūō Kōron-sha.

Schlesinger, Jacob M. 1997. *Shadow Shoguns: The Rise and Fall of Japan's Postwar Political Machine*. New York: Simon & Schuster.

"Seiji kaikaku minkan rinchō: Kon aki medo ni bappon-an" (Nongovernmental Ad Hoc Council for Political Reform aims to publicize its reform plan). 1992. *Asahi Shimbun* (21 April): 4.

Serizawa Hirofumi. 1988. *Habatsu saihensei* (Reorganization of LDP factions). Tokyo: Chūō Kōron-sha.

"Shakaitō tōsen ikkai no daigishi ga nibun: Seisaku no teigen de kyōsō" (JSP freshmen divided into two groups: Compete in policy recommendations). 1990. *Asahi Shimbun* (19 November): 2.

"Shikin atsume anote konote: Jimin ichi-nensei daigishi no shūshi" (Varied fund-raising channels: Accounting report by LDP rookies). 1989. *Asahi Shimbun* (4 March): 2.

"Shōsenkyoku hireidaihyō ren'yō-sei nimo sukunakunai mondaiten" (Problems with the proposal of the Nongovernmental Ad Hoc Council for Political Reform). 1993. *Asahi Shimbun* (1 May): 4.

Tejima Ryūichi. 1993. *1991-nen Nippon no haiboku* (Japan's defeat of 1991). Tokyo: Shinchō-sha.

Uchida Kenzō. 1983. *Habatsu* (LDP factions). Tokyo: Kōdan-sha.

Uezumi Mitsuhiro. 1995. *Bunretsu seikai no mitori-zu* (Sketch of a divided political world). Tokyo: Jiji Tsūshin-sha.

"Uriagezei zōhan-giin e kibishiku taisho (The LDP decides to deal strictly with rebels opposing the sales tax)." 1987. *Asahi Shimbun* (3 March): 1.

Wada Shūichi. 1999. "Gunji ni taisuru seiji no minshuteki kontorōru towa? Anzenhoshō seisaku ni okeru Kokkai no yakuwari" (What is democratic control over military affairs? The role of the Diet in security policy-making in Japan). *Kaikakusha*, no. 463: 28–31.

Yamagishi Akira. 1995. *'Renritsu' shikake-nin* (Mastermind behind the coalition governments). Tokyo: Kōdan-sha.

Yano Jun'ya. 1994. *Nijū kenryoku, yami no nagare: Yano Jun'ya kaisō-roku* (The double power structure and passages in the darkness: Yano Jun'ya's memoir). Tokyo: Bungei Shunjū-sha.

Yomiuri Shimbun Sengoshi-han, ed. 1981. *"Sai-gumbi" no kiseki* (The course to rearmament). Tokyo: Yomiuri Shimbun-sha.

Yomiuri Shimbun-sha Seiji-bu, ed. 1993. *Seikai saihen no makuake* (Prelude to political reorganization). Tokyo: Yomiuri Shimbun-sha.

Appendix 1. Chronology of Pertinent Political Events since 1980

1980

June 22   Lower and Upper House elections are held on the same day. The LDP wins by a landslide.

1981

March 16   Second Rinchō is launched with Dokō Toshiwo, former chairman of Keidanren, as chairman.

1982

July 30   Second Rinchō publishes its first report of basic recommendations.

November 24   LDP primary election for president is held. Nakasone Yasuhiro wins, receiving 57 percent of votes.

November 27   Nakasone cabinet is installed.

1983

March 14   Second Rinchō publicizes its final recommendations.

June 26   First Upper House general election under the proportional representation system is held.

October 12   Tokyo local court pronounces former Prime Minister Tanaka Kakuei guilty in the Lockheed affair.

December 18   Lower House general election is held. The LDP loses the majority.

December 20   JSP Chairman Ishibashi Masashi announces his view that the SDF is legal but unconstitutional.

December 27   The LDP and the NLC agree to form a coalition government.

1984

October 27   Former LDP presidents Suzuki Zenkō and Fukuda Takeo support Nikaidō Susumu as a candidate for party president. Kōmeitō and the DSP also back Nikkaidō, but his bid for the party presidency fails. Nakasone begins his second two-year term as LDP president on October 29.

December 14   The Denden-kōsha privatization bill is passed in the Diet. An addendum to the bill stipulates review of the corporation's breakup within five years.

1985

February 7   Takeshita faction first meets. On February 27, Tanaka suffers a stroke.

April 1   Denden-kōsha and the Japan Tobacco and Salt Public Corp. are privatized as NTT and Japan Tobacco.

December 16   The JSP convention shelves ratification of the 1986 Manifesto.

1986

January 22   The JSP convention adopts the 1986 Manifesto.

July 6   Lower and Upper House elections are held on the same day. The LDP wins by a landslide. Nakasone's term as LDP president is extended for one year. The number of JSP Lower House members falls to 85. Ishibashi announces his resignation as JSP chairman.

August 12   The NLC decides to disband. Its members rejoin the LDP.

September 6   Doi Takako is elected as JSP chairperson.

1987

April 1   Japanese National Railways is privatized and divided into seven companies.

April 23   The sales tax bill is tabled in the Lower House.

October 20   Nakasone appoints Takeshita Noboru as his successor.

November 6   Takeshita becomes prime minister.

November 20   Rengō is established as the national center of private labor unions. Dōmei is disbanded.

1988

July 29   Takeshita cabinet drafts the Tax Reform Bill and introduces it in the Diet.

October 19   The Tokyo Prosecutor's Office investigates Recruit Company in a stock-for-favors scandal.

December 9   The minister of finance resigns amid criticism for having received stock from Recruit Company.

December 24   A bill to introduce a 3 percent consumption tax is passed in the Diet after a 25-hour "cattle-walk" vote in the Upper House chamber.

1989

January 7   Emperor Hirohito dies.

April 28   Prime Minister Takeshita announces his resignation.

June 2   Uno Sōsuke is appointed prime minister.

July 23   Upper House election is held. The LDP is defeated. The JSP wins 46 seats. Rengō candidates defeat LDP candidates in 12 single-seat districts. On July 24, Uno announces his resignation.

August 9   Kaifu Toshiki is appointed prime minister.

November 21   Rengō is enlarged by the inclusion of public labor unions.

| | Yamagishi Akira becomes president of Rengō. Sōhyō disbands. Anti-Rengō labor unions organize Zenrōkyō. |
| December 21 | The Ministry of Health and Welfare publicizes a "Ten Year Strategy on Health and Welfare for the Elderly," known as the Gold Plan. |

1990
February 18	Lower House election is held. The LDP maintains its majority with 275 seats. The JSP wins 136 seats, the most it has won since 1967.
February 22	Ozawa Ichirō becomes LDP secretary-general.
March 2	The Telecommunications Council submits a report recommending NTT be divided in two. On March 30, the cabinet decides to shelve the issue until March 1996.
April 26	The Advisory Council on Electoral Reform recommends to the prime minister that a single-seat district system combined with proportional representation be introduced in the Lower House.
August 2	The Gulf crisis starts with Iraq's invasion of Kuwait.
August 30	The Kaifu cabinet announces its plan to contribute US$1 billion to multinational efforts for peacekeeping in the Middle East. On September 14, Kaifu announces an additional US$3 billion contribution.
October 16	The United Nations Peace Cooperation Bill is introduced in the Diet. On November 8, the bill is tabled in the Lower House.
October 31	The Third Provisional Council for the Promotion of Administrative Reform is launched.

1991
January 17	The Gulf War breaks out. On January 24, the Kaifu cabinet announces a US$9 billion contribution to the multinational peacekeeping effort.
April 7	An LDP-Kōmeitō-DSP–backed candidate is defeated in the Tokyo gubernatorial election. On April 8, Ozawa resigns as LDP secretary-general.
April 26	Maritime Self-Defense Force minesweepers are dispatched to the Persian Gulf.
June 21	Doi announces her resignation as SDPJ chairperson.
July 23	Tanabe Makoto is elected SDPJ chairman.
September 19	The Kaifu cabinet authorizes the International Peace Cooperation Bill and introduces it in the Diet.
September 30	The Political Reform Bill is tabled in the Lower House.
October 27	Miyazawa Kiichi is elected LDP president. On November 5, Miyazawa is appointed prime minister.

1992

January 9	Miyazawa and U.S. President George Bush publicize the Tokyo Declaration for U.S.-Japan Global Partnership.
April 20	The Nongovernmental Ad Hoc Council for Political Reform is launched.
May 20	Hosokawa Morihiro, former governor of Kumamoto Prefecture, establishes the JNP.
June 15	The International Peace Cooperation Bill is passed in the Diet.
July 26	Upper House election is held. The LDP wins 68 of the 127 seats up for election. The SDPJ wins 22 and the newly established JNP wins 4 seats.
September 2	The United Nations requests the Japanese government to dispatch Self-Defense Force personnel to assist the peacekeeping activities in Cambodia. From September 17 to October 13, 683 SDF members are sent to Cambodia.
October 14	Kanemaru Shin announces his resignation both as head of the Takeshita faction and as a Lower House member, amid criticism for receiving donations from Tokyo Sagawa Kyūbin.
October 28	Obuchi Keizō is selected as head of the Takeshita faction. Ozawa organizes an anti-Obuchi group.
November 3	Sirius is established with the SDPJ, Shaminren, and Upper House Rengō as members.
December 18	The Takeshita faction splits into the Obuchi and Hata/Ozawa factions.

1993

January 6	Yamahana Sadao is elected SDPJ chairman. On January 19, Yamahana appoints Akamatsu Hirotaka as the SDPJ's secretary-general.
March 6	Former LDP Deputy President Kanemaru is arrested for violation of the income tax law.
April 8	The SDPJ and Kōmeitō introduce a political reform bill in the Diet.
May 31	Prime Minister Miyazawa promises on television to enact political reform.
June 7	An SDPJ working group decides the final draft of the 1993 Manifesto. But the party never ratifies it.
June 18	A vote of no confidence against Prime Minister Miyazawa is passed in the Lower House. Miyazawa dissolves the Lower House.
June 18	Members of the Utopian Politics Study Group leave the LDP. On June 21, they launch the New Party Sakigake.
June 23	The Hata-Ozawa group forms the JRP.

July 18	Lower House general election is held. Winning 223 seats, the LDP loses its majority. The SDPJ loses 64 seats, falling from 134 to 70 seats. The JRP wins 55, and the JNP secures 35.
July 22	Prime Minister Miyazawa announces his resignation.
July 29	Eight parties agree to form a non-LDP coalition government.
July 30	Kōno Yōhei is elected LDP president.
August 6	Hosokawa is appointed prime minister. On August 9, the Hosokawa coalition government is installed.
September 8	Yamahana announces his intention not to run for the SDPJ chairmanship.
September 17	The Hosokawa cabinet authorizes the Political Reform Bill and introduces it in the Diet.
September 20	Murayama Tomiichi is elected SDPJ chairman.
October 27	The Third Provisional Council for the Promotion of Administrative Reform submits its final report to Prime Minister Hosokawa.
November 16	Prime Minister Hosokawa and LDP President Kōno meet to discuss revision of the Political Reform Bill. Kōno rejects Hosokawa's proposal.
November 18	The Political Reform Bill is passed in the Lower House.
December 16	The Hosokawa cabinet decides on the partial opening of the rice market.
December 21	SDPJ reformers organize The Democrats, a transfactional group, and Yamahana becomes chairman.
1994	
January 20	The Upper House Special Committee on Political Reform approves the Political Reform Bill by a vote of 18 to 16. On January 21, the Upper House chamber rejects the bill by a vote of 118 to 130. Seventeen SDPJ members vote against the bill and five LDP members favor the bill.
January 28	Prime Minister Hosokawa and Kōno meet and agree to revise the Political Reform Bill. On January 29, the Political Reform Bill is passed through the Diet.
February 3	Prime Minister Hosokawa announces the introduction of a 7 percent "national welfare tax" in a press conference at midnight. On February 4, the ruling parties agree to withdraw the national welfare tax plan.
February 11	Prime Minister Hosokawa meets U.S. President Bill Clinton. They agree to cooperate against North Korea's nuclear development, but they fail to reach an agreement on the trade issue.
February 25	The Hosokawa cabinet decides the General Program on Administrative Reform.

April 8	Hosokawa announces his resignation as prime minister.
April 15	Sakigake announces its intention not to send ministers to the next cabinet. Five LDP members leave the party to form Mirai (New Vision Party).
April 18	Five members of the Watanabe faction leave the LDP. On April 20, they form the Liberal Party.
April 25	Hata Tsutomu is appointed prime minister. The JRP, Kōmeitō, JNP, and DSP form a parliamentary group, Kakushin. The SDPJ, criticizing the parliamentary group, decides to break from the coalition.
April 28	Hata forms a minority cabinet.
May 16	Yamasaki Taku, Koizumi Shin'ichirō, and Katō Kōichi organize a transfactional group, the New Century, in the LDP.
June 25	The Hata cabinet resigns, threatened by the introduction of a vote of no confidence against the prime minister.
June 29	The LDP, SDPJ, and Sakigake agree to form a coalition government. SDPJ Chairman Murayama is appointed prime minister.
July 20	Prime Minister Murayama, in response to questions in the Lower House chamber, declares the SDF constitutional and expresses his intention to maintain the U.S.-Japan Security Treaty.
September 3	The SDPJ's extraordinary convention authorizes Murayama's position on the SDF and the U.S.-Japan Security Treaty by revising its long-standing security and foreign policies.
September 8	Yamagishi announces his intention to resign as Rengō's president.
September 19	The three-party coalition adopts the Basic Plan for Administrative Reform.
October 6	Rengō selects Ashida Junnosuke as president.
December 10	The New Frontier Party is formed with the merger of the JRP, Kōmeitō, JNP, and DSP. Kaifu is selected president.
1995	
January 17	The Great Hanshin-Awaji Earthquake strikes Kobe. Six thousand people die.
February 24	The Murayama cabinet decides to reorganize 14 public corporations into seven. On March 14, the coalition parties agree to merge two additional public corporations, the Export-Import Bank of Japan and the Overseas Economic Cooperation Fund, within four years.
March 20	The sarin gas attack on the Tokyo subway system occurs. Five thousand people's lives are threatened.

April 9	Local elections are held. Nonpartisan candidates win in gubernatorial elections in Tokyo and Osaka.
May 27	The SDPJ adopts the 1995 Manifesto.
June 9	The Diet passes a resolution on the 50th anniversary of the end of World War II. The NFP boycotts the plenary session.
July 23	Upper House election is held. Turnout is the lowest ever. The NFP defeats the LDP under the proportional representation system. The three ruling parties lose seats.
September 22	Hashimoto Ryūtarō is elected LDP president.
November 28	The Murayama cabinet authorizes the New National Defense Program Outline.
December 15	The Murayama cabinet decides on a bill to compensate sufferers of Minamata disease not yet officially recognized.
December 27	Ozawa defeats Hata in the NFP presidential election.
1996	
January 5	Prime Minister Murayama announces his resignation. On January 11, Hashimoto forms the LDP-SDPJ-Sakigake coalition government. He is the first LDP president since the end of one-party rule in July 1993 to form a government.
January 19	The SDPJ ratifies the new party platform and changes its name to the SDP.
March 4	NFP members use sit-down tactics in the Lower House to criticize public financing of the housing loan companies (jūsen). Budget deliberations are deadlocked for 23 days.
March 29	The Hashimoto cabinet postpones the issue of the division of NTT.
April 8	The SDP and Sakigake abandon their plan to merge.
August 4	In a referendum at Makimachi in Niigata Prefecture, a majority of residents vote against the plan to construct a nuclear power plant.
August 28	Hatoyama Yukio leaves Sakigake and announces his intention to form a new party.
September 28	The Democratic Party of Japan is established and Hatoyama and Kan Naoto become coleaders.
September 28	Doi begins a second term as chairperson of the SDP.
October 1	Six of 16 designated public corporations are reorganized into three.
October 20	The first Lower House general election under the new election law is held. The LDP wins 239 of the chamber's 500 seats. The NFP wins 156 seats, and the DPJ 52.
November 7	Hashimoto forms his second cabinet. The SDP and Sakigake do not send cabinet members.

November 8	Prime Minister Hashimoto announces a plan to reorganize ministers and agencies by 2001.
December 6	The minister of posts and telecommunication publicizes the NTT division plan.
December 26	Thirteen NFP members leave the party to form the Taiyō Party.

1997

April 3	Hashimoto agrees with NFP President Ozawa to cooperate on a bill to extend leases on land for U.S. military bases. On April 17, the bill is passed in the Diet.
June 18	Former Prime Minister Hosokawa leaves the NFP.
September 5	The LDP regains a majority in the Lower House with the return of former LDP members.
September 8	Hashimoto begins a second term as LDP president.
September 11	Hashimoto reshuffles his cabinet. His appointment of Satō Kōko, who was convicted in the Lockheed affair, draws public criticism. On September 22, Satō steps down.
September 23	Japan and the United States sign the new Guidelines for U.S.-Japan Defense Cooperation.
October 3	Washio Etsuya becomes president of Rengō.
December 9	The Long-Term Health Care Bill is passed through the Diet.
December 18	Ozawa is reelected NFP president. On December 27, the NFP members decide to disband the party.

1998

January 4	The NFP splits into six groups: Liberal Party, New Peace Party, Yūai (New Party Fraternity), Voice of the People, Reform Club, and Reimei (Club of Dawn).
January 23	The Good Governance Party is established with the merger of the Taiyō Party, Voice of the People, and a group of Hosokawa followers.
March 19	Law to Promote Specified Nonprofit Activities is passed in the Diet.
April 27	The DPJ is reorganized with the merger of four parties: DPJ, Yūai, Good Governance Party, and Democratic Reform Party.
June 1	The SDP and Sakigake leave the coalition with the LDP. The LDP forms a single-party government for the first time since the end of one-party rule in August 1993.
July 12	Upper House election is held. The LDP suffers a stinging defeat and loses its majority in the Upper House. The DPJ wins 27 seats, and the JCP 15. On July 13, Hashimoto announces his resignation.
July 24	Obuchi Keizō is elected LDP president. On July 30, Obuchi is appointed prime minister.

October 12	The Diet passes a bill to stabilize Japan's financial system. The bill is revised based on a bill opposition parties submit.
October 20	Sakigake disbands.
November 7	Kōmeitō is reestablished with the unification of the New Peace Party and Kōmei.
November 19	Prime Minister Obuchi agrees with Ozawa, head of the Liberal Party (LP), to create a coalition government.

1999

January 13	The LDP and the LP agree on policies for forming a coalition. On January 14, the LDP-LP coalition cabinet is installed.
May 24	The Diet passes a bill to activate the new Guidelines for U.S.-Japan Defense Cooperation.
July 1	NTT is divided into three carriers: two for regional services and one long-distance and international service under the control of a stock company.
July 24	The Kōmeitō convention authorizes the formation of a coalition with the LDP and LP.
August 9	The Diet approves a bill to recognize the Hinomaru (sun flag) and "Kimigayo" as the national flag and anthem.
October 5	The LDP-LP-Kōmeitō coalition cabinet is launched.

Appendix 2. Administrations
since 1989

Administration	Ruling Side	Opposition Side
Kaifu (Aug. 8, 1989–Nov. 5, 1991)	LDP	JSP/SDPJ, Kōmeitō, DSP, JCP, and Shaminren
Miyazawa (Nov. 5, 1991–Aug. 5, 1993)	LDP	SDPJ, Kōmeitō, DSP, JCP, Shaminren, and JNP
Hosokawa (Aug. 9, 1993–April 25, 1994)	SDPJ, Kōmeitō, JRP, JNP, DSP, Sakigake, Upper House Rengō/DRP, and Shaminren	LDP and JCP
Hata (April 25, 1994–June 25, 1994)	Kōmeitō, JRP, JNP, DSP, Shaminren, Mirai, Liberal Party*	LDP, SDPJ, Sakigake, and JCP
Murayama (June 30, 1994–Jan. 11, 1996)	LDP, SDPJ, and Sakigake	Kōmeitō, JRP, JNP, DSP, and JCP
Hashimoto (Jan. 11, 1996–June 1, 1998)	LDP, SDPJ/SDP, and Sakigake	NFP, JCP, and DPJ
Hashimoto (June 1, 1998–July 30, 1998)	LDP	NFP, DPJ, JCP, New Socialists, SDP, and Sakigake
Obuchi (July 30, 1998–Jan. 14, 1999)	LDP	DPJ, Liberal Party,† Kōmeitō, JCP, SDP, and Sakigake
Obuchi (Jan. 14, 1999–Oct. 5, 1999)	LDP and Liberal Party†	DPJ, Kōmeitō, JCP, and SDP
Obuchi (Oct. 5, 1999–)	LDP, Liberal Party,† and Kōmeitō	DPJ, JCP, and SDP

NOTE: A new administration begins with the interchange of coalition partners.
* Established by former LDP members in April 1994.
† Established by Ozawa Ichirō in January 1998.

Appendix 3. Election Results

Table A. *Lower House Election Results since 1958*

Date of Election	LDP	JSP/SDPJ/ SDP	DSP	Kōmeitō	NLC	Shamin- ren
May 22, 1958	287	166	–	–	–	–
Nov. 20, 1960	296	145	17	–	–	–
Nov. 21, 1963	283	144	23	–	–	–
Jan. 29, 1967	277	140	30	25	–	–
Dec. 27, 1969	288	90	31	47	–	–
Dec. 10, 1972	271	118	19	29	–	–
Dec. 5, 1976	249	123	29	55	17	–
Oct. 7, 1979	248	107	35	57	4	2
June 22, 1980†	284	107	32	33	12	3
Dec. 18, 1983	250	112	38	58	8	3
July 6, 1986†	300	85	26	56	6	4
Feb. 18, 1990	275	136	14	45	–	4
July 18, 1993	223	70	19	51	–	4
Oct. 20, 1996	239	15	–	–	–	–

SOURCES: Foreign Press Center/Japan, *The Diet, Elections, and Political Parties* (Toyko: Foreign Press Center/Japan, 1995); *Asahi Shimbun* (21 October 1996).

*Others includes minor parties and independents.
† The Lower House elections of 1980 and 1986 were held the same day as the Upper House elections for those years.

JCP	JNP	Sakigake	JRP	NFP	DPJ	Others*	Total No. of Seats
1	–	–	–	–	–	13	467
3	–	–	–	–	–	6	467
5	–	–	–	–	–	12	467
5	–	–	–	–	–	9	486
14	–	–	–	–	–	16	486
38	–	–	–	–	–	16	491
17	–	–	–	–	–	21	511
39	–	–	–	–	–	19	511
29	–	–	–	–	–	11	511
26	–	–	–	–	–	16	511
26	–	–	–	–	–	9	512
16	–	–	–	–	–	22	512
15	35	13	55	–	–	30	511
26	–	2	–	156	52	10	500

Table B. Upper House Election Results since 1956

Date of Election	LDP	JSP/SDPJ/SDP	DSP	Kōmeitō*	NLC	JCP
July 8, 1956	61	49	–	–	–	2
June 2, 1959	71	38	–	–	–	1
July 1, 1962	69	37	4	9	–	3
July 4, 1965	71	36	3	11	–	3
July 7, 1968	69	28	7	13	–	4
June 27, 1971	63	39	6	10	–	6
July 7, 1974	62	28	5	14	–	13
July 10, 1977	63	27	6	14	3	5
June 22, 1980‡	69	22	6	12	0	7
June 26, 1983	68	22	6	14	2	7
July 6, 1986‡	72	20	5	10	1	9
July 23, 1989	36	46	3	10	–	5
July 26, 1992	68	22	4	14	–	6
July 23, 1995	46	16	–	–	–	8
July 12, 1998	45	5	–	9	–	15

SOURCES: Foreign Press Center/Japan, *The Diet, Elections, and Political Parties* (Toyko: Foreign Press Center/Japan, 1995); *Asahi Shimbun* (13 July 1998).

NOTE: In the Upper House, half of the seats are up for election for six-year terms every three years. Since 1983, 50 seats have been contested under the proportional representation system. Until 1983, 50 seats were contested in the nationwide district.

* Kōmeitō was called the Kōmei Political League in 1962.

† Others includes minor parties and Independents.

‡ The Upper House elections of 1980 and 1986 were held the same day as the Lower House elections for those years.

JNP	Sakigake	NFP	DPJ	LP	Others'	Total No. of Seats
–	–	–	–	–	15	127
–	–	–	–	–	17	127
–	–	–	–	–	5	127
–	–	–	–	–	3	127
–	–	–	–	–	5	126
–	–	–	–	–	2	126
–	–	–	–	–	8	130
–	–	–	–	–	8	126
–	–	–	–	–	10	126
–	–	–	–	–	7	126
–	–	–	–	–	9	126
–	–	–	–	–	26	126
4	–	–	–	–	9	127
–	3	40	–	–	13	126
–	0	–	27	6	19	126

About the Contributors

ŌTAKE HIDEO is Professor of Political Science at Kyoto University. He graduated from Kyoto University in 1966 with a degree in political science. He received a Ph.D. in political science from the University of Tokyo in 1978. Professor Ōtake started his career as lecturer at Senshū University, after which he became a professor at Tohoku University. He has been in his current position since 1992. He has also served as a visiting professor at Nanyang University in Singapore, Hamburg University in Germany, Dhaka University in Bangladesh, and the Institut d'etudes politiques de Paris in France. His major publications include *Jiyū shugi teki kaikaku no jidai* (The era of neoliberal reform, 1994), *Sengo Nihon no ideorogī tairitsu* (Ideological confrontation in postwar Japan, 1996), *Gyōkaku no hassō* (The ideology of administrative reform, 1997), and *Nihon seiji no tairitsu jiku* (The axis of conflict in Japanese politics, 1999).

ETŌ MURASE MIKIKO is Professor of Law at Hōsei University. She graduated from the Nursing College of Yamaguchi University and Ōita College for Health Science in 1972 and 1974, respectively, and worked as a health officer at the Osaka City Office. In 1986, she went back to school to study law. She earned a B.A. in law from Rikkyō University in 1990, and in 1993 received an LL.M. from the Graduate School of Law, Chūō University. Upon graduation, she served as a researcher at the Tokyo Metropolitan Neurology Institute; she took up her current position in 1995. Professor Etō's publications include *Iryō no seisaku katei to juekisha* (Policy process and recipients in health care, 1993); *Chihō bunken no senryaku* (The strategy of decentralization, coauthored, 1996); and "Seisaku no renzoku to hen'yō: Nihon iryō seido no kōzō" (Continuity and change in medical policy: Structure of the Japanese medical system), in *Nempō seijigaku 1997* (Annual of the Japanese Political Science Association, 1997).

NONAKA NAOTO is Professor of Political Science at Gakushūin University. He earned a B.A. in Western history in 1984 and an M.A. and a Ph.D. in international relations from the University of Tokyo in 1987 and in 1993, respectively. Professor Nonaka served as researcher at the Asia Pacific Association of Japan from 1990 to 1994, and then as research associate at the University of Shizuoka. In 1995, he moved to Gakushūin University as associate professor. He has been in his current position since 1996. His major publications include *Jimintō seiken ka no seiji erīto* (Political elites under the LDP government, 1995); *Seiji katei no hikaku bunseki* (Comparative analysis of policy process, coauthored, 1999); and "Jimintō shikkōbu" (Party executives of the LDP), in *Seiji kaikaku 1800 nichi no shinjitsu* (The truth of the 1,800 days of political reform, 1999).

SHINKAWA TOSHIMITSU is Professor of Modern Political Analysis at Hokkaido University. He received his Ph.D. in political science from the University of Toronto in 1990. He taught political science at Niigata University as assistant professor from 1988 to 1992, then as professor until he took up his current position in 1995. His recent publications include *Nihongata fukushi no seiji keizaigaku* (The political economy of Japanese-style welfare, 1993); "Miki Takeo: Rinen to seron ni yoru seiji" (Prime Minister Miki Takeo: Politics of ideals through the mass media), in *Sengo Nihon no saishō tachi* (Prime ministers in postwar Japan, 1995); "Occupational Welfare and the Japanese Experience," in *The Privatization of Social Policy* (coauthored, 1996); and *Sengo Nihon seiji to shakai minshu-shugi* (Social democracy in postwar Japan, 1999).

TATEBAYASHI MASAHIKO is Assistant Professor of Law at Kansai University. He earned an LL.D. from Kyoto University in 1999, after receiving an M.A. in political science from the University of California, San Diego, in 1994. His major publications include "Kokka-ron apurōchi o koete—hikaku seiji keizaigaku ni okeru gōriteki sentaku seido-ron no shatei" (Beyond the statist approach: Rational choice institutionalist approach toward comparative political economy), in *Kōkyō sentaku no kenkyū* (no. 26, 1995); "Senkyo seido to chūshō kigyō seisaku" (Electoral institutions and public policy for small and medium-sized enterprises), in *Nempō Seijigaku 1997* (Annuals of the Japanese Political Science Association, 1997); and "Atarashii seido-ron to Nihon kanryōsei kenkyū" (New institutionalism and the study of Japanese Bureaucracy), in *Nempō Seijigaku 1999* (Annual of the Japanese Political Science Association, 1999).

TOYONAGA IKUKO is Associate Professor in Comparative Politics at Kyushu University. She graduated from the University of Tokyo with a B.A. in law and political science in 1989. She remained at the university as a research associate and later as a lecturer until 1995, while she also studied at the University of Cambridge as Nitobe-Daiwa Fellow from 1993 to 1995. In 1995, she briefly worked as special researcher at the Japan Research Institute for Local Government. Professor Toyonaga took up her current position in 1996. She is currently working at Georgetown University as a visiting researcher on an Abe Fellowship. She is the author of *Sacchārizumu no seiki: Sayō no seijigaku e* (The paradigm of Thatcherism: Introducing a new method for political science, 1998), which in 1998 won the Suntory Academic Award in the field of best books on history and ideas. Her other works include "Sacchārizumu to jūtaku seisaku: Popurā kyapitarizumu to eikoku kokka kōzō no setten" (Thatcherism and housing policy: The interface between popular capitalism and the British state structure), in *Kokka gakkai zasshi* (1994, 1995); and "Seijigaku ni okeru kūkan gainen: Metafā o koete" (The concept of space in political theory: Beyond metaphorical usage), in *Kūkan e no pāsupekutibu* (A perspective toward space, 1999).

WADA SHŪICHI is Program Officer at the Japan Center for International Exchange (JCIE). He earned a B.A. in social science in 1980 and an M.A. in political science in 1984 from Waseda University. He worked as the first assistant on legislative affairs to Seki Yoshihiko, member of the House of Councillors, from 1983 to 1989. He moved to the Research Institute for Peace and Security as a staff researcher in 1990 and joined JCIE in 1996. In 1995, he was a visiting researcher at the International Institute for Strategic Studies in London. His publications include *Nihon no Anzen-hoshō to kempō* (Japanese security policy and the Constitution, coauthored, 1998); *Kokusai seiji no kisochishiki* (Basics in international relations, coauthored, 1997); and "Amerika gikai to anzen-hoshō" (U.S. Congress and U.S. security policy), in *Gaikō Jihō* (no. 1296–1297, 1993).

Index

Japan Center for International Exchange

FOUNDED in 1970, the Japan Center for International Exchange (JCIE) is an independent, nonprofit, and nonpartisan organization dedicated to strengthening Japan's role in international affairs. JCIE believes that Japan faces a major challenge in augmenting its positive contributions to the international community, in keeping with its position as one of the world's largest industrial democracies. Operating in a country where policy making has traditionally been dominated by the government bureaucracy, JCIE has played an important role in broadening debate on Japan's international responsibilities by conducting international and cross-sectional programs of exchange, research, and discussion.

JCIE creates opportunities for informed policy discussions; it does not take policy positions. JCIE programs are carried out with the collaboration and cosponsorship of many organizations. The contacts developed through these working relationships are crucial to JCIE's efforts to increase the number of Japanese from the private sector engaged in meaningful policy research and dialogue with overseas counterparts. JCIE receives no government subsidies; rather, funding comes from private foundation grants, corporate contributions, and contracts.